INSPIRE / PLAN / DISCOVER / EXPERIENCE

SARDINIA

DK EYEWITNESS

SARDINIA

CONTENTS

DISCOVER 6

EXPERIENCE 54

NEED TO KNOW 200

Left: The Sant'Efisio festival in Cagliari
Previous page: The medieval town of Bosa
Cover: An idyllic beach on the Costa Paradiso

DISCOVER

The scenic hillside town of Jerzu

WELCOME TO
SARDINIA

An untamed coastline with heavenly slips of soft sand and sparkling turquoise bays. Mysterious ancient ruins and characterful medieval cities. Spirited festivals, featuring age-old traditions and flowing with food and wine. Whatever your dream trip to Sardinia includes, this DK Eyewitness travel guide is your perfect companion.

1 Colourful buildings in the medieval town of Bosa.

2 A traditional costume at the Festa di Sant'Efisio.

3 Relaxing at an outdoor café in Olbia.

4 The golden sands and turquoise sea at Muravera.

Surrounded by the Mediterranean Sea, the shores of Sardinia have seen the arrival of many invaders. Each power has left behind traces of their cultural legacy, creating an enticing blend of architecture, customs and cuisines. From the stone structures left by the enigmatic nuraghic people to the wealth of intriguing local festivals, you'll find evidence of the island's rich history wherever you look.

Sardinia's wind-shaped landscape holds many natural treasures, too. The island is justly famed for its idyllic beaches, but there's more to explore than just the coast. Encounter herds of wild horses high up on the plateau of the mountainous interior and stroll through fragrant maquis vegetation to marvel at the otherworldly rock formations of Capo Testa.

No less captivating are the island's urban areas. Cagliari, the capital, is awash with compelling museums and fine restaurants, while medieval towns such as Alghero and Bosa charm with their picturesque settings. Tradition remains strong in more remote regions, where shepherd's villages like Berchidda and Gavoi produce tangy cheeses and flavourful wines.

With so many things to see and do, any visit to Sardinia requires some thoughtful planning. We've broken the island down into easily navigable chapters, with detailed itineraries and comprehensive maps to help plan the perfect visit. Add insider tips and a Need To Know section with all the practical essentials to be aware of, and you've got an indispensable guidebook. Enjoy the book, and enjoy Sardinia.

REASONS TO LOVE
SARDINIA

Lazy days on secluded beaches and energetic mountaintop treks past wild horses and ancient ruins. Stunning roads that lead to pretty villages where you can sip fine wine and feast on fresh seafood. Sardinia is so easy to love.

1 SCENIC ROADS

Twisting around mountain tops, skirting along stunning coastline and weaving down into forested valleys, Sardinia's highways could be straight out of a sports car advertisement.

THE MADDALENA ARCHIPELAGO 2

Dip into the warm bays of the Maddalena Archipelago (p172), where the sea ripples in perfect shades of turquoise, offset by wind-sculpted rocks and pristine white-sand beaches.

3 FESTIVALS

Whatever time of year you visit, there's always a colourful celebration to join. Expect a rich feast of eye-catching costumes, mouth-watering food and free-flowing wine.

BOSA'S PASTEL HOUSES 4

Watched over by the ruins of a 12th-century castle, the pretty riverside town of Bosa *(p148)* is lined with row upon row of pastel-coloured houses that blush in the setting sun.

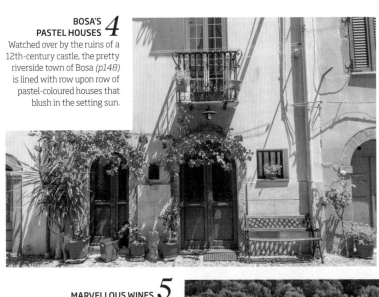

MARVELLOUS WINES 5

Great wine has been bottled and sipped in Sardinia for millennia – for proof, just ask the local centenarians, who attribute their longevity to the local red Cannonau.

SEAFOOD FEASTS 6

Surrounded by water, Sardinia is a haven for lovers of fresh seafood. Dig into grilled tuna steak on San Pietro *(p74)* and indulge in juicy saffron-infused prawns in Oristano *(p154)*.

DISCOVERING WILDLIFE 7

A wealth of captivating wildlife roams the length and breadth of the island, from the wild horses of La Giara di Gesturi *(p91)* to the colourful flamingos that nest near Cagliari *(p65)*.

SECRET COVES 8

Set sail around Sardinia's wild coast in search of your own hidden idyll. A bounty of secluded beaches fringe the island, providing the perfect opportunity to play castaway.

9 THE MAQUIS

The sweet aroma of maquis vegetation is a sensory delight. Immerse yourself in its unforgettable fragrance at the Parco Nazionale dell'Asinara *(p157)* or the Piscinas Dunes *(p72)*.

10 HIKING IN CODULA DI LUNA

Follow the age-old trails that snake through this craggy canyon and marvel at the tenacity of the shepherds who tend to their flocks in its sun-scorched lands *(p98)*.

PECORINO CHEESE 11

Sardinia's best known cheese is the salty and firm pecorino. Try it savoury style, stuffed in pockets of ravioli, or enjoy it melted with honey and lemon as a buttery *seada* (dumpling).

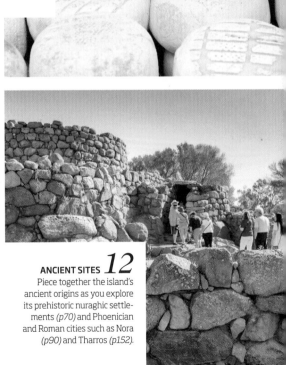

ANCIENT SITES 12

Piece together the island's ancient origins as you explore its prehistoric nuraghic settlements *(p70)* and Phoenician and Roman cities such as Nora *(p90)* and Tharros *(p152)*.

EXPLORE
SARDINIA

This guide divides Sardinia into five
colour-coded sightseeing areas, as
shown on the map below. Find out more
about each area on the following pages.

Isola Asinara

Cala d'Oliva

Stintino

Porto
Torres

Argentiera

Sassari

Alghero

Capo
Caccia

**THE
WESTERN
COAST**
p134

Capo Marargiu

Bosa

*Mediterranean
Sea*

Tramatza

San Salvatore

Oristano

Tharros

Golfo di Oristano

Arborea

San Nicolò
d'Arcidano

Guspini

Arbus

Campidano

Fluminimaggiore

Iglesias

Isola
San Pietro

Carbonia

Calasetta

Giba

Sant'Antioco

*Isola di
Sant'Antioco*

Capo Teulada

WESTERN EUROPE

NORWAY SWEDEN

*North
Sea* DENMARK

IRELAND

UNITED
KINGDOM

NETHER-
LANDS

GERMANY

POLAND

BELGIUM

CZECH
REP.

SLOVAKIA

*Atlantic
Ocean*

FRANCE

SWITZ.

AUSTRIA HUNGARY

ITALY

SPAIN

PORTUGAL

SARDINIA

Mediterranean Sea

MOROCCO

ALGERIA

TUNISIA

Isola della
Maddalena

Isola di
Caprera

Santa Teresa
Gallura

Palau

Porto Cervo

Golfo
dell' Asinara

Arzachena

Capo Figari

G a l l u r a

Tavolara

Trinità d'Agultu
e Vignola

Olbia

Isola Molara

Casterlsardo

**THE NORTH AND
THE COSTA SMERALDA**
p168

San Teodoro

Ploaghe

Oschiri

Alà dei Sardi

Budoni

Ozieri

Siniscola

Bitti

G o c e a n o

Orosei

Bono

Nuoro

Dorgali

Macomer

Oliena

Ottana

Tiscali

*Golfo
di Orosei*

Abbasanta

*Lago
Omodeo*

**CENTRAL SARDINIA
AND BARBAGIA**
p112

*Capo di
Monte Santu*

Fordongianus

Arzara

Arbatax

Laconi

Bari Sardo

Àles

Nurallao

*T y r r h e n i a n
S e a*

Su Nuraxi

*Lago del
Flumendosa*

Orroli

**THE
EASTERN COAST**
p92

Sanluri

*Lago
Mulargia*

Senorbi

Sarrabus

**CAGLIARI AND
THE SOUTH**
p56

San Priamo

Siliqua

*Capo
Ferrato*

Uta

Quartu Sant' Elena

Costa Rei

*Stagno di
Cagliari*

Cagliari

Geremeas

Villasimius

Golfo di Cagliari

*Capo
Carbonara*

Pula

Nora

Capo Spartivento

| 0 kilometres | 25 |
| 0 miles | 25 |

N
↑

GETTING TO KNOW
SARDINIA

Famous for its beaches, Sardinia is also cloaked in thick oak forests and vineyard-filled valleys, with an interior marked by sprawling plateaus, deep canyons and towering granite ridges. Scattered throughout are villages, towns and cities, the most populous of which are near the coast.

PAGE 56

CAGLIARI AND THE SOUTH

Less crowded than more northerly regions, the south is home to Sardinia's capital. Cagliari's elegant architecture lends the city an easy charm, and its museums provide a fascinating introduction to the island's past – a subject that can also be explored at prehistoric Su Nuraxi and the Roman city of Nora. On the Costa Verde, flamingos nest in lagoons edged by shifting sand dunes and flowering maquis, while Baia Chia and the island of San Pietro lure sunseekers with their gorgeous beaches.

Best for
Dunes, ancient ruins, museums, eating out

Home to
Cagliari, Su Nuraxi, the Piscinas Dunes, island of San Pietro, Iglesias

Experience
Walking through the medieval Castello district in Cagliari and stopping at a traditional ristorante for a seafood lunch

THE EASTERN COAST

Mile after mile of serene pastures and rocky summits characterize the east of the island, a remote region where authentic Sardinia thrives in humble farming villages. Many areas here are still relatively isolated, but they're rich in rewards for those who make the journey. The almost inaccessible Golfo di Orosei coastline is riddled with secluded caves and coves – some, such as Cala Luna, are reachable only by boat or on foot. And the wild Gennargentu National Park is a haven for hikers, who might catch sight of soaring golden eagles and nimble mouflon on its craggy peaks.

Best for
Secluded coves, caves, mountain treks

Home to
Gennargentu National Park, Codula di Luna

Experience
A scenic journey on the Trenino Verde, the little green tourist train that skirts around the mountains with jaw-dropping views along the way

$\rightarrow$

PAGE 112

CENTRAL SARDINIA AND BARBAGIA

With rugged mountains marked by shepherds' trails and age-old villages perched over steep valleys, the central region of Sardinia vividly reflects the ancient character of the island. The inhabitants of this isolated area have retained many aspects of their traditional way of life, most visibly in their pageantry-filled festivals. The countryside here is equally enchanting, with the mysterious cave dwellings of Tiscali and shady forest hiking trails among the many attractions.

Best for
Red wine, pecorino cheese, festivals

Home to
Nuoro, Tiscali

Experience
Watching the lively parade of costumed participants during Carnival in Mamoiada

PAGE 134

THE WESTERN COAST

The natural harbours and fertile land of this windblown region have attracted foreign ships for centuries – as attested by the ruins of the ancient city of Tharros. Still-thriving settlements here include the fine medieval city of Alghero (a top spot to feast on lobster) and the photogenic town of Bosa. Further scenic delights include the promontory of Capo Caccia, with its atmospheric caves and glittering underground lakes; the idyllic beaches of the Sinis region; and the verdant vineyards around the charming city of Oristano, the heart of Vernaccia wine production.

Best for
Seafood, caves, ancient ruins, white wine

Home to
Alghero, Capo Caccia, Bosa, Tharros, Oristano

Experience
Exploring the fascinating temple ruins of the ancient Roman city of Tharros

THE NORTH AND COSTA SMERALDA

The Costa Smeralda is Sardinia at its most classically picture-perfect: rocky coastline, sparkling turquoise sea and stunning beaches of brilliant white sand. Unsurprisingly, the resorts here are hugely popular with holidaymakers, but you can find unspoilt calm on the islands of the Maddalena Archipelago, a stone's throw from Corsica. The windswept valleys of the interior also offer a more peaceful retreat, with a sprinkling of impressive Romanesque churches to discover.

Best for
Beaches, island hopping, fine dining, medieval churches

Home to
The Maddalena Archipelago, Santissima Trinità di Saccargia, Sassari

Experience
A cruise around the incredible islands of the Maddalena Archipelago, with a swim at one of the beautiful beaches

←

1 Looking over the rooftops of Cagliari's old town.

2 The grand interior of Cagliari's cathedral.

3 An evening walk along the beach at Poetto.

4 A stall at the Mercato Civico di San Benedetto.

2 DAYS
in Cagliari

Day 1

Morning Sardinia's capital has a rich selection of sights, most of which are located in the atmospheric old town. The best place to begin exploring is the well-preserved Castello district, which dates back to the medieval era. Start by fuelling up for the day with breakfast from the Mercato Civico di San Benedetto, a spacious covered food market where you can pick up fresh bread, pastries, fruit, cheeses and more. Next, seek out the ornate 13th-century cathedral *(p61)*, with its distinctly Pisan design, before passing through the imposing gateway at the far end of Piazza Palazzo to the Cittadella dei Musei *(p62)*. This complex of museums offers a wealth of archaeological finds, Renaissance art and Asian treasures.

Afternoon Savour an authentic Sardinian lunch at Pani e Casu *(Via Santa Croce 51)*, where you'll find delicious local dishes such as roast lamb and wild mushroom pasta on the menu. After letting your meal settle, climb up one of the medieval defensive towers that punctuate the old city walls – either Torre di San Pancrazio or Torre dell'Elefante – for superb panoramas over the city and out to the sea.

Evening Saunter over to Bastione San Remy *(p60)* for more sweeping vistas – the view over the port and Cagliari's marshes and salt flats is especially magnificent at sunset. This wide esplanade was built in the 19th century and is now lined with elegant bars. Sip away the evening at Caffe degli Spiriti *(Via Torino 16)*, where you can gently swing in a hammock while drinking classic cocktails and nibbling on freshly shucked oysters and salty olives.

Day 2

Morning Stroll around Corso Vittorio Emanuelle II, stopping at one of the cafés for a typical Sardinian breakfast of coffee and a croissant. When you're ready to move on, make your way to the leafy Orto Botanico *(p63)* for a stroll among the local and exotic plants, keeping an eye out for hidden grottoes and Roman remains. Just above this shady sanctuary are the ruins of the Roman Amphitheatre *(p60)*, once a grand arena for popular entertainment. From there, it's a short walk over the brow of the hill to the Galleria Comunale d'Arte *(p63)*, with its wonderful collection of modern Sardinian art.

Afternoon Head to the modern Villanova district, where EXMA *(p65)* – a former slaughterhouse converted into an arts centre – hosts frequent art exhibitions. The nearby modern eatery MangioGiusto *(Via XX Settembre 51)* makes a great spot for a light lunch. Just a short walk west is San Saturnino *(p65)*, one of Sardinia's oldest churches, dating from the 5th century. The building suffered bomb damage during World War II, but you can still see some Roman remnants. From here, walk to Via Dante Alighieri to catch a bus to Poetto *(p64)*, alighting at whichever stop takes your fancy along the 7-km (4-mile) stretch of sandy beach.

Evening After a refreshing dip in the teal-coloured sea, feast on seafood at Frontemare *(Viale Lungomare del Golfo)*, which has a gorgeous beachside terrace with private cabanas. Finish off with an Aperol spritz or two, then take a barefoot walk in the soft sand to watch a southern Sardinian sunset.

7 DAYS
in Northern Sardinia

Day 1

Drive north out of Olbia towards Porto Rotondo *(p186)* for your first taste of the stylish Costa Smeralda. Secluded Spiaggia del Principe is one of the best beaches in the area, and is well worth a stop before continuing along the coast to glitzy Porto Cervo *(p189)*. Grab lunch at Ristorante Pizzeria la Rocca da Chiara *(www.ristorante-larocca-bajasardinia.com)* en route to Arzachena *(p190)*, where there are several interesting archaeological sites that can be easily visited in an afternoon. End the day back on the coast in Palau *(p188)*.

Day 2

Board an early ferry for La Maddalena, the main island of the gorgeous Maddalena Archipelago *(p172)*. Take some time on arrival to wander around the pretty port area, with a break for brunch at Zi Anto *(p172)*. Spend the rest of the day soaking up the scenery on a boat tour of the surrounding islands. Return to Palau come evening to dine at beachside Ristorante Faro *(www.ristorantefaropalau.com)*.

Day 3

Venture down Sardinia's northwestern coast, stopping in the quiet seaside village of Isola Rossa *(p197)* for a lunch of grilled fish and mussels at Bar Ristorante Il Cormorano *(Localita' Marinedda)*. Continue from there to Castelsardo *(p196)* and spend the rest of the afternoon meandering along the town's steep lanes, pausing to admire the ancient churches and the castle, and browse the shops selling local basketwork. Round off the day with a romantic dinner at Ristorante L'Incantu *(www.ristoranteincantu.it)*.

Day 4

A short drive inland brings you to Sassari, Sardinia's second-largest city *(p180)*. Fuel up with a pizza lunch at Il Quirinale *(p185)*, before seeking out the Spanish-inspired Duomo, with its flamboyant façade. Refresh with a gelato at Gelateria Bosisio Passione Bio *(Via Camillo Cavour 26)*, then make your way past the Piazza d'Italia to the Museo Nazionale, containing a wealth of nuraghic and Roman finds. If you have

5

① The charming harbour at Porto Rotondo.

② Spiaggia del Principe beach, surrounded by maquis.

③ The turquoise waters at La Pelosa beach, near Sassari.

④ Archaeological remains at Palmavera Nuraghe.

⑤ Pastel-coloured houses in the attractive town of Bosa.

time, squeeze in a trip to the lovely La Pelosa beach north of Stintino *(p157)*, before retiring for the evening in Sassari.

Day 5

Make the short drive southwest to the charming port city of Alghero *(p138)*. Spend the rest of the morning walking the city walls, browsing the jewellery shops and peeking inside the cathedral. After lunch at La Piadina del Pozzo *(p139)*, travel north out of town to enjoy more sandy beaches and explore the remains at Palmavera Nuraghe. If the weather permits, take a boat tour to view the striking rock formations in the Grotta di Nettuno at Capo Caccia *(p146)*. Back in Alghero, dine on Catalan-style lobster at Nautilus *(p139)* then spend the night at Maracaibo *(Via Lido 14)*, the city's top beach bar.

Day 6

Follow the scenic coastal road from Alghero to the picturesque town of Bosa *(p148)*. Take in the views from the top of the

12th-century castle, then enjoy a leisurely stroll around the Sa Costa medieval quarter. A great spot for lunch here is Bacco Bistrot *(Corso Vittorio Emanuele II)*, serving tasty focaccia sandwiches. Continue down to the Temo river, following it through town and out to the beaches at Bosa Marina for a lazy afternoon by the sea. For dinner, head back to cosy Sa Nassa *(Lungo Temo Alcide De Gasperi 13)* on the river.

Day 7

Drive east to the city of Nuoro *(p116)* for a fascinating insight into Sardinian culture. The Museo del Costume is the perfect place to start, with displays of traditional masks and costumes. You can also visit the Museo Deleddiano, devoted to local writer Grazia Deledda, and the city's art museum, MAN, if you're keen to learn more. After lunch, drive a short distance east to Monte Ortobene, which has great trails for an afternoon hike. End the day back in Nuoro, with a well-earned meal at one of the cheerful restaurants around Corso Giuseppe Garibaldi.

7 DAYS
in Southern Sardinia

Day 1

Start on the west coast in Oristano (p154). You can see evidence of this town's long and glorious history at the Antiquarium Arborense, one of the island's foremost museum collections, and in its cathedral, with its octagonal bell tower. After a late brunch at DriMcafé (Via Cagliari 316), make an afternoon trip to Santa Giusta, where you can admire the Romanesque Basilica di Santa Giusta (p166) and enjoy a tasting of local wines at Entio (Via Giovanni XXIII).

Day 2

Stock up on picnic supplies before setting out to explore the beautiful Sinis peninsula. The most prominent attraction here is the ancient city of Tharros (p152), best toured with a guide. Close by are San Giovanni di Sinis (p166), one of the oldest churches on the island, and San Salvatore (p164), a double-level church surrounded by pilgrims' lodgings. The beachside terrace of Il Lido Restaurant (Lungomare Eleonora d'Arborea 6) at Torre Grande is a good spot for dinner on the way back to Oristano.

Day 3

Set off along the Carlo Felice highway to Su Nuraxi, Sardinia's largest nuraghic site (p68). It's best to visit the museum for an overview before embarking on a guided tour of the extensive complex. For lunch, drive south to the friendly Agriturismo Su Stai (www.agriturvalbella.it). You can also stop the night here, so drop off your bags before jumping back in the car for an excursion to nearby Sanluri (p78). Its castle is home to an entertaining collection of militaria and quirky historical items.

Day 4

Drive west towards Guspini and follow the S126 south to the well-preserved Temple of Antas (p82). After spending the morning exploring its nuraghic, Carthaginian and Roman remains, continue south to Iglesias (p76) and pay a visit to the Museo dell'Arte Mineraria, dedicated to the town's mining heritage. You can then carry on this theme with a jaunt to Porto Flavia, a remarkable 1920s mining port built into rocky cliffs. Not far from here is clifftop 906 Operaio

5

☐ The lush landscape of the Sinis peninsula. ↑

② Nuraghic ruins at Su Nuraxi.

③ The town of Carloforte on the island of San Pietro.

④ Diners at Ristorante Mirage near Baia Chia.

⑤ Cagliari's picturesque Castello district.

(Passeggiata del belvedere di Nebida), where you can enjoy pizza and sunset views before returning to Iglesias for the night.

Day 5

Make your way to Portovesme to catch a ferry to the island of San Pietro *(p74)*. Try the local tuna for lunch at Ristorante da Andrea *(www.ristorantedaandrea.it)* in Carloforte, the island's only town, then hop on another ferry to the neighbouring island of Sant'Antioco *(p86)*. The main town here, also called Sant'Antioco, holds an array of interesting Phoenician and Punic finds – make sure to explore the museum and the catacombs below the basilica. As evening falls, seek out the welcoming Agriturismo Sa Ruscitta *(www. saruscitta. com)* for a traditional dinner and a comfortable bed for the night.

Day 6

Cross the land causeway that connects Sant'Antioco with the Sardinian mainland and follow the scenic southern coast road,

pausing for a dip at one of the beautiful beaches of Baia Chia *(p88)*. Feast on seafood for lunch at Ristorante Mirage *(www. miragechia.it)*, before continuing northeast to Nora *(p90)*, an important Carthaginian and Roman site. Cool off afterwards with a gelato from Gelateria Sottozero *(Viale Nora 91)* in nearby Pula, before a final 30-minute drive to Cagliari *(p60)*, the island's capital. Relax for the rest of the evening with refreshing craft beer and live music at Muzak *(Via Stretta 3)*.

Day 7

Spend your last day exploring the bounties of culture-rich Cagliari. After a lazy start, get brunch at the Mercato Civico di San Benedetto, then amble through the historic Castello district to the Cittadella dei Musei. Here, you can take your pick of the excellent art and archaeological exhibits. In the evening, stroll southwest to the Marina district to sample the 11-course set menu at Dal Corsaro *(www.stefano deidda.it)* – a Sardinian culinary delight, and the perfect treat to end your stay.

Roman Relics

Sardinia became a province of Rome in 238 BC, and you can still see evidence of its mighty empire today – sometimes in surprising places. When placing your towel down on the beaches of Santa Teresa Gallura *(p188)*, take a closer look at the huge granite slabs that are lying around: these unfinished columns were once destined to be used for grand Roman structures on the mainland. For the best-preserved sights, head to the ancient cities of Nora *(p90)* and Tharros *(p152)*, the baths at Fordongianus *(p163)* and the still-used amphitheatre in Cagliari *(p60)*.

←

The 2nd-century AD Roman amphitheatre in Cagliari

Did You Know?

Some scholars believe Sardinia might be Plato's fabled island of Atlas – the lost island of Atlantis.

SARDINIA FOR
HISTORY

A string of civilizations have left their mark on Sardinia, from the mysterious stone structures of the prehistoric nuraghic peoples to the imposing cathedrals and austere castles of the Spanish. Take a trip through time as you explore this legacy at the island's myriad historical sites.

Antique Architecture

As various medieval conquerors infiltrated Sardinia, the local architecture transformed. Pisan influence can be seen in the churches of the Logudoro region *(p198)*, with their arcaded façades and Gothic details – the striped Santissima Trinità di Saccargia *(p178)* is particularly impressive. Elsewhere, you'll find traces of Spanish rule in the cathedrals of Alghero *(p138)* and Sassari *(p180)*, and in Cagliari's Castello district *(p66)*.

Santissima ↑
Trinità di
Saccargia,
and *(inset)*
the frescoes
decorating
its apse

Enigmatic Nuraghi

Little is known about the builders of the unique stone structures known as nuraghi, which flourished on the island from about 1800 to 500 BC *(p68)*. One thing that's for certain, however, is that they were highly prolific: the remains of over 7,000 nuraghi have been found across Sardinia. Some have been developed into protected sites, including Maiori Nuraghe in Tempio Pausania *(p193)* and Su Nuraxi at Barumini *(p68)*, but you can stumble upon nuraghi anywhere – look out for them in the middle of farmers' fields, blending in at the edges of towns and hidden in forests.

←

Visitors on a tour of the
well-preserved nuraghic
site of Su Nuraxi

TOP 4 ARCHAEOLOGY MUSEUMS

Civico Museo Archeologico Villa Abbas, Sardara
Modest but informative, with a collection of Neolithic ceramics *(p79)*.

Museo Archeologico Nazionale, Cagliari
Exhibits on subjects ranging from Neolithic tools to the history of the Roman era *(p62)*.

Museo Civico Giovanni Marongiu di Cabras
Home to the mysterious Giants of Mont'e Prama statues *(p164)*.

Museo Archeologico Nazionale "G A Sanna", Sassari
Phoenician scarabs and Roman javelins feature in this collection *(p184)*.

A train snaking along the picturesque Costa Smeralda ↑

SARDINIA FOR
SCENIC JOURNEYS

Sardinia may be synonymous with beach breaks, but there are plenty of reasons to stray beyond your sun lounger. Pack your bags, stock up on picnic supplies from a local delicatessen, and get ready for a breathtaking adventure by road, rail or sea.

Road Tripping

With a good system of paved roads meandering across the entire island, the possibilities are endless when it comes to exploring by car. Marvel at the magnificent scenery as you wind over craggy mountains and across verdant plains, passing crumbling nuraghi and pausing at farmstead restaurants to sample the local produce. Particularly scenic areas to tour include Monte Albo (p130), with its fantastic rural mountain views, and the Logudoro (p198), sprinkled with delightful Romanesque churches.

↑ Mountain roads winding across Monte Albo

Touring by Train

There are few more relaxing ways to enjoy Sardinia's stunning countryside than on a train journey. The state-run company Trenitalia operates budget-friendly rail services across the length of the island *(p205)*, but for something a little more special take a ride on the Trenino Verde *(p110)*. This vintage train runs along five different sightseeing routes, conjuring up the atmosphere of a forgotten age as it chugs through an unspoilt landscape of steep hillsides and timeless villages.

💬 INSIDER TIP
Boat Tour Supplies

Many boat tours will include a meal with drinks, but it's advisable to pack a few extra snacks and water, especially for full day trips. A parasol can also be useful for providing much-needed shade.

↑ Boats docked in the attractive harbour of La Maddalena

Island Hopping

Sardinia is surrounded by numerous smaller islands, so taking a boat trip here seems only natural. There are more than enough companies from which to rent a boat or, better yet, take you out on one. One of the best day trips on offer is a serene sailboat tour around the picturesque Maddalena Archipelago, run by Fil Rouge Sail *(p174)*. Other top island excursions include Asinara *(p157)* - great for wildlife lovers - and the scuba-diving paradise of Tavolara *(p74)*.

↑ Sailing through the turquoise waters of the Maddalena Archipelago

Lunar Landscapes

Much of Sardinia's landscape is made up of exposed granite rock, often resembling something from another planet. Make like Neil Armstrong as you venture into the Codula di Luna - the "Valley of the Moon" - on one of the island's top hiking trails (p98). The trek through the Valle della Luna at Capo Testa (p188) is equally otherworldly, with footpaths winding between boulders that gradually change shape according to the prevailing wind and sea.

→

Walking through the wind-sculpted landscape of the Valle della Luna

SARDINIA FOR
NATURAL WONDERS

Wild and weathered, Sardinia is bejewelled with stunning caves, soaring sand dunes, aromatic flowers and extraordinary rock formations. Marvel at the power of nature as you roam these unforgettable terrains, with your camera at the ready to capture their splendour.

Stalactites and Stalagmites

Speckled with caves, subterranean Sardinia is a magical realm of shimmering limestone formations. The most enchanting of all is the vast Grotta di Nettuno (p146), which encases the crystal-clear waters of Lake Marmora - once home to monk seals. You can explore this atmospheric space on foot, along illuminated walkways, or experience a seal's-eye view of its depths on a diving excursion.

←

Unique limestone formations inside the Grotta di Nettuno

📷 PICTURE PERFECT
Pan di Zucchero

Sardinia's highest and most magnificent sea stack is Pan di Zucchero (Sugarloaf). Rising out of the bright blue sea, this dramatically steep limestone rock is only a few hundred metres from the shore. Capture it from the cove of Masua at sunset, when it almost appears to glow.

Fragrant Wildflowers
No trip to Sardinia is complete without a walk through the maquis, with its sweet-smelling carpet of scented flora. You'll find this typical Mediterranean vegetation in coastal and mountainous regions, including Gennargentu National Park (p96) and the island of San Pietro (p74). Visit in spring, when the aroma is at its strongest.

→

Common asphodel, a flower frequently found in the maquis

Dramatic Dunes
There's no shortage of spectacular scenery on the coast, but the dazzling Piscinas Dunes (p72) are in a league all of their own. These massive mounds of sand can reach heights of up to 60 m (196 ft), and provide a habitat for Sardinian deer and loggerhead turtles.

→

Strolling across the ever-shifting sands of the Piscinas Dunes

Issohadore characters at the annual Carnival celebrations in Mamoiada ↑

SARDINIA FOR
TRADITIONAL CULTURE

Centuries-old traditions are an integral part of life in Sardinia, whether it's making cheese, creating fine crafts or singing folk songs. Delve into this unique culture at the island's rural mountain villages, where you'll find a warm welcome at the many annual festivals.

Shepherd's Lunch

For a truly immersive taste of local life, take a tour of the mountain village of Orgosolo *(p125)*. Organized by operators such as Jebel Sardinia *(www.jebel sardinia.com)*, the experience usually includes an interpretive walk around the local murals, a scenic hike to old ruins, and a splendid picnic lunch in the forest, prepared by the shepherds who live there. The typical menu features *pane carasau* (flat bread), olives, pecorino cheese, roasted meats, seasonal fruit and wine.

→

Enjoying lunch with the local shepherds in the forest near Orgosolo

Steadfast Villages

High up in the mountains, in the heart of Sardinia, lies the tranquil village of Ollolai (p122), famed for its basket weaving. Eager visitors flock here for Ollolai's colourful, costume-filled festivals, guaranteed to be flowing with good wine and food. The nearby village of Mamoiada (p122) also comes alive during festival time – especially Carnival – though its traditions can be explored year round at the excellent Museo delle Maschere Mediterranee. Both villages are good places to purchase Cannonau wine and local pecorino cheese.

← A Mamuthone, one of the Carnival figures in Mamoiada

TOP 3 TRADITIONAL FESTIVALS

Barbagia Carnival
Expect age-old rituals, bonfires, bizarre masks and local delicacies to eat from early February to early March in the Barbagia region.

Cavalcata Sarda
Exciting horseback races, stunning costumes and throat singing are all part of this spring festivity in Sassari (p46.

Sagra del Redentore,
A massive late-summer pilgrimage to the top of Monte Ortobene near Nuoro, accompanied by beautiful choir music (p47).

> **INSIDER TIP**
> **Informative Overview**
>
> For an introduction to the island's traditional culture, head to the Museo del Costume in Nuoro (p116), which has detailed exhibits on life in a rural village.

↑ A group of throat singers at the Sherden Overtone Singing School

Singing School

Performed in Sardinia since nuraghic times, throat singing (cantu a tenòre) is a style of traditional folk singing that is practised mainly in the mountainous Barbagia region. It's usually performed by a group of four standing face to face, with each singer using a distinct tonal range. You can often hear this intimate song at festivals, though impromptu sessions may spring up any time. Try it for yourself at the Sherden Overtone Singing School in Mogoro (www.canto difonico.eu), which offers workshops and summer camps.

Forests and Fields

Not only is Sardinia's flora beautiful to look at, but it's tasty, too. Wild herbs from the forest and the maquis are often used to flavour roasted meats such as *porceddu* (spit-roasted whole suckling pig) and *agnello* (lamb), while figs, honey and almonds are popular ingredients in desserts and sweets. You'll also find hundreds of varieties of bread made with local durum wheat; the most common is the crispy, flat *pane carasau* that's often served with main meals.

$\longrightarrow$

Croccante alle mandorle, a type of brittle made with locally grown almonds

SARDINIA FOR
FOODIES

The flavours of Sardinia are similar to mainland Italian cuisine, but have a noticeable twist that makes them distinctly their own. Savour hearty dishes with humble origins, created by farmers and lovingly made from ingredients grown and nurtured on the island.

Tangy Pecorino

Sardinia's most famous cheese is pecorino, which is made of sheep's milk and comes in three main varieties: *sardo, romano* and *fiore sardo*. You can taste all three and more at roadside cheese markets, or on a tour of a dairy farm such as Argiolas Formaggi in Dolianova *(www.argiolasformaggi.com)*.

Wheels of fresh pecorino cheese, a Sardinian speciality $\uparrow$

Raise a Glass

Wine has been made in Sardinia ever since the Phoenicians introduced the first grapevines. Popular varieties include red Cannonau, rich and bold and the perfect accompaniment for roasted meat; white Vermentino, made from vines that grow primarily in the north; and the sweeter, mature white Vernaccia, which is generally taken as an aperitif. The island's most iconic drink, however, is not wine – it's a strong liqueur known as Mirto, made with wild myrtle leaves and local berries.

← Locals enjoying a glass of the island's renowned Cannonau wine

SU FILINDEU

In early May and early October, for the Feast of St Francis festival, numerous pilgrims head to the Santuario di San Francesco in Lula to dine on the rarest pasta in the world – *su filindeu* ("threads of God"). It is made by only a few local women, who have mastered the intricate art of creating the super fine noodles from a secret recipe that's over 500 years old. These savoury strands are served in a hot sheep broth with cheese and are said to nourish the soul as well as warm the body.

Did You Know?

Cannonau wines are rich in procyanidins, one of the chemicals known to contribute to a longer life span.

Coastal Catches

Although Sardinians were traditionally farmers rather than fishermen, today seafood is a prominent feature on menus throughout the island. Classic dishes to try include grilled lobster, *pizza ai frutti di mare* (seafood pizza) and octopus salad, but if you're feeling adventurous you can sample more unusual delicacies such as *bottarga* (sliced mullet roe), *orziadas* (deep-fried sea anemones) or *spaghetti ai ricci* (sea urchin pasta).

→ A bowl of *spaghetti ai ricci*, made with freshly caught sea urchins

Focus on Flamingos

Every year, between late summer and early spring, thousands of shocking-pink flamingos descend on the island's western coast, where they settle in marshes and salty lagoons to nest and raise their chicks. Known locally as *sa genti arrubia* (the pink people), these distinctive birds are best observed around Oristano – particularly the Sale Porcus Reserve *(p165)* – and on the outskirts of Cagliari *(p65)*. You can also find them nesting in the Stagno di San Teodoro *(p194)*, a coastal marsh that can be explored by boat or along well-marked walking trails.

Flamingos gathered in a flock on the coast near Cagliari

SARDINIA FOR
WILDLIFE

The mountains, valleys and coastal waters of Sardinia are teeming with wildlife, including a surprising number of rare species. Encounter herds of stocky wild horses and vivid flocks of pink flamingos as you explore the varied habitats of this natural wonderland.

Wild Giara Horses

Unique to the island, Sardinia's wild Giara horses may have been introduced by the Phoenicians as early as the 9th century BC. Compact and sturdy, these sure-footed creatures today roam only on the high plateau of the rocky Giara di Gesturi *(p91)*. Take a tour of this spectacular area with Giara Country *(www.giaracountry.it)* or Parco della Giara *(www.parcodellagiara.it)*, and witness these spirited animals grazing freely amid the cork trees and ancient nuraghe, pausing to drink from rainwater ponds.

A wild stallion cantering among the cork oaks on the Giara di Gesturi plateau

THE RETURN OF THE MONK SEAL

Once widespread, with a range extending from the Mediterranean to the Madeira Islands in the Atlantic Ocean, monk seals have fallen victim to human activities since the Roman era. Today thought to be the world's rarest pinniped (fin-footed) species, with less than 800 in existence, monk seals have promisingly begun to return to the Golfo di Orosei. They live there in coastal caves; sightings are possible but rare.

The Shy Mouflon

The mouflon, with its thick coat and curved horns, is an ancient inhabitant of the island. Until recently it was an endangered species, but now its population is on the rise in Sardinia thanks to concerted conservation efforts. You're most likely to spot one in arid mountainous regions such as Gennargentu *(p96)*, where they graze around the rocky cliffs.

→

A hardy mouflon cautiously peering out from behind a tree

The Asinara Donkey

This feral breed of albino donkey is indigenous to the island of Asinara *(p157)*, once the site of a prison and now a national park. About 100 of the creatures live there, sharing the landscape with wild boars and mouflon. The only way to visit is on a tour, which can be arranged from Stintino *(p157)* or Porto Torres *(p156)*.

→

Endemic white donkeys on the island of Asinara

Family-Friendly Beaches

To be confident of good facilities and safe swimming, look for beaches with Green Flag status. There are more than 25 of these on the island, the best of which include the shallow waters of Santa Giusta in Oristano *(p154)*, the ever-popular resort of Santa Teresa Gallura *(p188)* and the sweeping sands of Bari Sardo *(p105)*. There are hundreds more beaches that are just as family-friendly, with the most idyllic spots including the golden sands of Chia *(p88)* and forest-fringed Maria Pia in Alghero *(p141)*.

→

Relaxing in the sunshine on Santa Giusta beach

SARDINIA FOR
FAMILIES

With its spectacular beaches, intriguing history and hearty food, it's little wonder that Sardinia is hugely popular with families. Whether you're lazing by the sea or letting off steam inland, a memorable day out is guaranteed.

Farm Stays

Farms make a great setting for families, with plenty of outdoor space to run around in and lots of friendly animals to meet – it's good news, then, that many of the farms in Sardinia double as hotels. Enjoy cosy accommodation, tasty meals, and a warm welcome from your hosts at Agriturismo Sa Mendhula near Olbia *(www.samendhula. com),* the Country Hotel Mandra Edera in Abbasanta *(www.mandraedera.cc)* or La Fattoria delle Tartarughe in Sinnai *(www.lafattoria delletartarughe.it).*

←

Playing outdoors at one of the island's friendly farms

TOP 3 **KID-FRIENDLY HIKES**

Porto Conte
Just west of Alghero (p138), the vast Porto Conte forest has many walking trails suitable for little ones.

Capo Testa
A maze of short trails lead through the low-shrub maquis here, each ending up at a secret cove (p188).

Cala Goloritzé
This easy 7.5-km (4.5-mile) hike along a plateau near Santa Maria Navarrese (p100) is great for teens.

Marvellous Museums

Kids with an interest in history will love the Parco Museo S'Abba Frisca in Dorgali (p101), an outdoor museum that offers an immersive insight into traditional island life. They'll also be captivated by the Museo dell'Arte Mineraria in Iglesias (p77), packed with mega machinery and old mine tunnels to explore.

↑ A demonstration by a guide at the Parco Museo S'Abba Frisca.

EAT

Here are two of the best spots for a gelato break.

Intenso Gelateria
Piazza Giuseppe Garibaldi 46, Cagliari

$⑤⑤

La Pecora Nera
Via Luigi Galvani 70, Olbia

$⑤⑤

Amusement Park Adventures

Too windy for a beach day? Try splashing around at a water park instead – top picks include Aquafantasy in Isola Rossa (www.aquafantasy.it) and BluFan near Pula (www.blufan.net). Alternatively, take a trip around the island in just a few fun hours at the Parco Sardegna in Miniatura in Tuili (www.sardegnainminiatura.it), which features impeccable scale replicas of the island's monuments.

↑ Gliding down a slide at the Aquafantasy water park

In the Saddle

Horses have been part of local life since Phoenician times, and are an integral part of the island's culture: many of the religious feast days feature horse races among their festivities. Saddle up and take a rural horseback tour with Centro Ippico Meurreddus a Cuaddu *(www.facebook.com/ Meurreddus)*, clopping around scenic Sant'Antioco *(p86)*.

→

Exploring the beautiful Sardinian countryside on a horseback tour

SARDINIA FOR
OUTDOOR ADVENTURES

With a sunny climate and no end of inspiring landscapes, it's hard to resist the lure of Sardinia's great outdoors. From scaling towering mountains to descending into secret caverns, a wealth of exciting adventures await.

Wild Walks

The interior of Sardinia is a beguiling blend of wild mountains and rolling hills, dotted with prehistoric ruins, shady forests and fragrant maquis (scrub vegetation). The best way to explore this rugged landscape is on foot, and you'll find a variety of trails catering to all ability levels. Head to the Supramonte, the Gennargentu massif *(p96)* and the Sulcis area for the most rewarding routes.

 HIDDEN GEM
Adventure Playground

Little adventurers will love Gregoland in Porto Cervo *(p189)*, a large and free playground that's suitable for all ages. It features several climbing structures, shady picnic benches and gorgeous views of the bay below.

Hiking across the breathtaking terrain of the Gennargentu massif ↑

Going Underground

Delve beneath the island's surface and uncover an intriguing world of hidden sights. Marvel at the ancient cave village of Tiscali *(p118)*, secreted inside a huge chasm, or seek out the diminutive *janas* (half-witches, half-fairies) that are said to inhabit the Grotte Is Janas near Sadali. Experienced spelunkers can venture into the depths of the Grotte del Bue Marino *(p99)*, named after the "sea oxen" *(bue marino)* – or monk seals – that once lived here. Unusually, this cave system is also a draw for music lovers – it is used as a venue for the Cala Gonone Jazz Festival, which takes place on the Golfo di Orosei every year in late July.

← Peering into the remains of the prehistoric cave village at Tiscali

TOP 4 CAVES WITHOUT CROWDS

Grotte di Su Mannau, Fluminimaggiore
Mammoth-sized, 540-million-year-old cave system used by the Romans for worship.

Grotte Is Zuddas, Santadi
During the Christmas season a magical nativity scene is set up in one of the large chambers *(p89)*.

Grotta Su Marmuri, Ulassai
Underground lakes, bats, and cool temperatures – ideal on a hot day *(p105)*.

Sa Oche 'e Su Bentu, Oliena
Named "the voice of the wind" for the magnificent sound of the wind howling through its caverns *(p124)*.

Thrilling Climbs

Sardinia's craggy landscape makes it a haven for climbers, with numerous challenging rockfaces to scale. Popular areas include Domusnovas near Iglesias and Cala Gonone near Nuoro, both of which have plenty of routes to attempt. If you're in a group with mixed abilities, then Gola di Gorropu is a good choice: it has a range of trails suited to different experience levels.

↑ Scaling the heights of the Gola di Gorropu gorge

SARDINIA FOR
BEACHES

Idyllic half-moon bays with soft white sand and sparkling turquoise waters, teeming with marine life and ancient treasures: Sardinia's beaches are among the most beautiful in the world. With over 1,600 km (1,000 miles) of coastline to uncover, your own slice of paradise is within easy reach.

Relaxing Resorts

For people-watching, seafood shacks and convenient facilities, most city and town beaches have got all you need. Among the most appealing options are the ever-popular La Pelosa beach in Stintino (p157) or Poetto beach in Cagliari (p64), with its miles of creamy white sand and a palm-tree lined boardwalk that buzzes with bars and eateries. Spiaggia del Principe in Porto Cervo (p189) is another crescent jewel, with a natural fjord setting as a backdrop, while the main beach at Santa Teresa Gallura (p188) is full of life on any balmy day.

Soaking up the sun at Spiaggia del Principe ↓

Secluded Beaches

Escape the crowds and find a secluded stretch of sand all for yourself. Reachable only by boat or long hike, the unspoilt Golfo di Orosei is littered with isolated coves – the breathtaking Cala Luna *(p98)* is one of the most renowned. The beach at Berchida *(p104)* is equally remote; lined with red rocks and junipers, it's also home to nuraghic ruins and flamingo nests. If those options aren't exclusive enough, then you can always seek out your own hidden gem amid the 300 beaches of La Maddalena *(p172)* – all you need is a map and a sense of adventure.

←

Relaxing on the idyllic Cala Luna beach on the Golfo di Orosei

The submerged Madonna del Naufrago by Sardinian sculptor Pinuccio Sciola ↑

Snorkelling Hotspots

The seas around Sardinia are some of the cleanest in Italy and are rich in flora and fauna. Pop on a snorkel and search the seabed for wonders: the best spots include the Golfo di Orosei, the beaches around Stintino *(p157)* and the warm lagoons of the Sinis peninsula. You'll find sunken treasure at the ancient city of Nora *(p90)*, where the seabed is littered with Roman remains, and at Villasimius *(p106)*, where a huge sculpture by Pinuccio Sciola rests on the sea floor.

↑ Snorkelling in the crystal-clear waters off the Sardinian coast

Dazzling Jewellery
Delicate filigree jewellery is a speciality in Sardinia and you'll often see ornate items being worn at the island's many festivals. One of the best places to buy your own is Alghero *(p138)*, which is famed for its coral pieces – make sure to ask for a certificate of authenticity as proof that the coral has been harvested sustainably.

←

An intricate piece of filigree being crafted by a goldsmith

SARDINIA FOR
LOCAL CRAFTS

Traditional handicrafts have been made here since antiquity, and you can still see artisans using centuries-old methods today. Each village and town has its own distinct style and speciality - choose your favourite from an array of cork products, ceramics, metal work and hand-woven baskets.

Organic Ceramics
Typically hand-thrown in fluid shapes and glazed in natural tones, Sardinian pottery still bears traces of its ancient roots. Oristano is the place to view the island's finest clay creations - the CMA Ceramica Maestri d'Arte *(www.cma-ceramica-maestri-darte.business.site)* has a particularly beautiful selection.

→

Artisan pottery featuring stylized natural motifs

INSIDER TIP
**Buying
Etiquette**

Bargaining is not
practised at shops in
Sardinia, unless it's
a market and no price
is listed. Most smaller
shops prefer cash
for payment.

Woven Wonders

For an insight into the ancient
art of basket weaving, head
to Castelsardo (p196). Not
only can you see numerous
skilled practitioners at work,
but you can also explore the
craft's history at the excellent
Museo dell'Intreccio. The town
is a great place to purchase
one of the colourful woven
vessels, especially during
the Basket and Handicrafts
Fair in August.

↑ A local basket-weaver
practising their craft
in Castelsardo

Sardinian Razors

The most prized examples of the
iconic Sardinian shepherd's knife,
the *resolza* (razor), are handmade
by blacksmiths in Pattada (p197).
Finding an authentic one isn't
always easy, so beware of imita-
tions; Coltelleria di Deroma Antonio
in Pattada (Piazza Vittorio Veneto 8)
offers a fine selection of the real thing.

←

A traditional shepherd's knife
with a wooden handle

Cork Crafts

As you're travelling through the
countryside, particularly in the arid
region around Calangianus (p191),
you might notice groves of gnarly
trees with bright red trunks that have
been stripped of their bark. These are
cork oaks, which have been supplying
wine stoppers for the island since pre-
Roman times. Imaginative artisans
have found countless other uses for
this versatile material, and today you
can buy bowls, boxes, and even pens.

→

Inspecting wine corks made
from local bark in Calangianus

A YEAR IN
SARDINIA

JANUARY

△ **Cap d'Any** *(early Jan)*. New Year's celebrations in Alghero, featuring live music, folk dancing, traditional food and plenty of wine.

Feast of Sant'Antonio Abate *(16–17 Jan)*. Huge bonfires and dramatic processions take place in several interior towns in honour of the Egyptian St Anthony, one of the first Christian monks.

FEBRUARY

Sagra del Bogamarì *(all month)*. A food-filled extravaganza in Alghero, honouring the sea urchin.
△ **Carnival** *(mid-Feb)*. Weeks of colourful parades, daring horse races and other entertainment.
Sa Sartiglia *(Shrove Tue)*. Celebrated especially in Oristano, this marks the end of Carnival.

MAY

Festa di Sant'Efisio *(1–4 May)*. A commemoration of the end of several 17th-century plagues, with a procession of costumed people and decorated ox-drawn carts that leads from Cagliari to Pula.

△ **Cavalcata Sarda** *(end of May)*. The streets of Sassari are filled with market stalls, music and horses in this celebration of spring.

JUNE

Festa di San Giovanni Battista *(24 Jun)*. A folk festival in Quartu Sant'Elena, featuring bonfires, almond cakes, and pagan rituals dating back some 3,000 years.

△ **Sardegna Pride** *(late Jun–early Jul)*. Cagliari hosts rainbow-coloured parades at this growing annual LGBT+ event.

SEPTEMBER

Corsa degli Scalzi *(first weekend)*. A barefoot race in Cabras, re-enacting the rescue of St Salvatore's statue from attack by the Moors.

Festa Manna *(7–15 Sep)*. Processions, concerts, dances and archaeological tours in Luogosanto, all in honour of the local patron saint.

△ **Autunno in Barbagia** *(7 Sep–mid-Dec)*. A celebration of autumn in the villages of Barbagia.

OCTOBER

Santa Vitalia Festival *(first Mon)*. Celebrated in Serrenti, this religious festival honours the martyrdom of St Vitalia in AD 120.

△ **Sagra delle Castagne e delle Nocciole** *(last Sun)*. Aritzo's streets are full of life during this nut festival, where roasted chestnuts, hazelnuts, craft beer and wine are offered.

MARCH

Holy Week (Sa Chida Santa) *(Mar/Apr)*. An important religious time for the whole island, where sombre processions, ancient rituals and chantings occur as part of the re-enactment of the last days of Jesus' life until the Resurrection.

△ **Easter Sunday** *(Mar/Apr)*. Austerity gives way to celebrations of Jesus' Resurrection, and music fills the air as families share a traditional meal together.

APRIL

△ **Festa Patronale** *(2nd Sat after Easter)*. One of the oldest religious festivals in Sardinia, held in honour of Sant'Antioco's patron saint, it includes a wonderful food and wine fair, fireworks and live music in the evenings.

Fiera di San Marco *(25 Apr)*. Held since 1839, this fair in Ollastra features farmers markets, equestrian shows, and best-of-breed contests for livestock.

JULY

△ **S'Ardia** *(5–8 Jul)*. A spectacular horse race around the village church in Sedilo.

L'Isola delle Storie *(early Jul)*. Three-day literary festival in Gavoi.

Festa della Madonna del Naufrago *(mid-Jul)*. A procession in Villasimius honouring shipwrecked sailors.

AUGUST

Sa Coia Maurreddina *(first Sun)*. The historic ritual of the Mauritanian wedding is revived in Santandi.

△ **Festa di Santa Maria del Mare** *(first Sun)*. Farmers and fishermen don their finery and descend on the Temo river in Bosa for a boat procession.

Sagra del Redentore *(29 Aug)*. Nuoro's big event, celebrating the day in 1901 when the massive bronze statue of Cristo Redentore (Christ the Redeemer) was placed on top of Monte Ortobene.

NOVEMBER

△ **Rassegna dei Vini Novelli** *(early Nov)*. Milis celebrates the latest wines produced in the town and the surrounding region, with tastings and food pairings.

Festa della Madonna dello Schiavo *(15 Nov)*. A statue of the Madonna is worshipped as it passes through the town of Carloforte.

DECEMBER

Sagra delle Salsicce *(first Sun)*. A sausage and wine festival in Siligo, with stalls serving up all manner of sausages along with various Italian wines and beers.

△ **Natale** *(25 Dec)*. Christmas is celebrated throughout Sardinia with craft markets, Santa Claus parades and elaborate nativity scenes.

A BRIEF
HISTORY

Set in the middle of the western Mediterranean Sea, Sardinia has been repeatedly invaded from all directions. This large island was difficult to subdue, however, and the rise and fall of subsequent occupiers left an impressive cultural and architectural inheritance.

Early Inhabitants

The first people to settle the island are thought to have crossed over a natural causeway that once linked Tuscany and Sardinia, some 450,000 to 150,000 years ago. Around 9000 BC, the island began to see populations arrive from Asia Minor, the African coasts, the Iberian peninsula and Liguria. These early settlers prospered from the fertile, mineral-rich land and the obsidian mines at Monte Arci.

By 3000 BC the Sardinians had grouped into tribes of shepherds and warriors. They lived in villages with thatched-roof huts and buried their dead in rock-cut tombs. By about

Did You Know?

The ancient ruins at Monte d'Accoddi bear similarities to the ziggurat temples of Mesopotamia.

Timeline of events

250,000 BC
Approximate date of hominid finger bone found in a cave in the Logudoro region.

150,000 BC
Earliest evidence of stone tools, found during modern excavations near Perfugas.

1800 BC
Rise of nuraghic civilization.

1000 BC
Phoenician ships moor along the coast.

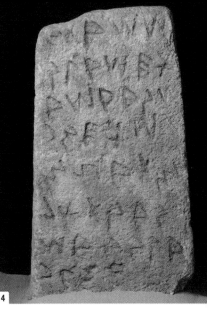

1800 BC this rural society had evolved into the nuraghic civilization (p70), which built thousands of circular stone structures (nuraghi) across the island. Many of these are still visible, though their true purpose remains a mystery.

Phoenicians, Carthaginians and Romans

Around 1000 BC, Phoenician ships from the Levant began to use inlets along the Sardinian coast as harbours. As commerce intensified, they founded the cities of Nora, Sulcis, Tharros, Olbia, Bithia and Karalis (today's Cagliari). After an initial period of peace, the nuraghic populations attacked the Phoenician settlements, who turned to Carthage (today's Tunis) for help in 509 BC. In 238 BC, following their defeat in the First Punic (Carthaginian) War, the Carthaginians ceded Sardinia to the Romans. The Sardinians were hostile to their new rulers, who collected the island's wheat, mined its metals, and coerced the local population into forced labour. Rebellions battled on for years, most notably in the interior. The Romans never succeeded in subduing the entire island, and the fall of the Western Roman Empire in the 5th century marked the end of their Sardinian rule.

1 A 17th-century map of Sardinia.

2 The ruins of a structure at Monte d'Accoddi, built in the 3rd millennium BC.

3 A bronze votive boat crafted by the nuraghic civilization.

4 An ancient stele from Nora, engraved with a Phoenician inscription.

730–700 BC
The first Phoenician harbours are built.

238 BC
The Carthaginians lose the First Punic War.

227 BC
Sardinia, together with Corsica, becomes a province of Rome.

550 BC
The Carthaginians arrive and found the first Punic cities.

AD 66
Roman Sardinia becomes an imperial province and is occupied by legions.

1

Middle Ages

As Rome's strength weakened, the Vandals – a Germanic people who maintained a kingdom in North Africa – seized the opportunity to conquer Sardinia in AD 456. Liberated shortly afterwards by Byzantium, the island became one of its seven African provinces. The subsequent power vacuum, aggravated by Arab invasions, gave rise to the four autonomous *giudicati*, or principalities, of Torres, Gallura, Arborea and Cagliari. After fierce campaigns against the Arabs, the Pisans and Genoese of the Italian mainland took over parts of the island in around AD 1000. A few centuries later, in 1295, Pope Boniface VIII gave James II of Aragon control of Corsica and Sardinia in exchange for the Spanish relinquishment of Sicily. James II's son, Alfonso IV of Aragon, arrived on Sardinia with his army in 1323.

Spanish Rule

By the end of the 14th century, Arborea was the only *giudicato* still resisting Spanish rule. However, it, too, lost its independence following the death of its ruler Eleonora d'Arborea in

ELEONORA D'ARBOREA

The remarkable Eleonora d'Arborea (1340-1404) inherited the Arborea *giudicato* from her father in 1383, and by 1394 had gained control of most of Sardinia. She published the *Carta de Logu* in 1392, Sardinia's first official code of law, which included provisions that defended women's rights. It remained in effect until 1827.

Timeline of events

456
The Vandals arrive during the fall of the Roman Empire.

534
Byzantium liberates Sardinia, which becomes one of its African provinces.

600
Pope Gregory the Great sets out to convert Sardinia to Christianity.

711
Arab invasions begin and continue for centuries afterwards.

1016
Pope Benedict VIII asks Genoa and Pisa to intervene in Sardinia.

2 3

1404. The Spanish era continued for a further 300 years; despite being somewhat tumultuous, this period saw the founding of the island's first universities, in Sassari in 1562 and Cagliari in 1620. The death of the childless Charles II of Spain in 1700 triggered the War of the Spanish Succession (1701–14), which resulted in control of the island being passed to Austria, who in turn ceded it to King Vittorio Amedeo II of the House of Savoy (a royal Italian family) in exchange for Sicily in 1718.

The Kingdom of Sardinia

One of the first acts of the Savoyard government was to expand the island's universities. However, a serious economic and social crisis led to unrest and the spread of banditry. After the Revolution of 1789, France made vain attempts to conquer Sardinia, but, by 1795, the island was overwhelmed by revolutionary fervour of its own and a short-lived rebellion broke out in Cagliari. Reforms were undertaken by the Savoys in the early 19th century, and in 1847 the kingdom of Sardinia was linked with the Savoyard territory of Piedmont in *"fusione perfetta"*. In 1861, both became part of the new Kingdom of Italy.

1 Alfonso IV of Aragon, ruler of Sardinia in the 14th century.

2 Antique books in the library of the University of Cagliari.

3 Relief dedicated to Carolo Felici Savoyard, King of Sardinia from 1821 to 1831.

1323

Alfonso of Aragon lands in Sardinia.

1402

Anno de Sa Mortagia Manna, the year of the great plague.

1718

Sardinia is ceded to the House of Savoy in the Treaty of London.

1857

Giuseppe Garibaldi, one of Italy's founding fathers, settles on Caprera.

1861

Sardinia, together with Piedmont, joins the Kingdom of Italy.

Growing Industrialization

Industrialization in Sardinia began to make progress after Italian unification: in 1871 the first railway line was built and the mines in Sulcis and Iglesiente became fully operational. The first daily newspapers were founded and Nuoro became the centre of a cultural movement that included the Nobel Prize-winning novelist Grazia Deledda. In World War I, the heroism of the Brigata Sassari infantry brigade emerged as a symbol of the island's new confidence, and led to the foundation of the Partito Sardo d'Azione political party in 1921. Between the wars, the mining industry continued to develop, and the town of Carbonia was founded by Mussolini in 1938. While Sardinia was not invaded during World War II, Allied bombs did destroy much of Cagliari in 1943 and ferry transport was halted until 1947, leaving the island isolated for several years.

A Changing Landscape

On 31 January 1948, Sardinia became an autonomous region of Italy. A wide-ranging programme of land reclamation and artificial lakes – such as Lake Omodeo, created by a dam on the

↑ An early Sardinian newspaper from 1899.

Timeline of events

1889–99
Arrival of army task force to combat rampant banditry in Sardinia.

1926
The Sardinian writer Grazia Deledda wins a Nobel Prize for Literature.

1950
Malaria is eradicated from the island.

1943
Allied bombing seriously damages Cagliari.

1962
Development of the Costa Smeralda begins, triggering a boom in tourism.

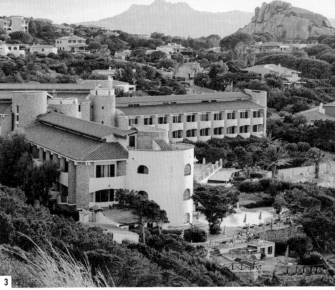

3

Tirso river – was carried out, significantly improving the health of previously malarial areas. This reclamation of the coastal marshes was crucial in kickstarting the modern development of the island. Sardinia's lovely shoreline, abandoned and shunned for millennia, was now ripe for tourism and the construction of seaside resorts. New luxury villas and holiday villages sprang up rapidly, and the Costa Smeralda, or Emerald Coast, became world-famous as an exclusive holiday area. Reclaimed land could also be used for agriculture for the first time, leading to the planting of market gardens and orchards.

1 The Tirso-Orzieri railway line under construction in the 19th century.

2 The village of Carbonia, built in 1938 by the Mussolini regime.

3 A luxury resort on the Costa Smeralda.

Sardinia Today

The island's economy has shifted, partly as a result of the changes to its topography: sheep-rearing is on the decline, while industry and services are developing with the increase in tourism, sometimes adversely affecting the environment. Sardinia at present appears to be at a crossroads, as modern life competes with the precious resources of unspoilt nature and habitat diversity. The island is nonetheless committed to sustainability, with a growing market in ecotourism.

1971

Industrial workers outnumber farmers for the first time.

1985

Francesco Cossiga from Sassari is elected President of Italy.

1998

Renato Soru founds Tiscali, which becomes one of Europe's biggest internet service providers.

2011

The first wind farms on the island get the go-ahead.

2017

Alghero hosts the 100th edition of the Giro d'Italia cycle race.

EXPERIENCE

A street in the Villanova district of Cagliari

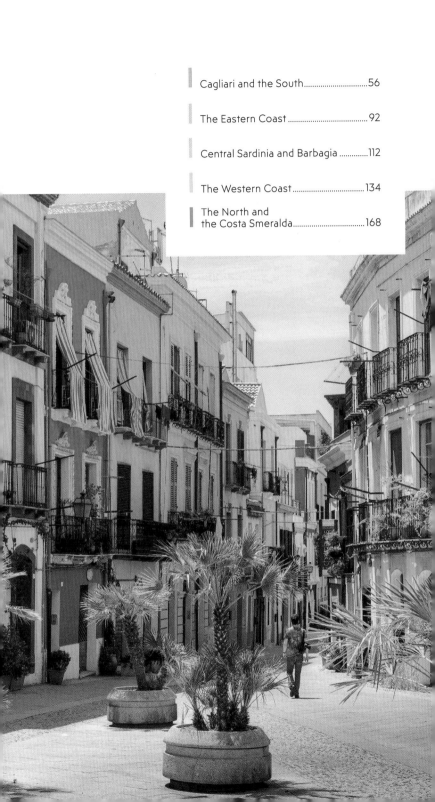

CAGLIARI AND THE SOUTH

Southern Sardinia has been a centre of mining since 5,000 BC, when the island's early inhabitants discovered how to extract and smelt copper and silver. The industry continued to play an important role in the 1st millennium BC with the arrival of the Phoenicians, who established Nora – the island's first official city – as a base from which to trade and ship mined ore across the Mediterranean. In the 8th–6th centuries BC the Phoenicians founded Cagliari, then known as Karalis ("rocky city"), as a stopover for trade ships en route between Lebanon and Iberia. The city soon became a major trade centre in the Mediterranean, prospering under Roman rule for almost 700 years before becoming part of the Byzantine Empire in 534. In 1258, the Pisans took over Cagliari and the rest of the region, bringing additional wealth with an expansion of the silver mines. The mineral-rich land continued to be exploited by various powers up to the Fascist era, but the mining industry declined after World War II as demand decreased. Cagliari underwent a significant reconstruction period following heavy bombing during the war, but its port today continues to be a leading transport hub.

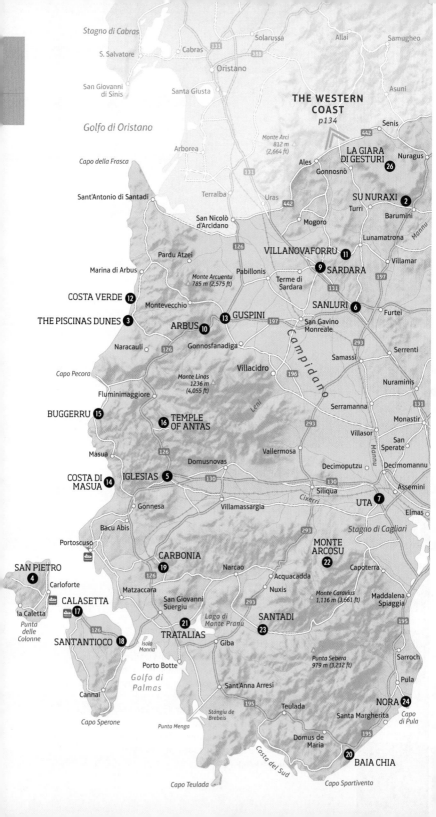

Stagno di Cabras
S. Salvatore
Cabras
131
388
Solarussa
Allai
Samugheo

San Giovanni di Sinis
Oristano

Golfo di Oristano

Santa Giusta

Asuni

Senis

THE WESTERN COAST
p134

442

LA GIARA DI GESTURI **26**

Nuragus

Capo della Frasca

Monte Arci 812 m (2,664 ft)

Ales
Gonnosnò

SU NURAXI **2**

Sant'Antonio di Santadi

131

Uras

Turri
Barumini

Terralba

442

Mogoro

Lunamatrona
Villamar

San Nicolò d'Arcidano

126

Pardu Atzei

VILLANOVAFORRU **11**

Marina di Arbus

Pabillonis
Terme di Sardara

SARDARA **9**

197

COSTA VERDE **12**

Montevecchio

Monte Arcuentu 785 m (2,575 ft)

SANLURI **6**

Furtei

THE PISCINAS DUNES **3**

ARBUS **10**

GUSPINI **13**

San Gavino Monreale

197

Serrenti

Naracauli

126

Gonnosfanadiga

Samassi

Nuraminis

Capo Pecora

Monte Linas 1236 m (4,055 ft)

Villacidro

196

Serramanna

131

Fluminimaggiore

Serramanna

Monastir

BUGGERRU **15**

TEMPLE OF ANTAS **16**

293

Villasor
San Sperate

Masua

126

Domusnovas

Vallermosa

Decimoputzu

Decimomannu

COSTA DI MASUA **14**

IGLESIAS **5**

130

Siliqua

130

Assemini

Gonnesa

Villamassargia

Cixerri

UTA **7**

Elmas

Bacu Abis

Stagno di Cagliari

Portoscuso

293

CARBONIA **19**

Narcao

MONTE ARCOSU **22**

Capoterra

SAN PIETRO **4**

Carloforte

Matzaccara

Acquacadda
Nuxis

Monte Caravius 1,116 m (3,661 ft)

Maddalena Spiaggia

195

la Caletta

CALASETTA **17**

San Giovanni Suergiu

Lago di Monte Pranu

SANTADI **23**

Punta delle Colonne

SANT'ANTIOCO **18**

Isola Manna

TRATALIAS **21**

Giba

Sarroch

Punta Sebera 979 m (3,212 ft)

Pula

Porto Botte

Golfo di Palmas

Sant'Anna Arresi

195

NORA **24**

Cannai

Stàngiu de Brebeis

Punta Menga

Teulada

Santa Margherita

Capo di Pula

Capo Sperone

BAIA CHIA **20**

Domus de Maria

195

Costa del Sud

Capo Teulada

Capo Spartivento

CAGLIARI AND THE SOUTH

Must Sees
1. Cagliari
2. Su Nuraxi
3. The Piscinas Dunes
4. San Pietro
5. Iglesias

Experience More
6. Sanluri
7. Uta
8. Serri
9. Sardara
10. Arbus
11. Villanovaforru
12. Costa Verde
13. Guspini
14. Costa di Masua
15. Buggerru
16. Temple of Antas
17. Calasetta
18. Sant'Antioco
19. Carbonia
20. Baia Chia
21. Tratalias
22. Monte Arcosu
23. Santadi
24. Nora
25. Parco dei Sette Fratelli
26. La Giara di Gesturi
27. Quartu Sant'Elena

CENTRAL SARDINIA AND BARBAGIA p112

THE EASTERN COAST p92

Nurallaó
Isili
SERRI 8
Mandas
Gesico
Guasila
Suelli
San Basilio
Ballao
Senorbi
San Nicolò Gerrei
Villasalto
Quirra
C. S. Lorenzo
Sant'Andrea Frius
Donori
San Vito
Villaputzu
Dolianova
Muravera
S a r r a b u s
Punta Serpeddi 1,067 m (3,500 ft)
San Priamo
Burcei
Sestu
Sinnai
V.gio di C. Ferrato
Capo Ferrato
Selargius
PARCO DEI SETTE FRATELLI 25
Monte dei Sette Fratelli 1,023 m (3,356 ft)
Cagliari Elmas Airport
27 QUARTU SANT'ELENA
Castiadas
Costa Rei
1 CAGLIARI
Poetto
Casa della Marina
Geremeas
Villasimius
Golfo di Cagliari
Capo Boi

CAGLIARI AND THE SOUTH

0 kilometres 15
0 miles 15
N

Looking out over the city from the Castello district ↑

❶

CAGLIARI

 D6 ⊠🚕🚌 **𝑖** Via Roma 145; www.cagliariturismo.it

The city's sheltered position, tucked into the Golfo di Cagliari, has long made it an important harbour. The Phoenicians first established Cagliari in the 8th–6th centuries BC, but its present appearance was largely the work of the Pisans, who developed the Castello district in the Middle Ages. Flanked on three sides by sea and marshes, this picturesque city offers delightful sights around every corner.

① Palazzo Civico

 Via Roma 📞 070 67 71

At the corner of Via Roma and Largo Carlo Felice is the elegant Palazzo Civico (town hall). Built in the early 20th century in Neo-Gothic style, the building was restored after it suffered bomb damage during World War II. Its façade is decorated with double lancet windows and turrets, while inside – hanging in the Sala della Giunta and in the Sala del Consiglio – are paintings by Filippo Figari and Giovanni Marghinotti that depict key moments in Sardinian history.

② Roman Amphitheatre

Viale Sant'Ignazio da Laconi ⏰ Summer: 10am–7pm daily; winter 9am–5pm daily 🌐 beniculturali cagliari.it

Northwest of the city centre is the most significant evidence of Roman Cagliari. The impressive 2nd-century AD amphitheatre was hewn out directly of the rock, in the style of Greek theatres. Circus acts with wild beasts were performed here, as well as *naumachiae* – popular recreations of naval battles. A canal system made it possible to fill the arena with water.

Much of the brick masonry collapsed during the Middle Ages and stone was taken from the tiers to build the Castello district. Still visible among the remains, however, are the *cavea* (the pit that held the wild beasts), the corridors behind the tiers and underground passageways, as well as some of the tiers where the spectators sat.

③ Bastione di San Remy

Terrazza Umberto I ⏰ 24 hrs

Built in the late 19th century over the Spanish ramparts, the Bastione di San Remy can be reached from Piazza Costituzione up a stairway that leads to a wide terrace,

 PICTURE PERFECT
City Panorama

With its spectacular views across the city, Bastione San di Remy is the perfect spot to snap some panoramic shots. The large arch here makes a useful device with which to frame the vista.

Terrazza Umberto I (which is also accessible from Porta dei Leoni if the stairway is closed). From here, there is a magnificent view over the seafront to the surrounding marshes.

> **Underneath the cathedral altar is a crypt containing the tombs of the princes of the House of Savoy, as well as relics of almost 200 martyrs.**

④

Cattedrale

⌂ Piazza Palazzo
🕐 8am–8pm daily
🌐 duomodicagliari.it

Cagliari's Cathedral of Santa Maria was built by the Pisans in the 11th and 12th centuries. Gradually transformed over the centuries – particularly with 17th-century additions – today's façade is the result of restoration in the 1930s, which reinstated the original Romanesque style. The four lions that guard the entrance all date from this period.

Inside, Santa Maria retains much Baroque decoration, as well as some original detail. Close to the entrance are two pulpits by Master Guglielmo, sculpted in 1162 for the cathedral of Pisa and donated to Cagliari by the Tuscan city. In the chapterhouse, paintings include a *Flagellation of Christ* attributed to Guido Reni.

Underneath the altar is a crypt containing the tombs of the princes of the House of Savoy, as well as relics of almost 200 martyrs. The Treasury, meanwhile, hosts the **Museo del Duomo**, which displays precious church items such as chalices and amphoras, as well as a large gilded cross.

Museo del Duomo

⌂ Via del Fossario 5 🕐 4:30–7:30pm Tue–Fri, 10am–1pm & 4:30–7:30pm Sat & Sun
🌐 museoduomodicagliari.it

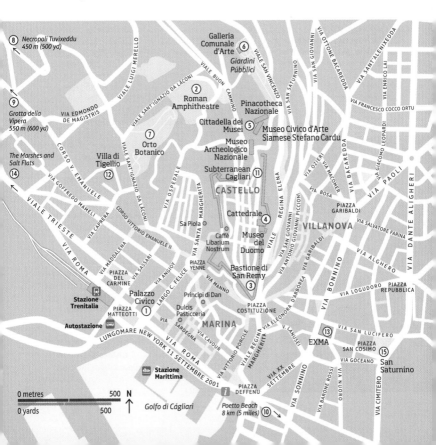

INSIDER TIP
Walking Tour

The main square in the Castello district, Piazza Yenne, is lined with boutiques, gelaterias and cafés. A free walking tour meets here at the obelisk, at 10am Monday to Friday – just look for the pink T-shirts.

⑤

Cittadella dei Musei

📍 Piazza Arsenale   📞 070 67 57 627

At the northern end of the Castello district is this modern museum complex. Fashioned from the former royal arsenal, which had been built on the site of the Spanish citadel, the complex houses a trio of excellent museums: the Museo Archeologico Nazionale, the Museo Civico d'Arte Siamese Stefano Cardu and the Pinacoteca Nazionale.

The **Museo Archeologico Nazionale** (National Archaeological Museum) is devoted to the history of Sardinia. The ground-floor exhibits are arranged in chronological order, from the Neolithic era

to the Middle Ages; the other floors are organized by archaeological site. In the Neolithic hall are fine alabaster statues of female divinities, including one in the shape of a cross from Senorbì. Objects from the late Bronze Age include axes with raised edges. There is an exceptional collection of nuraghic bronze figurines, found in the Tempio di Teti at Abini. The collection includes a particularly striking votive sword decorated with deer and the figure of a tribal chief or warrior. In the third hall is a statuette of a musician playing the *launeddas*, a Sardinian woodwind instrument.

The Phoenician and Roman periods are represented by objects found mostly at sites around Cagliari, Tharros and Nora. These include jewellery and amulets, small coloured glass heads and terracotta votive statuettes. Among the loveliest pieces of jewellery are an embossed golden bracelet and gold earrings from Tharros.

The early Christian pieces, such as jugs, lamps and gold jewellery, give an insight into the island's medieval culture, displaying influences from various Byzantine, Vandal and Moorish invaders.

The **Museo Civico d'Arte Siamese Stefano Cardu** (Stefano Cardu Siamese Art Museum) exhibits most of the 1,300 objects donated to the city in 1917 by Stefano Cardu, a Sardinian who served at the court of the King of Siam (modern Thailand). The collection includes imperial gold and silver objects, ivory statues and vases, mostly dating from the 11th century.

The three-storey **Pinacoteca Nazionale** (National Art Gallery) contains a mixture of art and ethnographic objects. Its entrance is on the upper floor,

←

Rest in Egypt by Michele Cavaro, on display in the Pinacoteca Nazionale

where 15th- and 16th-century paintings include Catalan and Sardinian altarpieces, like the *Annunciation* by Joan Mates (active 1391–1431), *Sant'Eligio* by the Master of Sanluri (early 16th century), and *Nostra Signora della Neve* (1568) by Michele Cavaro.

The middle floor houses 17th- and 18th-century paintings and reveals the original Spanish fortification wall (1552–63). The lower floor features the restored *Retablo di San Cristoforo*, rescued from the Chiesa di San Francesco di Stampace, which was damaged by lightning in 1871.

Museo Archeologico Nazionale

♿ 📍 Cittadella dei Musei   🕘 9am–8pm Tue–Sun   🌐 museoarcheocagliari. beniculturali.it

Museo Civico d'Arte Siamese Stefano Cardu

♿ 📍 Cittadella dei Musei   🕘 10am–6pm Tue–Sun   🌐 sistemamuseale.musei civicicagliari.it

Pinacoteca Nazionale

♿ 📍 Cittadella dei Musei   🕘 9am–8pm Tue–Sun   🌐 pinacoteca.cagliari.beni culturali.it

A display at the Museo Archeologico Nazionale, part of the Cittadella dei Musei *(inset)*

Galleria Comunale d'Arte

🏛 Giardini Pubblici, Largo Giuseppe Dessì ⏰ 10am-8pm Tue-Sun (to 6pm Sep-May) 🌐 sistemamuseale.museicivicicagliari.it

The Municipal Art Gallery has a collection of significant works by Sardinian artists from the late 19th century to the 1970s. On the ground floor are works by Francesco Ciusa. The first floor features contemporary art.

Orto Botanico

🏛 Viale Sant'Ignazio da Laconi 11-13 ⏰ Apr-Oct: 9am-6pm Tue-Sun; Nov-Mar: 9am-2pm Tue-Sun 🌐 sites.unica.it/hbk

Founded in 1866, the botanical gardens contain over 500 species of tropical plants from the Americas, Africa, Asia and the Pacific, as well as from the Mediterranean region. The grounds are full of small caves such as the Grotta Gennari, used to cultivate ferns, as well as the remains of Roman tunnels constructed to supply water to the gardens, a Roman gallery and a well.

Necropoli Tuvixeddu

🏛 Via Falzarego ⏰ 7am-sunset daily

West of the botanical gardens are hundreds of underground burial chambers belonging to the Punic necropolis. The area is rather overgrown with brambles, but the funerary paintings on the tombs are worth a visit, especially the *Tomba del Sid* (Tomb of Sid) and the *Tomba dell'Ureo* (Tomb of the Uraeus).

Grotta della Vipera

🏛 Viale Sant'Avendrace 🕐 For restoration; check website for details of reopening 🌐 beniculturali cagliari.it

This tomb belongs to Attilia Pomptilla, wife of Cassius Philippus, exiled here in the 1st century AD. Two snakes adorn the façade – giving rise to the name "viper's cave" – and on the walls are inscriptions in Greek and Latin.

DRINK

Caffè Libarium Nostrum

Relax under a shaded canopy at this popular bar, surrounded by old city walls, and sip an Aperol Spritz while taking in the spectacular views over the city and the sea. Visit at sunset, when the setting is at its most atmospheric.

Via Santa Croce 33
346 522 0212

Reached by a short and easy bus ride from the centre of Cagliari, this vast, white sandy stretch overlooking the Golfo deli Angeli has clear turquoise water and long, shallow edges, perfect for kids to frolic in. There are five bus stops along the length of the beach, as well as full facilities – including bike and boat rentals and dozens of eateries and bars. This is a highly popular place with locals, who jog along the boardwalk, play beach volleyball in the soft sand, and kite-surf in the waves further out. Nearby are the salt marshes, where flamingos sometimes reside, and the site of Saline di Molentargius – an old salt mine once used by the Romans.

Did You Know?

Buenos Aires, the capital of Argentina, is named after the Virgin of Bonaria shrine in Cagliari.

chamber named after King Vittorio Emanuele II. It is accessed from the Casa di Riposo in Viale Sant'Ignazio via a dingy stairway, which leads into the eerie chamber. The walls, around 2,500 sq m (26,900 sq ft), are covered with thick facing to protect them from the humidity.

---

⑩
Poetto Beach

Viale Lungomare del Golfo Line PF, PQ, Poetto Express
cagliariturismo.it

Cagliari's famous beach extends for more than 8 km (5 miles), from the Roman ruin-topped promontory of Sella del Diavolo (Devil's Saddle) to the town of Margine Rosso on the Quartu Sant'Elena coast.

---

⑪
Subterranean Cagliari

Viale Sant'Ignazio
For guided tours only; see website cagliari tour.com

In the area below the Roman amphitheatre, the hospital and the Orto Botanico, there are a number of underground chambers and passageways cut out of the rock by the Phoenicians. The most spectacular of these is the vast

---

⑫
Villa di Tigellio

Via Giovanni Carbonazzi
Summer: 10am-2pm, 3-7pm; winter: 9am-5pm
beniculturalicagliari.it

Southeast of the botanical gardens, Villa di Tigellio is a group of three Roman villas and baths dating from the imperial era. The first house has a *tablinum*, the room used to receive guests, which opens onto the central atrium.

← Sunbathers and watersports enthusiasts enjoying the delights of Poetto beach

EXMA

⊗⊚ 🚻 **Via San Lucifero 71**
🕐 **9am–1pm & 4–8pm Tue–Sun** 🌐 **consorziocamu.it/spazi/exma**

On the eastern side of the Castello district stands the former municipal slaughter-house, built in the mid-19th century and closed in 1964. This dark-red building, decorated with sculpted heads of cows, has been restructured to house the city's contemporary arts centre, EXMA (Exhibiting and Moving Arts).

The centre's cultural calendar offers temporary exhibitions of photography, painting and sculpture, as well as courses for children and adults. Classical music concerts are held in the courtyard in the summer and in the auditorium in the winter.

The Marshes and Salt Flats

📌 **Molo Sanità; 070 37 91 92 16** 🚌 **P from Via Roma for Poetto; 8 for Santa Gilla**

An expansive network of marshes and lakes extends around the outskirts of Cagliari, particularly along the western shore of the bay. The vast lagoon of the Santa Gilla marsh stretches over 40 sq km (15 sq miles), including the ancient Macchiareddu salt flats. These saltworks are now the only ones in operation in the area.

After years of neglect and environmental deterioration, the marshy areas around Cagliari have finally become reserves, and the area once again has a rich and varied fauna. To the east of the city, the Molentargius marsh is a favourite refuge for migratory birds. At least 170 species have been identified here, which is one-third of the entire bird population of

Europe. Between August and March, flamingos attract dozens of naturalists. Since 1993 these creatures have begun once again to nest along the banks of the Molentargius marsh.

San Saturnino

🏛 **Piazza San Cosimo** ☎ **070 201 03 01** 🕐 **9am–1pm Mon & Thu–Sat**

East of the EXMA building is the church of San Saturnino, also known as Santi Cosma e Damiano. Restored in the late 20th and early 21st centuries, but still not completely refurbished, this simple church is one of the oldest Christian buildings on the island. It was begun in the 5th century to commemorate the martyrdom of Saturnino (also known as Saturno), the city's patron saint, who was decapitated in AD 304 for refusing to renounce his Christian faith.

In the Middle Ages, San Saturnino, together with its adjacent monastery, became an important religious and cultural centre. The Greek cross plan of the church was enlarged in the 11th century

↑ The Basilica of San Saturnino, dedicated to Cagliari's patron saint

by French Victorine friars from Marseille, who constructed three aisles with barrel vaults. Inside, a marble ex voto holds the oldest representation of San Saturno.

Glass windows have been placed in the sturdy tufa (limestone) construction to prevent further damage and decay from humidity and air, and this has given the church a rather modern appearance. Nonetheless, it is still a fascinating place to visit.

WILDLIFE OF THE MARSHLANDS

Many migratory and endemic bird species populate the marshes around Cagliari. These feed upon the small creatures, such as the brine shrimp *Artemia salina*, which thrive in the salt-rich water. In addition to the colony of flamingos, which sometimes exceeds 10,000, you will also see many other species of water bird such as black-winged stilts, avocets, cormorants and teal. The waters of Macchiareddu salt flats, on the other hand, are populated by mallards, coots and pintail ducks.

A SHORT WALK
CASTELLO

Distance 1 km (half a mile) **Nearest bus stop** Indipendenza **Time** 20 minutes

The Castello district, the oldest part of Cagliari, was built by the Pisans and Aragonese. Positioned at the top of a hill, and protected by ancient city walls, it consisted of aristocratic mansions and the city's cathedral. With time, its function as a centre of power waned, and the elegant buildings gradually deteriorated. It is nonetheless a delightful place for a stroll today, with imposing watchtowers dominating the entrance gates and a grand esplanade along parts of the former fortifications.

The richly decorated interior of Cagliari's elegant cathedral

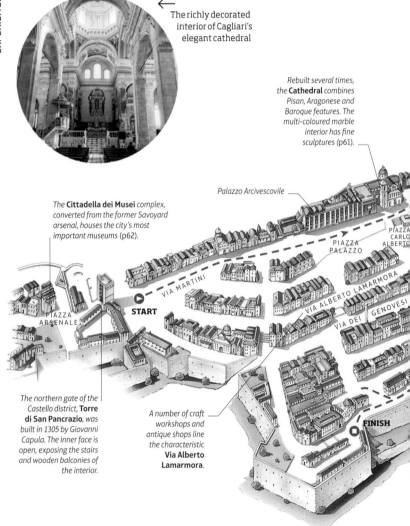

Rebuilt several times, the **Cathedral** combines Pisan, Aragonese and Baroque features. The multi-coloured marble interior has fine sculptures (p61).

Palazzo Arcivescovile

The **Cittadella dei Musei** complex, converted from the former Savoyard arsenal, houses the city's most important museums (p62).

The northern gate of the Castello district, **Torre di San Pancrazio**, was built in 1305 by Giovanni Capula. The inner face is open, exposing the stairs and wooden balconies of the interior.

A number of craft workshops and antique shops line the characteristic **Via Alberto Lamarmora**.

↑ The grand limestone arch at the entrance to Bastione di San Remy

Locator Map
See p61

*Overlooking the Bastione di San Remy, **Palazzo Boyl** was built in 1840. It incorporates the remains of the Torre dell'Aquila (Eagle's Tower), one of the large Pisan towers that stood over the entrance gates of the ancient city.*

*In the early 1900s, the Spanish defensive walls were transformed into the **Bastione di San Remy**, opening out onto a wide esplanade with spectacular views (p60).*

*The **Porta due Leoni** gate that leads into the lower Marina district owes its name to the two Romanesque lions' heads (leoni) above the arch.*

Did You Know?

The severed heads of executed prisoners used to be hung from the Torre dell'Elefante.

*The **Torre dell'Elefante**, or Elephant's Tower, was built by local architect Giovanni Capula in 1307. The mechanism for opening the gates is still visible and an elephant statue, after which the tower was named, can be seen on the façade.*

| 0 metres | 50 |
| 0 yards | 50 |

 N

→

The remains of the defensive fortress that overlooked the village and its surrounds

Did You Know?

Su Nuraxi is the only UNESCO World Heritage Site in Sardinia.

 ② ⊘ ⊘

SU NURAXI

🅰 D5 🚗 1 km (0.5 miles) W of Barumini 🚌 To Barumini then 1 km (0.5 miles) on foot ⏱ 9am-7:30pm daily (to 4pm in winter); Museum: summer: 10am-8pm daily, winter: 10am-5pm daily 🌐 fondazionebarumini.it

Containing the remains of the largest and most complete nuraghic fortress in all of Sardinia, this archaeological site is truly fascinating. Scenically surrounded by fertile countryside, and featuring a labyrinthine village built around an imposing central tower, it is deservingly one of the island's most popular attractions.

💬 INSIDER TIP
Family Fun

A few minutes down the road from Su Nuraxi is the Parco Sardegna in Miniatura *(www. sardegnainminiatura. it)*. This family attraction features scale models of the island's monuments, as well as a life-size reconstruction of a nuraghic village.

Su Nuraxi is one of a number of nuraghic sites that have been uncovered during excavations in the area around Barumini. The original settlement here dates from 1500 BC, during the Middle Bronze Age. Built on a hill, the 19-m- (62-ft-) high fortress occupied an excellent vantage point, with clear views over the surrounding plains. In the 7th century BC, with the threat of Phoenician invasion, the central section of the fortress – consisting of a tower connected to four external nuraghi – was further protected by a thick outer wall with turrets and a sentinel's walkway. The village gradually developed outside the main fortifications with single- and multi-room dwellings, including a flour mill and bakery. The area was inhabited for almost 2,000 years, although after the Carthaginian conquest, the upper parts of the fort were demolished and the site lost its strategic importance.

↑ Exploring the inside of one of the towers

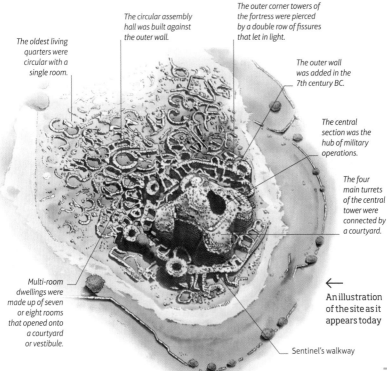

The circular assembly hall was built against the outer wall.

The outer corner towers of the fortress were pierced by a double row of fissures that let in light.

The oldest living quarters were circular with a single room.

The outer wall was added in the 7th century BC.

The central section was the hub of military operations.

The four main turrets of the central tower were connected by a courtyard.

Multi-room dwellings were made up of seven or eight rooms that opened onto a courtyard or vestibule.

← An illustration of the site as it appears today

Sentinel's walkway

THE NURAGHI

There are over 7,000 nuraghi in Sardinia, forming a familiar feature of the landscape with their distinctive truncated cones. They were built by a civilization that flourished on the island from 1800 to 500 BC (in some areas the nuraghic peoples resisted the Romans long after this date), but many of the workings of their society remain a mystery. Nuraghi served as both dwelling and fortress, and the towers were often surrounded by a village and wall. There is no trace of any written language, but over 1,500 bronze figures have been found in tombs and near holy wells. The figures, and other finds, are now on display in Sardinia's archaeological museums.

NURAGHIC STRUCTURES

Initially a nuraghe consisted of a single tower with a chamber made of inwardly stepped circular stone tiers. Built without mortar, these simple structures are the most commonly seen form of nuraghe on the island. Later, more towers were added, with connecting ramparts, resulting in more complex structures such as the Losa nuraghe at Abbasanta *(p160)*, the Su Nuraxi at Barumini *(p68)* and the Arrubiu Nuraghe near Orroli *(p106)*.

BRONZES

The distinctive bronze statuettes range in size from a few centimetres to almost half a metre. Most of the figures are men – many of which are warriors – but they also include women, animals and everyday objects such as boats and furnishings. They are thought to have been mainly used as votive offerings.

Examining the inside of a nuraghe at Su Nuraxi ↑

A Tomba dei Giganti
near Dorgali ↑

←
A bronze figure
of a tribal chief

NURAGHIC BURIALS

The nuraghic peoples built monumental tombs known as Tombe dei Giganti (Giants' Tombs) in which to bury their dead. The name refers to the tombs' large size - some are big enough to have held several hundred bodies. Each tomb consisted of a long covered corridor constructed with huge slabs of stone. The shape represented the horn of the bull god. A monolithic oval stele, with an opening at the base, formed the front face. Two rows of stones on either side, forming an arch, completed the burial chamber. The central, arched stele could sometimes be as much as 3 m (10 ft) tall, and is thought to have possibly represented a door to the underworld. The area around a typical Tomba dei Giganti was often surrounded by long rows of menhirs. The tombs can be found throughout Sardinia, but are particularly concentrated in the centre of the island.

The remains of the massive fortress at Arrubiu Nuraghe ↓

Did You Know?

The nudist beach at the southern end of the Piscinas Dunes is one of the largest in Europe.

3

THE PISCINAS DUNES

⚠ C6 🚌 To Arbus then private car along rough road via Ingurtosu

Stretching for 7 km (4 miles), the golden sands at Piscinas beach form an undulating dunescape of wild beauty that is ever changing with the wind.

The hills of sand at Piscinas and Is Arenas ("the sands" in Sardinian) are "moving" dunes, sometimes up to 50 m (164 ft) high, that rise up around the estuary of the River Piscinas. Wind erosion by the mistral – the cold north wind that blows in from France – continually changes the landscape, while strongly rooted pioneer plants work their way across the sand. The robust roots of marram grass (Ammophila arenaria) gradually stabilize the dune slopes, which are then covered by other salt-resistant plants such as juniper and lentiscus. This unique eco-logical niche is also the habitat for many animals, and tracks of foxes, wild cats, partridges and rabbits are a common sight on the sand. Remains of the 19th-century mines that were once the mainstay of the Sulcis regional economy are also still visible.

TOP 3 OTHER DUNES

Torre dei Corsari
This gorgeous beach on the Costa Verde is overlooked by a 17th-century watch-tower and features golden dunes edged with strawberry trees and junipers.

Sabbie d'Oro of Pistis
Also on the Costa Verde, these sculpted hills reach up to 30 m (98 ft) in height. At one end of the beach is an old Punic-Roman quarry.

Is Arenas Biancas
An impossibly white sandy beach near Teulada, with sugary dunes that extend for miles.

↑ The golden dunes of Piscinas beach, carpeted with maquis vegetation

1 The strongly rooted, perennial plant, *Ammophila arenaria* (also known as European marram grass), is typical of sandy environments.

2 Remnants of the 19th-century narrow-gauge railway that once used to transport material from the mines to the sea, are visible near the beach.

3 The Sardinian partridge favours sunny habitats with diverse vegetation. It was introduced to the island from North Africa by the Romans.

SAN PIETRO

⚑ B7 🚢 Delcomar from Calasetta or Portovesme **ℹ️** Via Garibaldi 72; www.sardegnaturismo.it/en/explore/san-pietro-0

The second-largest island in the Sulcis Archipelago, San Pietro is home to the captivating town of Carloforte and features a dazzling coastline fringed with towering cliffs and idyllic coves.

The only town on the island, Carloforte, is a delightful place to wander, with colourful alleys leading down to the port. Named after the apostle Peter, who is said to have taken refuge here during a storm, the island of San Pietro was virtually uninhabited until 1736, when Carlo Emanuele III offered it to a community of Ligurian coral fishermen whose ancestors had been exiled to the island of Tabarka, off the Tunisian coast. San Pietro's Ligurian origins can be seen in the architecture, dialect and cuisine, which also bears traces of North African influences. The rugged coast has spectacular coves that can be reached only by sea, and is a haven for snorkelling, diving and fishing. Its cliffs provide a habitat for several bird species, including the peregrine falcon, Corsican gull and the rare Eleonora's falcon.

> **INSIDER TIP**
> **Pedal Power**
>
> The island is ideal for exploring by bicycle – try the 14.5-km (9-mile) southeastern loop along the SP103, passing through farmland and maquis and along high sea cliffs. Bikes can be rented in Carloforte.

① Walls of silver rock on one side and brown rock on the other enclose the sheltered inlet of Cala Fico, which is home to the Eleonora's falcon.

② The Colonne di Carloforte, or Cape of Columns, is named after the trachytic stacks that jut out from the sea.

③ Protected from rough seas by Punta Spalmatore, the sheltered bay of La Caletta has a white, sandy beach lapped by crystal-clear waters.

Did You Know?

The locals on San Pietro speak Tabarchino, a 16th-century Genoese dialect.

↑ A colourful street in Carloforte, the only town on the island

5

IGLESIAS

A C6 **i** Piazza del Municipio; www.visitiglesias.it

Iglesias was founded in the 13th century by Count Ugolino della Gherardesca. Former Roman mines in the area were also reopened around this time, and by the mid-19th century the city had grown into an important mining centre. The industry declined after World War II, however, and many of the mines were abandoned. Evidence of the city's industrial past can still be seen today, creating a striking contrast with the well-preserved historic centre.

The attractive Piazza Lamarmora in Iglesias' historic old town

① Castello di Salvaterra

A Via Monte Altari
C 0781 27 45 07 (tourist office) **O** By appointment only, call the tourist office for details

A short walk north from the central Piazza Quintino Sella is the Castello di Salvaterra, a square Pisan tower built in 1284 as part of the city's medieval defensive walls. The tower is named after the hill on which it stands, from where there are expansive views over the city.

Further remains of the defensive walls are also visible along Via Eleonora d'Arborea and Via Roma. Originally, there were 23 towers along the walls, with four main gates, all to protect Iglesias (then called Villa di Chiesa) from the Aragonese invaders who ultimately conquered and renamed the city in 1324.

> **INSIDER TIP**
> **Take a Tour**
> Local operators offer tours to a number of intriguing nearby sights, including the Porto Flavia mining port, the sprawling Monteponi mining complex and the Grotte di Su Mannau cave.

② Chiesa di San Francesco

A Piazza San Francesco
C 0781 27 45 07 **O** 8.30am-11:30am & 5-7pm daily

The church of San Francesco was built between the 14th and 16th centuries and has remarkably intact Catalan Gothic details. It was built out of locally quarried pink granite, and features several side chapels dedicated to noble families. The church's original altarpiece has been relocated to the Pinacoteca Nazionale in Cagliari (p62).

③ Orto Botanico Linasia

A Località Case Marganai
C 0781 220 97 **O** 9am-noon & 4:30-7:30pm Tue-Sun

Located in the national forest of Marganai, 10 km (6 miles) northeast of Iglesias, the Linasia Botanical Gardens extend over a large area with various examples of local plants on display.

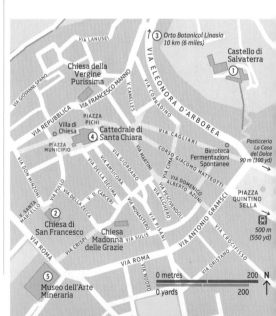

former local industry. Tours take visitors to underground tunnels, which were dug out by mining students in the 1930s as part of their training in different techniques. During World War II the tunnels found temporary use as air-raid shelters and an infirmary.

The museum is housed in the Asproni Mining Institute, an elegant Art Nouveau building that also contains an old geological museum with a vintage collection of fossils and minerals.

Nearby is the Grotta di San Giovanni and the sa Dom'e s'Orcu nuraghe site. The forest has several good walking trails and is littered with old mining relics.

---

 ④

Cattedrale di Santa Chiara

🏛 **Piazza del Municipio**
📞 **0781 221 42** ⏰ **9am–12:30pm & 3-8pm daily**

Opposite the Palazzo del Municipio is the cathedral of Santa Chiara. Completed in the late 17th century, the cathedral has a Romanesque façade dating from 1288. The bell tower accommodates a bronze bell from 1337, crafted by Andrea Pisano, who was known for his work on the grand Duomo in Florence. Inside the cathedral's crypt is a collection of unusual religious art.

The narrow, winding streets around the cathedral are lined with buildings adorned with wrought-iron balconies in typical Aragonese fashion.

---

 ⑤

Museo dell'Arte Mineraria

🏛 **Via Roma 47** ⏰ **Hours vary, check website**
🌐 **museoartemineraria.it**

Dedicated to the city's mining history and run by volunteers, this museum is just outside the old centre of Iglesias. It houses a fascinating collection of photographs, machinery and tools relating to the

←

The simple brick façade of Cattedrale di Santa Chiara and its bell tower

General Nino Villa Santa's well-preserved study in the Castello di Sanluri

monastery) on a hill above the town, displays a collection of tools and archaeological finds.

Museo Risorgimentale Duca d'Aosta

 Castello di Sanluri
070 930 71 05 Jul-Sep: 4:30–9pm Tue-Fri, 10am–1pm & 4:30–9pm Sun; Sep-Jun: 9:45am–1pm & 3-7pm Sun

Museo Storico Etnografico

Via San Rocco 6
070 930 71 07 Appt only: 9am–noon & 3:30-7pm daily

EXPERIENCE MORE

❻ Sanluri

D5 Via Mazzini 74; www.prolocosanluri.eu

Sanluri grew up around the 14th-century castle of Eleonora d'Arborea (p50), also known as Castello di Sanluri. This strong-hold changed hands several times before it was taken by the Aragonese in 1409. The massive square structure has towers on its four corners and an ornate wrought-iron gate.

Today the castle is owned by the descendants of General Nino Villa Santa, a decorated veteran of the Italo-Turkish war, and houses a series of museums, including the **Museo Risorgimentale Duca d'Aosta**, which holds a fine collection of World War I memorabilia. Other historical exhibits include fine furniture such as a 16th-century bed. On the upper floor is the interesting Museo delle Ceroplastiche, in which there are 343 artistic wax models from 1500 to 1800, and in the entrance hall stands a sculpture of San Michele.

The **Museo Storico Etnografico**, in the restored 16th-century Convento dei Cappuccini (still a working

❼ Uta

D6 Via Nuova; www.prolocouta.it

The flourishing agricultural town of Uta is situated at the edge of the Campidano plain, a vast fertile corridor that stretches northwards from Cagliari to Oristano. On the outskirts of town is the church of **Santa Maria**, built in 1140 by French Victorine friars from Marseille. The façade is made of light-coloured stone, with blocks of a darker hue, and is decorated with blind arches and a small bell gable. Intricate sculptures of human heads, deer, calves and geometric patterns adorn the arches.

The village of **San Sperate**, some 8 km (5 miles) northeast of Uta, is a living museum with hundreds of murals inspired by the town's history adorning the houses and shops. There are also sculptures by local artist Pinuccio Sciola.

Santa Maria

Via Santa Maria 070 754 94 43 By appt only

San Sperate

Via Sassari 12; www. sansperate.net

THE SAFFRON OF SARDINIA

Derived from the flower of the *Crocus sativus* and known as "red gold", the exquisite spice saffron is prized throughout the world. Most of the saffron in Sardinia is grown around the Campidano plain, in small farming communities outside of Sanluri, such as Turri, San Gavino Monreale and Villanovafranca. In early November, these communities celebrate the precious spice with lively festivals. During this time, visitors can tour the flowering fields, observe the careful harvesting process and sample traditional dishes flavoured with saffron, including *fregula* pasta, lamb stews and even gelato.

8

Serri

D5 🚌🚉 **ℹ** Via Municipio 5, 0782 80 60 81; Pro Loco, Via Roma 36, 0782 80 51 42

This sheep-farming centre lies on the edge of a plateau dominating the Trexenta hills. Right on the spur of the promontory is the **Santuario Nuragico di Santa Vittoria**, one of Sardinia's most fascinating nuraghic sites. The ruins here have yielded some important bronze votive statuettes, now housed in the Museo Archeologico Nazionale in Cagliari (p62).

Pilgrims once came here to worship the god of water at the sacred well, which is in an excellent state of preservation, and is reached via 13 amazingly precise basalt steps. A short walk from the entrance is the Recinto delle Feste (festivities area). This elliptical building has a porticoed courtyard surrounded by rooms for the pilgrims. This is possibly a predecessor of the many rural sanctuaries (cumbessias or muristeni) found today in Sardinia's country churches.

Santuario Nuragico di Santa Vittoria

🏛 7 km (4 miles) NW ⏰ 9am–dusk daily 🌐 santuario nuragicoserri.it

9

Sardara

D5 🚌 **ℹ** Piazza Gramsci 1; www.provincia.medio campidano.it

Situated at the edge of the Campidano plain, the town of Sardara lay on the border between the medieval principalities of Arborea and Cagliari. Stone houses from this period have been preserved around the Chiesa di San Gregorio. This Romanesque church was built in the 13th–14th centuries, and its tall, narrow façade shows the initial influence of Gothic architecture. On the western outskirts of town is the 16th-century church of Beata Vergine Assunta, worth a look for its sculpted columns and arches, and its star-patterned vault.

Nearby are the remains of a nuraghic well-temple, the sanctuary of Sant'Anastasia. This underground chamber, from the 9th–10th centuries BC, was known as the Funtana de is Dolus (Fountain of Pain) and was where worshippers came to take the curative spring waters. The water was carried to the temple from an ancient underground well via a canal. The small but informative **Civico Museo Archeologico Villa Abbas**, in Piazza Libertà at the edge of the nuraghic

ruins, features archaeological finds from this site and others nearby. Particularly interesting are a pair of replica bronze archer statues. The originals can be seen at the Museo Archeologico Nazionale in Cagliari (p62). Fine views from its balcony extend beyond the Castello di Monreale and the surrounding countryside.

Ruins of the medieval Castello di Monreale, a fortification of the principality of Arborea, stand on a hill 1 km (half a mile) southwest of town. A little further west are the remains of Roman baths, and nearby is the Gothic church of Santa Maria de Is Acquas.

Civico Museo Archeologico Villa Abbas

🏛 Piazza Libertà 7 ⏰ 9am–1pm & 4–7pm Tue–Sun 🌐 coopvillabbas.sardegna.it

↑ The austere stone exterior of the church of Santa Maria de Is Acquas near Sardara

⑩
Arbus

🅐C6 🚌 𝒊 Via Repubblica 40; www.proloco.arbus.it

Granite houses characterize the village of Arbus, set on the slopes of Monte Linas. Arbus is known for the production of traditional knives with curved blades, known locally as *arresojas arburesa*.

Southwest down the N126 for 7 km (4 miles), then due west across a winding mountain road, is the mining village of Ingurtosu. Once home to over 1,000 mine workers, the houses, office building and church are now abandoned. The pine forest surrounding the dilapidated buildings was planted by the mine workers.

A dirt road runs among the old mines, abandoned buildings and former dumping area as far as Naracauli, where there are ruins of a more modern mine complex built shortly after World War I. A train once transported the extracted lead and zinc to the coast, where it was loaded onto ships. Sections of the narrow-gauge track and some carriages can be seen on the Piscinas beach *(p72)*.

↑ Exploring traditional knife-making in the Museo del Coltello Sardo in Arbus

 HIDDEN GEM
Beautiful Blades

On Via Roma in Arbus, just off Piazza Mercato and adjacent to a master cutler workshop, the Museo del Coltello Sardo *(museodelcoltello.it)* is just the spot for knife enthusiasts. The brainchild of artisan Paolo Pusceddu, it displays hundreds of masterful Sardinian blades, both old and new, and there's a shop on site. You'll also find an extraordinary specimen that once held the title of "Largest Pocket Knife in the World", as recognized in the 1986 *Guinness Book of Records*.

⑪
Villanovaforru

🅐D5 🚌 𝒊 Piazza Costituzione 1; www.villanovaforru.gov.it

This agricultural centre was founded in the 1600s by the Spanish and has retained much of its original layout. Many houses have kept their decorative features. Today, a 19th-century building, the former Monte Granatico (grain store), in the town's central square, houses the small but excellent **Museo Civico Archeologico Genna Maria**. Finds from the nearby nuraghic site of Genna Maria are on display, including bronze, iron and ceramic objects from the 9th century BC on the ground floor. On the first floor are several votive items dedicated to Demeter and Persephone from the Roman era.

On the road to Collinas, 1 km (half a mile) west of the town, is the **Genna Maria Parco Archeologico**. Discovered in 1977, the nuraghic village, which is still being excavated, sits on a prominent hilltop. This nuraghe has a typical design *(p70)*. Thick walls with three towers form a triangle that encloses a central tower and courtyard with a well.

Another wall with six corner towers surrounds the entire village area.

Museo Civico Archeologico Genna Maria
Ⓐ Piazza Costituzione 4
📞 070 930 00 50 🕐 9:30am-1pm & 3:30-6pm Tue-Sun (Apr-Sep: to 7pm)

Genna Maria Parco Archeologico
Ⓐ 1 km (half a mile) W of Villanovaforru
🕐 Seasonal; check website
🌐 gennamaria.it

⑫ Costa Verde

📍 C5-6 🚌

Costa Verde, the Green Coast, is an apt name for this wild and solitary stretch of coastline edged with wind-sculpted maquis and scented juniper trees. Extending some 50 km (30 miles) from Capo Pecora in the south to Capo Frasca in the north, the beaches here are known for their soft dune landscapes, mining ghost towns and shy *Cervo sardo* (Sardinian deer). The emerald-and-teal-coloured sea is utterly pristine, so much so that loggerhead turtles still come to the shores to lay their eggs, and you can sometimes spot bottlenose dolphins leaping about in the distant crests. Kite-surfers, too, enjoy the waves here, especially in the spring, and kayakers are often seen paddling from cove to cove in the summer.

The nearest towns are Arbus and Guspini, situated further inland, with little else around. Highlights in the area include the Piscinas Dunes (*p72*) and the secluded Scivu beach, both of which have a decent array of facilities in spite of their rural location, and which offer unparalleled Mediterranean sunsets.

⑬ Guspini

📍 C6 🚌 ℹ Town Hall, Via Don Minzoni 10; www. comune.guspini.vs.it

Overlooking the flat and fertile Campidano plain, Guspini is surrounded by olive groves and backed by the gradually rising foothills of Monte Arcuentu. The 17th-century church of San Nicolò di Mira, in the main square, boasts a large rose window and is the hub of local life. Events in town include the annual Festa di Santa Maria del Mare, celebrated with a procession and horse race.

The **Montevecchio Mine**, 8 km (5 miles) west, was one of the largest in Europe from the mid-1800s until the 1950s, eventually ceasing operations completely in the early 1990s. Despite its state of abandon, the miners' houses, headquarters, church, school and hospital are worth a visit. There are guided tours of the mine and the office building as well as an exhibition on the life of the miners in the past.

Montevecchio Mine

🖌 🚶 📍 8 km (5 miles) W of Guspini ⏰ Seasonal; check website 🌐 miniera montevecchio.it

← Ruined buildings of the Montevecchio Mine complex near Guspini

 GREAT VIEW
Coastal Vista

For the best panoramas of Costa di Masua and the rocky island of Pan di Zucchero, head to the old Porto Flavia mine. Whether looking out to sea from the cliffs above or from the beach down below, the views are just splendid.

14

Costa di Masua

 C6

The corniche road between Fontanamare and Masua, some 12 km (7 miles) north, follows a wild and splendid coastline. At Masua, the little beach of Porto Flavia is overlooked by pillars of eroded limestone and, offshore, the distinctive Pan di Zucchero ("Sugarloaf") island. This sheer rock rises 132 m (433 ft) from the sea.

At Nebida you can see the abandoned mines of the industrial archaeological area. A panoramic path along the coast leads to the abandoned remains of Lamarmora mine buildings and shafts.

15

Buggerru

C6

Situated in a valley opening out onto the sea, Buggerru was founded in the mid-18th century in a mineral-rich area. It soon became a flourishing mining town with a small theatre, and the headquarters of the French Société Anonyme des Mines de Malfidano. In the lower part of the town, a sculpture by Pinuccio Sciola is dedicated to the miners who died in the strikes of 1904. The mines are now closed, but some of the abandoned tunnels and caves can still be seen.

Today, the town is a popular resort and its harbour – the only one between Carloforte and Oristano – is usually filled with pleasure boats. The docks, where boats were once loaded with local minerals for export, now serve as a port for visitors to the wild western coast of the island and its long stretches of sandy, sheltered beaches. To the south is the long and secluded Cala Domestica, a rocky bay overlooked by a Spanish watchtower.

16

Temple of Antas

C6 Fluminimaggiore
Via Vittorio Emanuele 225; 0781 58 09 90
9:30am-7:30pm daily (to 4:30pm in winter)

First discovered in 1966, the ancient Temple of Antas is believed to have been a sacred nuraghic site. It was adopted by the Carthaginians in the 4th century BC and dedicated to the deity Sid Addir Babai. A century later, the temple was restructured with an atrium and a central chamber and decorated with Egyptian and Ionic symbols.

In the 3rd century AD, the Romans rebuilt the temple using some of the existing

Although only six of the columns remain standing today, the Temple of Antas's isolated position amid the wild maquis makes it an enchanting place to visit.

↑ A secluded beach hidden in Cala Domestica bay near Buggerru

material, such as the Ionic capitals of the columns. This temple was dedicated to the god and "creator of Sardinians", Sardus Pater. Although only six of the columns remain standing today, the temple's isolated position amid the wild maquis makes it an enchanting place to visit.

Southwest of the temple are the remains of a nuraghic village whose inhabitants were likely attracted to the area's rich metal deposits. A bit further down, remnants of Roman limestone quarries used for the construction of the temple can be seen. Workers, likely Sardinians under forced labour, would have had only simple hammers and chisels to carve out the huge blocks, transporting them up the hill with oxen-pulled carts. An ancient trail leads out from the temple and connects to the Grotte di Su Mannau, a sacred cave with underground lakes where rituals would have taken place.

In the fertile valley of the River Mannu, 9 km (5 miles) north, is the small agricultural village of Fluminimaggiore, founded in the 18th century. The road west towards the sea proceeds 9 km (5 miles) to Portixeddu beach, protected by extensive sand dunes. The headland of Capo Pecora offers stunning views of the coast.

Calasetta

 www.comune.calasetta.ci.it

The second-largest village on the island of Sant'Antioco (p86), Calasetta was founded in 1769. The straight streets with their two-storey houses lead to the main square. Here, the parish church has a bell tower of Arab derivation. The road heading south along the western coast offers a panoramic view of cliffs, coves and beaches.

↑ Ruins of the Carthaginian-Roman Temple of Antas amid the Iglesiente mountains

Capo Malfatano, at the island's southern tip

18 Sant'Antioco

C7 ▪ **Town Hall;**
Pro Loco, P'za Repubblica 41
comune.santantioco.ca.it

The island of Sant'Antioco is connected to Sardinia by a causeway, and the remains of a Roman bridge are still visible from the road. The *faraglioni*, two large menhirs, stand on one side. According to legend these are the petrified figures of a nun and a monk, turned to stone as they tried to elope.

Sant'Antioco town was founded by the Phoenicians in the 8th century BC and named Sulki. It soon became a major port in the Mediterranean, due to the trade in minerals mined from the area, including gold. Ptolemy, the Greek astronomer, gave it the name Insula Plumbaria (Island of Lead). The Carthaginians used the port during the Second Punic War (218–201 BC), but this alliance was harshly punished by the victorious Romans. Under the Roman Empire the town flourished, but continuous pirate raids in the Middle Ages led to its gradual decline.

The picturesque town centre climbs away from the sea and its characteristic houses have small wrought-iron balconies. The main street, Corso Vittorio Emanuele, is shaded by an avenue of trees. High above the town is the **Basilica of Sant'Antioco**, built in the 6th century with a Greek cross plan and central dome, but

↑ Burial urns in the ancient Phoenician sanctuary and necropolis of Tophet

modified in the 11th century. According to tradition, the remains of St Antiochus are buried in the catacombs, reached via the transept. The body of the martyr is said to have floated here after he was killed by the Romans in Africa.

The **Museo Archeologico** houses Phoenician and Roman earthenware, jewels and other objects uncovered in the area, including burial urns from the nearby Tophet necropolis.

The **Museo Etnografico** is housed in a former wine-making plant. The central hall holds equipment used to make cheese and cultivate grapevines, and the weaving section features spindles and looms. Under the arcade outside, wine-making equipment and implements used to raise livestock are on display.

Dominating the town is the red stone Castello Sabaudo, rebuilt by the Aragonese in

the 16th century. Just outside the town, on a cliff overlooking the sea, is the bleak **Tophet**, a Phoenician sanctuary and necropolis. This burial ground was used for the ashes of still-born babies, or those who died shortly after birth. Nearby is the Carthaginian necropolis, with about 40 underground tombs. This area was later used by the Romans for the ashes of their dead. The tombs occupy the upper part of town and were used as catacombs in the early Christian period.

INSIDER TIP
Carolina Ranch

Explore the island of Sant'Antioco on horseback via the family-friendly Carolina Ranch outfit *(carolinaranch.it)*. Follow scenic trails along the coastline, through valleys dotted with nuraghi remains, or opt for one of their exhilarating quad bike tours.

→
Frammento di Vuoto (2005) by Giò Pomodoro in Piazza Roma, Carbonia

Basilica of Sant'Antioco

⊕⊕ ☐ Via Necropoli
📞 0781 830 44 🕐 9am-noon
& 3-8pm Mon-Sat, 10-11am
& 4-8pm Sun

Museo Archeologico

⊕⊕ ☐ Piazza Sabatino
Moscati 🕐 9am-7pm daily
🌐 mabsantantioco.it

Museo Etnografico

⊕ ☐ Via Necropoli
🕐 9:30am-1pm & 3-6pm
daily (summer: 9am-8pm)
🌐 mabsantantioco.it

Tophet

⊕ ☐ Piazza S Moscati
🕐 9am-7pm daily
🌐 mabsantantioco.it

Carbonia

🅰 C7 🚌 🛈 Town Hall,
Piazza Roma 1; www.
comune.carbonia.su.it

Carbonia, located in the mining region of Sulcis, was founded by Fascist prime minister Benito Mussolini in 1938. The town has retained its Fascist-style plan and architectural conception, with imposing buildings and broad streets that converge at the central Piazza Roma. The majority of the town's important public buildings are found here, including the Town Hall, the Torre Civica tower and the parish church of San Ponziano.

Among the other notable sights in Carbonia is the **Museo dei Palaeoambienti Sulcitani E A Martel**, which has a collection of fossils dating back 600 million years. Villa Sulcis, the former residence of the director of the mines, has become the **Museo Archeologico**. On display are earthenware and jewels from local *domus de janas* (literally "houses of fairies" – prehistoric caves used as burial sites), and finds from the archaeological site at Monte Sirai.

The archaeological site itself lies to the west of Carbonia along the SS126, from which it is accessed via a signposted road. The stunning view alone is worth the visit, taking in the islands of Sant'Antioco and San Pietro. The fortified **Parco Archeologico di Monte Sirai** was built by the ancient Phoenicians in 750 BC. The thick outer wall protected the acropolis and the surrounding garrison town, which could house 500 foot soldiers and 100 mounted military. The ruins of this ancient military camp were discovered in 1962 and archaeological excavations are still under way.

The necropolis, northwest of the main citadel, is mainly Carthaginian, but there is also a Phoenician area with common graves, as well as an area of Punic tombs.

EAT & DRINK

Rubiu Birrificio Artigianale

Modern artisan brewery with refreshing white beers, golden ales and porters, plus speciality wood-fired pizzas with a choice of not only toppings but organic doughs as well.

🅰 C7 ☐ Via Bologna 25, Sant'Antioco
🕐 For dinner only
🌐 rubiubirra.it

€€€

Museo dei Palaeoambienti Sulcitani E A Martel

⊕ ☐ Grande Miniera di Serbariu 🕐 Apr-Sep: 10am-1pm & 3-6:30pm Tue-Sun; Oct-Mar: 10am-1pm & 2-4pm Tue-Sun 🌐 pasmartel.it

Museo Archeologico

⊕ ☐ Villa Sulcis, V. Campania
🕐 Apr-Sep: 10am-1pm & 3-6:30pm Tue-Sun; Oct-Mar: 10am-1pm & 2-4pm Tue-Sun
🌐 carboniamusei.it

Parco Archeologico di Monte Sirai

⊕⊕⊕ ☐ 3 km (2 miles) S of Carbonia 🕐 Apr-Jun & Sep: 9am-7pm Tue-Sun; Jul-Aug 9am-8pm daily; Oct-Mar: 9:30am-4:30pm Tue-Sun 🌐 carboniamusei.it

Baia Chia

🅐D7 🚌 ℹ️ Via Garibaldi 2, Domus de Maria; www.comune.domusdemaria.ca.it

The Southern Coast (Costa del Sud) is an area of sand dunes and beaches that extends as far as the Capo Spartivento headland. Junipers grow here, and the marshland is frequented by egrets, purple herons, grebes and other migratory aquatic birds. There are plans to turn the area into the centre of a regional nature reserve.

Along the coastal road is the hamlet of Chia, a popular tourist destination set among orchards and fig trees. A rough road leads to the sheltered bay of Chia, flanked on one side by the 17th-century Torre di Chia, and on the other by red cliffs covered with maquis vegetation. At the foot of the tower it is possible to visit the remains of Phoenician **Bithia**. This ancient city, which features in the writings of Ptolemy and Pliny the Elder, was covered by the sea for centuries.

Remains of a Punic and Roman necropolis are visible, as are the ruins of a temple thought to be dedicated to the god Bes. Earthenware pots and amphorae from the 7th century BC have been discovered in the sand, and traces of Roman wall paintings and mosaics decorate porticoed houses. Ancient Punic fortifications can be seen near the base of the watchtower and an elliptical cistern has also been found. Excavations are still ongoing.

Along the coast as far as the promontory of Capo Spartivento, where there are spectacular views, is a series of bays, dunes and pine forests that can be reached on foot.

Bithia

🅐Domus de Maria, Località Chia 🕐24 hrs daily

Tratalias

🅐C7 🚌 ℹ️ www.comune.tratalias.ca.it

This village in the Sulcis region was the seat of the diocese until 1413. The façade of the Pisan Romanesque **Cathedral of Santa Maria di Monserrato**, consecrated in 1213, is divided horizontally by a row of arches surmounted by a rose window. The tympanum is curious, in that the last section of a stairway juts out from it. The sides and apse are decorated with pilasters and blind arches.

Inside, the three naves are separated by large, octagonal pillars. An altarpiece from 1596 depicts St John the Baptist and St John the Evangelist with the Madonna and Child.

Cathedral of Santa Maria di Monserrato

⊗ 🅐Via d. Angeli 18
📞078 168 80 46
🕐Summer: 9am-1pm & 4-8pm Tue-Sun; winter: 9am-1pm & 3-5pm Wed-Sun

←

Statue of the Madonna in the Cathedral of Santa Maria, Tratalias

Monte Arcosu

🅐D7 🚗E of Santadi on SP1 🕐9am-6pm Sat & Sun 🌐wwf.it/oasi/sardegna/monte_arcosu

The Monte Arcosu reserve includes one of the largest expanses of maquis in the Mediterranean basin. Until 1985, it served as a private game reserve, depleted of wildlife by poachers. Part of the area is now protected by the World Wide Fund for Nature (WWF), and it is home to significant species of native flora and fauna. The mountain forests are covered in cork oak, holm oak, strawberry trees and junipers, from which dramatic granite peaks emerge. The area extends for miles, interrupted only by a rough road that connects the towns of Santadi and Capoterra along the Mannu and Gutturu Mannu river valleys.

Sardinian deer, which roamed the entire island until the late 1890s, are in high numbers once again. Other forest mammals include fallow deer, wild boar, wild cats and martens. Among the birds found here are the golden eagle, peregrine falcon and the goshawk. There are two well-marked nature trails: the easier Perdu Melis trail and the more challenging Sa Canna trail. Both take about 2 hours and require proper footwear and plenty of water. Maps of all of routes can be picked up at the visitor centre. Guided tours, including overnight trips, can be arranged at the visitor centre as well.

219

The number of species of lichen discovered (so far) in the Monte Arcosu reserve.

→ Prehistoric cave tombs of the Montessu Necropolis in Villaperuccio, near Santadi

 INSIDER TIP
Local Specialities

Santadi is known for its Carignano wine, but don't overlook the cheeses, breads and pastries that can be found on the local *agriturismo* farms.

㉓

Santadi

△C7 ▦ **𝘪** www.comune.santadi.ci.it

Built on the banks of the River Mannu, Santadi's old town sits on the higher, north side. Some traditional architecture made from rough volcanic rock is still visible in the medieval centre. Evidence that the area has been inhabited since the nuraghic age can be seen in the copper, bronze, gold and earthenware objects found here, which are now on display in the Museo Archeologico in Cagliari (*p62*). Local tools and furniture are kept at the **Museo Etnografico Sa Domu Antiga**, which has shop selling a range of typical Sulcis handicrafts.

A notable tradition in Santadi is the Sa Coia Maurreddina (Mauretanian Wedding), a ceremony held in August. These celebrations, featuring local costumes and food, are thought to have started with the North Africans who settled in the area during the Roman era.

On a plateau southwest of the town is the 7th-century BC Phoenician fortress of Pani Loriga. Continuing south for 5 km (3 miles) will bring you to two caves: **Grotte Is Zuddas**, with splendid formations of stalagmites and stalactites, and Grotta Pirosu (now closed), where archaeological finds such as a votive lamp and a Cypriot-style tripod were made. Roughly 3 km (2 miles) north of Villaperuccio, the **Montessu Necropolis** has typical *domus de janas* rock-cut tombs, some of which still have traces of the original yellow and red wall facing. Other tombs were probably used for worship.

Museo Etnografico Sa Domu Antiga

△Via Mazzini 37 **☎**340 507 48 81 **⊙**8:30 am-1:30pm & 3:30-6:30pm Tue-Sun

Grotte Is Zuddas

⊛⊛ △Benatzu
⊙Seasonal; check website
🅆grotteiszuddas.com

Montessu Necropolis

⊛⊛ △Villaperuccio, Località Montessu **☎**340 743 35 21 **⊙**Summer: 9am-8pm daily; winter: 9am-5pm daily

---

DRINK

Cantina Santadi

Come into the barrel room for tastings and purchases of Santadi's award-winning Carignano reds and Vermentino whites, along with a range of other locally grown and produced wines. Contact the cantina in advance for tours.

△C7 △Via Cagliari 78, Santadi ⊙Sun
🅆cantinadisantadi.it

← Columns and mosaic flooring in the ancient Phoenician city of Nora

Nora

📍D7 🏛Viale Nora, Capo di Pula 🕐10am–sunset daily 🌐nora.sardegna.it

Founded by the Phoenicians in the 9th–8th centuries BC, the ancient city of Nora was built on a spit of land jutting out to sea, an enviable location that was perfectly suited for sailing off in all directions. Nora was Sardinia's first official city, and continued to enjoy its auspicious status under the Romans, who started most of their roads from here. However, repeated Saracen raids and the lack of fertile land finally forced the inhabitants to abandon the city in the Middle Ages; the three ports were gradually covered up by the incoming sea, and the submerged city became something of a legend. Divers and snorkellers can still admire the Roman roads, fragments of amphorae (ceramic jars), and other remains underwater via a special licence that can be obtained from the **Fralomar Diving Centre**.

The ruins on land, essentially an open-air museum, extend to the headland of Capo di Pula, dominated by the Spanish Torre di Coltellazzo.

An impressive vestige of the Carthaginian city is the Temple of Tanit, dedicated to the goddess of fertility. Little else remains of the Punic period, although rich findings in the tombs testify to active trading.

Left of the main entrance are the 2nd–3rd-century AD Terme di Levante – Roman baths decorated with mosaics. Nearby is a 2nd-century AD amphitheatre, which was once lined with marble, and the rectangular forum behind it. South of the theatre, the mosaics in the *frigidarium* and *caldarium* of the baths are decorated with white, black, and ochre tesserae. Paved roads and the city's sewage system are also still visible.

Many finds, including the Nora Stone with Punic inscriptions in which the name of the island of Sardinia is first mentioned, can be seen in Cagliari's Museo Archeologico Nazionale (p62). Some earthenware objects found at the site are on display in the small **Museo Archeologico Patroni** in Pula, the colourful village close by. Pula's many cafés and gelaterias are buzzing during the summer months, and the nearby Romanesque church of Sant'Efisio, built on top of a Phoenician funerary by French Victorine monks in the 11th century, is the site of an annual procession from Cagliari in early May (p46). At the shore, the Lagoon of Nora is a great spot for bird-watchers and there's a small aquarium and turtle rehabilitation centre that is worth a visit.

Fralomar Diving Centre
🏛Santa Margherita di Pula
📞070 924 10 42

Museo Archeologico Patroni

 Corso Vittorio Emanuele 67, Pula 🞔070 920 96 10 🞔9am-8pm Tue-Sun (to 5:30pm in winter)

25

Parco dei Sette Fratelli

E6 🛈Visitor centre: SS125 to Muravera, junction of SP21 N to Burcei 🞔Park: dawn-dusk daily; visitor centre: Jun-Sep: 9am-6pm daily; Oct-May: 9am-noon Mon-Fri 🖥sardegna foreste.it

The mountainous "Park of the Seven Brothers" was named after the seven peaks visible from Cagliari which tower over the holm oak forests and maquis. The vast forest reaches an altitude of 1,067 m (3,500 ft) at the peak of Serpeddì, which is dusted with snow during the winter months. Strawberry trees, myrtle, thyme, lavender, juniper and eucalyptus scent the air while providing cover for wild boar, wild cats, mouflon and deer. Up above, peregrine falcons and golden eagles soar through the crisp mountain air. The whole area is dotted with ancient nuraghic settlements to discover, caves to peek into, canyon vistas to admire and old mule paths to follow. The visitor centre has maps of hiking trails, directions to the botanical garden inside the park, and some exhibits on the local flora and fauna.

26

La Giara di Gesturi

D5 🛈Visitor centre: 6km (4 miles) NE of Tuili 🞔Dawn-dusk daily 🖥parcodellagiara.it

Famed for its herds of wild horses, the verdant plateau of La Giara di Gesturi is a captivating landscape for trekkers. Formed by lava flows around 3 million years ago, the area is peppered with clusters of ancient, crooked oak and cork trees, interspersed by sturdy maquis that's especially beautiful in the spring. Well-worn paths lead to several seasonal and essential rainwater lakes (*paùli*). Here the *cavallini della Giara* (little horses of the Giara) come to quench their thirst, along with stray cattle. Other points of interest are nuraghi ruins, mostly set along the perimeter of the plateau. Guided tours are recommended, though not required, and can be arranged at the park's visitor centre.

27

Quartu Sant'Elena

D6 🛪Elmas 🚌🚉Cagliari 🛈Via Cavour 56; 070 233 46 57

Situated on the outskirts of Cagliari, Quartu Sant'Elena has grown to become one of the island's largest cities, though for some it is something of a suburb of Cagliari, given its proximity to the capital. It lies at the edge of the salt flats and marshes of the same name, which are a favourite breeding and nesting ground for flamingos.

The medieval church of Sant'Agata stands in the town's main square, Piazza Azuni. From here Via Porcu leads to the Casa Museo Sa Dom'e Farra, literally "the house of flour". This large country house has been converted into a museum with over 14,000 traditional farm and domestic tools and equipment collected over the years by Gianni Musiu, a former shepherd.

A short bus ride southwest brings you to the stunning beach resort of Poetto (*p64*), a popular spot with locals.

 INSIDER TIP
Local Wine

Quartu Sant'Elena is renowned for its Malvasia, a sweet white dessert wine with a deep golden colour and a rich flavour. You'll find it on the menu at many of the city's restaurants.

↑ Native horses roaming the forests of La Giara di Gesturi

THE EASTERN COAST

Relatively inhospitable, the eastern coast has remained largely unpopulated for much of its history. The region's early Neolithic inhabitants adapted the rocky terrain to their advantage, using the natural caves that pit the karst landscape of the Golfo di Orosei as dwellings. The high peaks of the Supramonte mountains also provided a safe haven with their elevated vantage point: it was here, on a plateau overlooking the sea, that the nuraghic village and sanctuary of Serra Orrios was constructed during the late Bronze Age. The later arrival of the Romans and subsequent invaders saw the construction of roads running inland, but settlements remained modest and their distance from the coast prevented most from growing to any great size. This situation remained unchanged for centuries, with the twin threats of constant pirate raids and endemic malaria deterring any further development. The postwar eradication of malaria-carrying mosquitoes has enabled the establishment of a number of seaside resorts, but for the most part the region is still the domain of its hardy shepherds and their flocks.

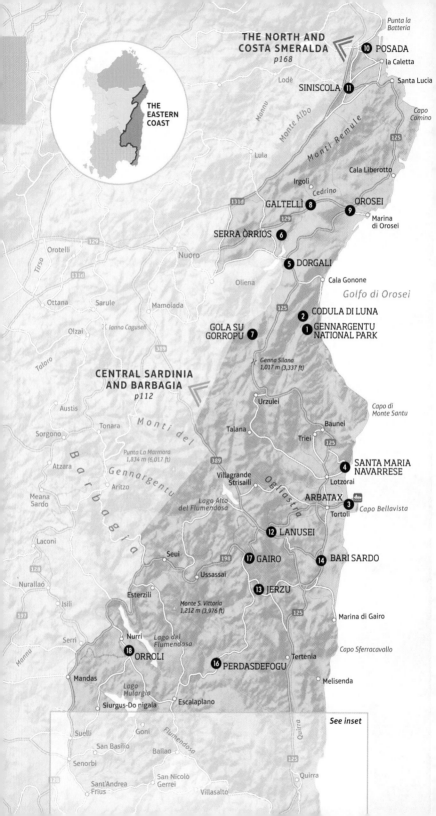

THE NORTH AND
COSTA SMERALDA
p168

Punta la Batteria

10 POSADA
la Caletta
Santa Lucia

Lodè

SINISCOLA **11**

Capo Comino

Monte Albo

Lula

Cala Liberotto

Irgoli
Cedrino
131d
GALTELLÌ **8**
OROSEI
9
Marina di Orosei

SERRA ÒRRIOS **6**

Nuoro

DORGALI
5
Cala Gonone

Golfo di Orosei

Oliena

2 CODULA DI LUNA
1 GENNARGENTU NATIONAL PARK

GOLA SU
GORROPU **7**

Genna Silana
1,017 m (3,337 ft)

CENTRAL SARDINIA
AND BARBAGIA
p112

Capo di
Monte Santu

Urzulei

Punta La Marmora
1,834 m (6,017 ft)

Baunei
Triei
125

Talana

4 SANTA MARIA
NAVARRESE
Lotzorai

Villagrande
Strisaili

ARBATAX
3
Tortolì

Capo Bellavista

Lago Alto
del Flumendosa

12 LANUSEI

17 GAIRO
14 BARI SARDO

Seui

Ussassai

13 JERZU

Esterzili

Monte S. Vittoria
1,212 m (3,976 ft)

Marina di Gairo

Capo Sferracavallo

Nurri

18 ORROLI

16 PERDASDEFOGU

Tertenia

Melisenda

Mandas

Lago del
Flumendosa

Lago
Mulargia

Siurgus-Do nigala
Escalaplano

See inset

Suelli
Goni
San Basilio
Ballao
Senorbì
San Nicolò
Gerrei
Sant'Andrea
Frius
Villasalto

Quirra

See inset

THE EASTERN
COAST

THE EASTERN COAST

Tyrrhenian
Sea

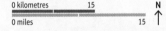

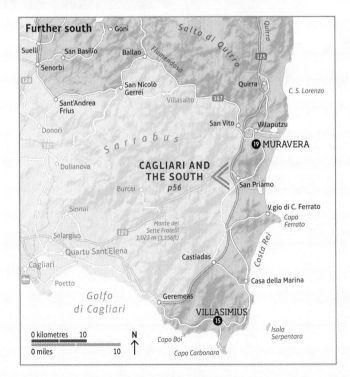

GREAT VIEW
Punta La Marmora

It's worth making the climb to the top of Punta La Marmora for the 360-degree views of the entire island. The sky is populated by raptors circling around in search of prey and with a bit of luck you might be able to see, in the distance, small groups of moufflon, or mountain sheep.

→ The edge of the park along the Golfo di Orosei coastline

❶

GENNARGENTU NATIONAL PARK

🅐 E4 🈺 Dorgali Pro Loco, Via La Marmora 108 or Desulo Town Hall; www.parcogennargentu.it

With a rugged landscape that encompasses forbidding mountains, verdant pastures, craggy plateaus and ancient forests – not to mention a spectacular stretch of coastline along the Golfo di Orosei – this park is a natural haven for wildlife and walkers alike.

The park extends over 590 sq km (228 sq miles) of some of the wildest, most mountainous terrain in Sardinia, and includes the island's highest peak, Punta La Marmora (1,834 m/6,015 ft). Established in 1988, most of the park lies in the province of Nuoro. There are 27 towns and villages in this protected area, but few tarmac roads, and the steep-sided valleys and bare peaks give the area an isolated air. The unspoilt nature of Gennargentu makes it enchanting for walkers, geologists and naturalists alike.

The climb up Punta La Marmora is rewarding, and the limestone landscape of Supramonte is one of Italy's spectacular sights. Monte Tiscali hides the fascinating prehistoric rock village of Tiscali (p118), and the ravines of Su Gorropu (p101) and the Su Gologone spring (p124) are among the park's unmissable natural wonders. The coast to the east, home to the endangered monk seal, is one of Europe's loveliest. When walking, it is advisable to take an up-to-date map and plenty of water.

↑ Looking over the scenic landscape of Gennargentu National Park

→ Hiking through the deep limestone canyon of Su Gorropu

← Looking down on Su Gorropu, hemmed in by towering rock faces up to 450 m (1,500 ft) high

WILDLIFE IN GENNARGENTU

The varied terrain of Gennargentu provides a thriving habitat for a wide range of wildlife. Stocky wild boars can be found throughout the park, as can foxes, weasels, dormice, hares and wild cats. Moufflon scale the rocky heights of some of Gennargentu's most seemingly inhospitable areas, while native Sardinian deer graze in the forests. The skies are populated by several different species of birds of prey, including the golden eagle, peregrine falcon, Eleonora's falcon, buzzard and Eurasian sparrowhawk.

2

CODULA DI LUNA

▲E4 ⏰Grotte del Bue Marino: Apr–Oct: tours daily; Nov–Mar: by appointment 🌐Tours: excursionscalagonone.com

Steep cliffs, rocky spires and deep caves dominate the phenomenal karst landscape of Codula di Luna, home to a stunning hiking trail that ends at the impeccably beautiful Cala Luna beach.

> 💬 INSIDER TIP
> **Camping Facilities**
>
> As the Codula di Luna is part of the Gennargentu National Park *(p96)*, wild camping is not permitted, even on the beaches. However, the proprietors of the seasonal Su Neulagi bar and restaurant *(339 598 04 07)*, located at Cala Luna beach, may give you permission to pitch a tent there.

Millennia of wind and water erosion has sculpted the Codula di Luna (Valley of the Moon). The hike through the gorge is long and strenuous, but the effort of the journey is more than rewarded by the secluded beaches that await at the end. The trail is accessed from the Orientale Sarda, or SS125, not far from the turn-off for Urzulei; take the road down the Codula valley for about 11 km (7 miles) and leave your car where the tarmac ends. A roughly 3-hour walk (one-way), marked by cairns, leads from the Supramonte mountains to the sea, following the path of the dry creek bed. The trail runs through aromatic maquis and passes old shepherds' huts *(pinnatu)*, as well as the entrances to enormous caves, many of which have not yet been fully explored. Further along, the valley widens and, finally, opens out onto Cala Luna bay, with a stunning, crescent-shaped beach backed by a ravine and pink-flowered oleander trees.

It is strongly advised to pack plenty of water and wear sturdy shoes for the hike. Gnarly old juniper trees offer the occasional shaded sanctuary, but most of the trail is exposed.

The end of the Codula di Luna gorge, on the final approach to Cala Luna beach ↓

← A rock climber scaling a cliff at Cala Luna beach

→ The tranquil interior of the Grotte del Bue Marino

Coastal Activities

Cala Luna beach is popular with rock climbers, who attempt the pock-marked vertical cliffs. During the summer months this spot can often be crowded because boats stop here, but other paths along the coastline lead to further coves. To the south is an unmarked trail to Cala Sisine, and to the north lies a well-used but challenging trail to Cala Fuili (2–3 hours).

In between Cala Luna and Cala Fuili are the Grotte del Bue Marino, which can be reached by boat from the village of Cala Gonone. Over 15 km (9 miles) in length, these caves branch into two main systems: north and south. The south branch is open to the public and is illuminated for the first 1 km (half a mile). Here, forests of stalagmites and stalactites sparkle in the dim light reflected off the underground saline lakes.

Did You Know?

Five-thousand-year-old petroglyphs have been found inside the Grotte del Bue Marino.

EXPERIENCE MORE

Arbatax

F4 ✈🚂🚌 **i** Pro Loco;
0782 62 28 24

The small town of Arbatax lies on the northern tip of the Capo Bellavista promontory, a red porphyry cliff that plunges into the Tyrrhenian Sea. The port, guarded by a Spanish tower, is the terminus for the narrow-gauge trains arriving from Cagliari. Ferries from Cagliari, Olbia and the Italian mainland also dock here.

This stretch of coast has clear, clean water and enticing coves such as Cala Moresca, south of Arbatax. Several tourist resorts now cover this small promontory, such as the popular Arbatax Park Resort and Spa, built to resemble a typical Mediterranean village. This eco-resort contains a large nature park, which is home to typical Sardinian plants and animals. Further to the south is Porto Frailis, also protected by a Spanish tower, and the long, sandy Orrì beach. Footpaths lead from Arbatax up to the 19th-century Faro (Lighthouse) di Capo Bellavista, high on the promontory. This attractive structure, with its crenellated tower and black-and-white-striped walls, still guides ships to safety to this day.

Did You Know?

Sardinia has one of the world's highest life expectancies. Locals credit this to the island's red wine.

Santa Maria Navarrese

F4 ✈🏛🚌 **i** www.
turismo.ogliastra.it

This seaside resort was named after the church around which it developed. It is said that the church – a three-aisle structure with a semicircular apse – was built in the 11th century by the daughter of the king of Navarra after she had been saved from a shipwreck. In its courtyard is a huge wild olive tree that is thought to be over a thousand years old.

The beautiful beach at Santa Maria Navarrese is bordered by a pine forest and protected by a Spanish watchtower. Facing this is the huge Agugliastra (or Sa Pedra Longa) rock, a slim limestone pinnacle that rises up from the sea. Boat services from the tiny port will take visitors to the stack, as well as to Cala Luna, Cala Sisine and Cala Goloritzé.

Dorgali

E3 🚌 **i** Viale Umberto 37; www.enjoydorgali.it

The charming town of Dorgali lies on a ridge that descends from Monte Bardia and is some 30 km (19 miles) from Nuoro and a little less than 10 km (6 miles) from the sea at Cala Gonone. Dorgali is predominantly an agricultural centre, but it is also important for locally produced crafts such as leather, ceramics and filigree jewellery, as well as rug- and carpet-weaving.

In the old town the buildings are made of a dark volcanic stone. These include several churches: Madonna d'Itria, San Lussorio and the Maddalena. The central square, Piazza Vittorio Emanuele, is dominated by the façade of the parish church, Santa Caterina.

The **Museo Archeologico di Dorgali** contains objects from nuraghic sites, as well as finds from sites dating back to Punic and Roman times. Some of the finest nuraghic pieces come from the nearby site of Serra Orrios. The museum also provides

→ The well-preserved ruins at the Serra Orrios nuraghic village

information on visits to the rock village of Tiscali, another major nuraghic site (p118). The town is known for its wine, and a visit to the local wine-making cooperative is a pleasant way to spend an afternoon.

Parco Museo S'Abba Frisca, some 6 km (4 miles) north of Dorgali, demonstrates how ancient rural people once lived. Visitors can also learn about the region's flora and fauna.

Museo Archeologico di Dorgali

 Via Lamarmora ⏱ May-Sep: 9:30am-1pm & 3:30-6pm Tue-Sun; Nov-Feb: 9:30am-1pm & 4-7pm Tue-Sun 🌐 museoarcheologico dorgali.it

Parco Museo S'Abba Frisca

🚶🚶 Strada Cartoe ⏱ Hours vary, check website 🌐 sabbafrisca.com

6 🚶🚶

Serra Orrios

 Località Biriddo, off SP38 ⏱ Apr-Jun & Sep: 9am-6pm daily; Jul-Aug: 9am-7pm daily; Oct-Mar: 9am-5pm daily 🌐 museo archeologicodorgali.it

High on a plateau with views of the sea, the remains of this well-preserved nuraghic village take visitors on a journey through time from the 16th to the 6th centuries BC. Over 70 small dwellings, each with a central hearth and connected by simple streets and plazas, perfectly illustrate proto-urban civilization. Dozens of other purpose-built structures

←
Sheer red rocks reaching into the clear waters of the Tyrrhenian Sea at Arbatax

include a space for livestock, a communal hut and temples. A variety of decorative artifacts excavated from the site can be viewed at the Museo Archeologico in Dorgali.

7

Gola Su Gorropu

 E4 🏠 Base camp 25 km (15 miles) N of Urzulei ⏱ Mar-Nov: dawn-dusk daily 🌐 gorropu.info

Eroded endlessly over time by the great Flumineddu river, this massive gorge is one of Europe's deepest and most spectacular. It's a 2-hour downhill walk from the base camp parking lot to the entrance of Gorropu along the Genna Silana pass, which can be taken part of the way by a jeep service. Colour-coded circles indicate the three trail levels; the third, red level, requires proper climbing equipment. To the west, reaching up into the clouds, is the massive grey wall of the Supramonte mountain range, where the ancient rock village of Tiscali (p118) hides in a giant chasm. Local legends about creatures lurking in the shadows and stars shining brightly during the day shroud this impressive gorge in further mystery.

STAY

Hotel Nettuno
Boutique hotel close to the beach, with complimentary breakfast and a swimming pool.

🅰 E3 🏠 Via Vasco De Gama 26, Cala Gonone 🌐 nettuno-hotel.it

€€€

Parco Blu Club Hotel Resort
Family-friendly hotel offering a playground, kids club and a pool.

🅰 E3 🏠 Viale Bue Marino, Cala Gonone 🌐 parcoblu.com

€€€

Hotel Villa Gustui Maris
Elegant, romantic hotel with impeccable sea views, inviting rooms and delicious breakfasts.

🅰 E3 🏠 Via Marco Polo 57, Cala Gonone 🌐 villagustuimaris.it

€€€

EAT

Gelateria Stracciatempo

Enjoy homemade, all-natural gelato and other enticing treats surrounded by a garden with sea views. Try the myrtle-flavoured gelato for something unusual.

F3 Viale Cala Liberotto 86, Orosei ⓦstracciatempo.it

€€€

8

Galtellì

E3 ⧉ ⓘPro Loco, Via Garibaldi 2; www.galtelli.gov.it

Lying on the slopes of Monte Tuttavista, Galtellì was the most important town in the region during the Middle Ages. Until 1496 it was the regional bishopric, as evidenced by the Romanesque San Pietro, the former cathedral built in the 12th century. After this era the town began to decline due to the ravages of malaria and frequent pirate raids, but traces of its glorious past have been preserved in the parish church of Santissimo Crocifisso.

The charming historic centre is a delightful place for a stroll, with its whitewashed buildings and well-kept houses. In August, the town throws a party for all foreigners and tourists living or staying there.

One of the most fascinating sights in this area is Monte Tuttavista. A short dirt road followed by a footpath takes you up to Sa Pedra Istampada ("The Perforated Rock"), a wind-sculpted arch 30 m (98 ft) high, with splendid views from the summit.

Near La Traversa, a village 12 km (8 miles) from Galtellì, is the Tomba dei Giganti (Giants' Tomb) of S'Ena 'e Thomes. This impressive monument from the Early Bronze Age (1800–1600 BC) features a 3-m (10-ft) stele hewn out of a single block of granite.

9

Orosei

F3 ⧉ ⓘwww.comune.orosei.nu.it

The historic capital of the Baronia region is situated about 5 km (3 miles) inland, and has a bustling, well-kept historic centre with several beautiful churches, stone archways and small, whitewashed buildings overlooking courtyards.

The town of Orosei was most likely founded in the early Middle Ages and its golden age occurred under Pisan domination, when it was ruled by the barons of the Guiso family. The town developed into an important harbour with moorings alongside the Cedrino river. After yielding to Aragonese rule,

The hilltop village of Posada, overlooked by Castello della Fava ↑

the town began to decline as a result of malarial disease, repeated pirate raids and the gradual silting up of the river.

A labyrinth of alleys leads to the central Piazza del Popolo, where three churches stand. At the top of a flight of steps is San Giacomo Maggiore with an 18th-century façade and terracotta-tiled domes. Opposite is the Chiesa del Rosario, with a Baroque façade, and the Chiesa delle Anime, founded by the brotherhood of monks that participates in the Easter Week ceremonies.

Sant'Antonio Abate, once an isolated rural sanctuary, is now surrounded by the expanding town. Local handicrafts are on display in the medieval Pisan tower inside the precincts of Sant'Antonio. The 17th-century Sanctuary of the Madonna del Rimedio is now part of the outskirts and is surrounded by *cumbessias*, the houses used by pilgrims each September.

The Bronze Age Giants' Tomb monument of S'Ena 'e Thomes, in a village near Galtellì

 HIDDEN GEM
Oasi Biderosa

A half-hour drive north from Orosei is the Oasis of Biderosa – a series of five secluded beach coves framed by a protected woodland and a pond frequented by flamingos.

Near the mouth of the Cedrino river is the church of Santa Maria 'e Mare, founded in the 13th century by Pisan merchants. The church is full of ex votos (votive offerings to a saint), and on the last Sunday in May it is the focus of an important pilgrimage, when a statue of the Madonna is taken down the river on a boat, followed by a flotilla.

At the mouth of the estuary the river divides into two. The northern part flows into an artificial canal, while the southern half feeds the Su Petrosu marsh. Here you will find coots, moorhens, mallards and purple gallinules. The shallows are home to avocets, stilts, grey herons and egrets.

 10
Posada

⌂ F2 🚌 ⓘ Via G. Garibaldi 4; www.comune.posada.nu.it

Perched on top of a limestone bank covered with euphorbia and lentiscus, this village is dominated by the ruins of Castello della Fava. The castle was built in the 12th century by the rulers of Gallura, who were later conquered by the principality of Arborea before passing into Aragonese dominion (p50). In the Carthaginian era this place was known as the colony of Feronia.

The town still retains much of its medieval character, with winding alleyways connected by steep stairways, arches and tiny squares. Wooden steps lead to the top of its square tower, where you will find a panoramic view of the sea, the mouth of the Posada river and the surrounding plain, covered with fruit orchards.

In the valley below, the Posada can be traversed by canoe, allowing you to admire the hordes of flamingos that frequent the area.

Siniscola

F3 ✉ ℹ Via Roma 125;
www.comune.siniscola.
nu.it

Set at the foot of Monte Albo, the once agricultural town of Siniscola was an important trading centre in the 14th century under the principality of Gallura. Since then, the town has grown somewhat haphazardly around the medieval centre. On the lively main street, Via Sassari, the 18th-century parish church of San Giovanni Battista is decorated with a fresco cycle depicting the life of St John the Baptist.

Siniscola is famous for its cultivation of the rare *pompia* fruit, a hybrid of lemon and citron. This monstrous-looking citrus is a key ingredient in some Sardinian desserts. The town is also well known for its local pottery studios.

A straight road northeast from Siniscola leads to La Caletta, a small tourist port with a wide sandy beach, 4 km (2 miles) long. Heading southwards from town, the SS125 passes the fishing village of Santa Lucia. Thought to have been founded by emigrants from the island of Ponza, the village is guarded by a Spanish watchtower. Today Santa Lucia is a popular summer resort, with a pine forest that extends behind the beach. Continuing southwards, a long walk along the shore will take you to the white sand dunes and juniper bushes of Capo Comino.

STAY

L'Essenza
Set in peaceful countryside north of Siniscola, this hotel offers accommodation in a rustic but cosy *pinnetos* – circular stone huts once used by shepherds. The breakfast is delicious.

F2 📍 Località Cuccu Ezzu, Torpè
🌐 essenzasardegna.com

€€€

GREAT VIEW
Star Gazing

In the evening, wrap up warm and head to the Osservatorio Astronomico Caliumi *(www.astroarmidda.it)* on Monte Armidda, just outside Lanusei, to witness one of the greatest starry spectacles on earth.

The headland of Capo Comino consists of rounded rocks and pebble beaches overlooked by a lighthouse. A 2-hour walk along the seashore will take you to Berchida beach, dominated by a huge rock known as S'incollu de sa Marchesa ("The Marquise's Throat"). Eels and grey mullet populate an area of marshland here.

An alternative excursion is to take the track that turns right from the SS125 after the Berchida river. Winding through the maquis, it leads to a splendid white sand beach and clear blue sea. On the way, the road passes the remains of the nuraghic settlement of Conca Umosa.

→ The "heels" of the rugged limestone mountain range rising above the hillside town of Jerzu

Lanusei

E5 🚌 🚏 *i* Via Roma 100;
www.comunedilanusei.it

This large, austere-looking town, situated on a hillside at 600 m (1,926 ft), overlooks the plain that descends to the sea. It was once a popular health retreat due to its excellent climate, high altitude and the many walking trails through the forest that surrounds it. The old town centre has retained many of its 19th-century aristocratic buildings, including Casa Mameli, the family home of poet and writer Goffredo Mameli, famous for authoring the words to the Italian national anthem.

Jerzu

E5 🚏 *i* www.comune. jerzu.og.it

The tall, sharp pinnacles of rock known locally as *tacchi* (heels) are an impressive sight as they emerge from the maquis on the approach to Jerzu. This modern town was built on several levels up the hillside, with tall townhouses overlooking the main street. Steep side streets in the lower quarter lead to older houses that retain many of their original features.

Jerzu's economy is based mainly on viticulture, and vineyards cling to the steep slopes surrounding the town. The area produces about 10,000 tonnes of grapes a year, from which the local wine cooperative makes Cannonau DOC, one of the most famous red wines in Sardinia.

Every year on 13 June, the town celebrates the festival of Sant'Antonio da Padova with a procession up to the medieval church that bears his name.

At Ulassai, 7 km (4 miles) northwest of Jerzu, is the limestone **Grotta Su Marmuri**. Stone steps descend to reveal spectacular pools and stalagmites. Wear warm clothes and sturdy shoes.

Grotta Su Marmuri

🚏 🚏 🚏 *i* Piazzale Grotta Su Marmuri ⏰ Apr–Oct; tours compulsory: 11am, 2:30pm (more in summer) 🌐 grottasumarmuri.it

↑ A cannon pointing out to sea from Torre di Bari, near Bari Sardo

Bari Sardo

E5 🚌 *i* www.comune dibarisardo.gov.it

This agricultural centre is set in fertile countryside filled with vineyards and orchards. The name of the town is derived from the Sardinian word for marshes, *abbari*. Original stone houses are still visible in the old town, around the district of San Leonardo to the southwest. Here, the parish church, Beata Vergine del Monserrato, has a Rococo bell tower dated 1813. The town is also known for its textiles: tapestries, rugs and bed linen.

On the coast, 5 km (3 miles) east of Bari Sardo, the pretty seaside resort of Torre di Bari developed around the 17th-century Spanish tower built to defend the town from pirates. Its sandy beach and pine forest make for a good day trip.

Did You Know?

During July's Su Nenniri festival in Bari Sardo, seedlings are cast into the sea to encourage a good harvest.

15
Villasimius

A E7 **·** *i* Piazza Giovanni XXIII; 070 79 20 76

This leading seaside resort on the southeastern coast lies on the northern edge of a promontory that extends to Capo Carbonara. At the centre of the headland is the Notteri marsh, separated from the sea by Simius beach. In the winter the marsh is a popular spot for migratory flamingos. On the very tip of the promontory, the lighthouse offers a sweeping view of the coast and the tiny islands of Serpentara and Cavoli. The stretch of water between the two islands has witnessed several shipwrecks over the years. Off Cavoli, at a depth of 10 m (33 ft), is the statue of the Madonna del Naufrago (Our Lady the Castaway). Excursions to view the submerged statue by glass-bottomed boat leave from the quay at Porto Giunco. This port is protected by the Fortezza Vecchia, a star-shaped fortress built in the 1600s. The waters around the headland are rich in sealife and are popular with scuba divers.

16
Perdasdefogu

A E5 **·** *i* www.comune. perdasdefogu.nu.it

An isolated mountain village in the lower Ogliastra area, Perdasdefogu lies at the foot of the striking *tacchi*, sheer limestone walls that tower over the maquis. The road that meanders northeast towards Jerzu is one of the most scenic in Sardinia. It runs along a plateau at the base of these dolomitic walls, offering a spectacular view of the sea and the Perda Liana peaks in the distance. Along the way is the church of Sant'Antonio, set in a meadow at the foot of Punta Coróngiu, one of the most impressive of the *tacchi*.

↑ A shepherd guiding his sheep through the abandoned village of Gairo Vecchio

17
Gairo

A E5 **·** *i* www.comune. gairo.og.it

Gairo Sant'Elena lies in the Pardu river valley, a deep ravine with limestone walls. The present-day village was built after 1951, when Gairo Vecchio had to be evacuated after excessive rain caused a series of landslides. All that remains of the abandoned village are gutted houses without doors and windows, giving this ghost town an eerie but fascinating character.

On the coast, the bay of Gairo is protected by headland covered with maquis. From here you can go to Coccorrocci, an attractive pebble beach with volcanic stones that range in colour from pink to dark grey. The coastal road runs along the seashore, which is characterized by sandy inlets and cliffs of pink rock.

18
Orroli

A E5 **·** *i* www.comune. orroli.ca.it

The town of Orroli lies on the rather barren Pranemuru plateau, at the edge of the

Flumendosa valley. The area is dotted with archaeological sites, such as the necropolis of **Su Motti**, where *domus de janas* tombs are cut out of the rock.

Other archaeological sites in the area include the ruins of the **Arrubiu Nuraghe**, 3 km (2 miles) southeast of Orroli. This complicated, pentagonal site rivals Su Nuraxi *(p68)* in sheer size. The complex, made of red stone, was built around a 14th-century BC central tower, which, according to experts, was 27 m (88 ft) high. Five towers connected by tall bastions, probably dating from the 7th century BC, were built around the complex, and an outer defensive wall was added in the 6th century BC. The ruins of the nuraghic village, consisting of round and rectangular dwellings, lie around the nuraghe.

Another impressive site is the nearby Su Putzu nuraghe, filled with numerous dwellings in excellent condition.

Su Motti
A 4 km (2 miles) SE of Orroli **·** 24 hrs daily **W** orroliproloco. com/parco-su-motti.html

Arrubiu Nuraghe
· **A** 6 km (4 miles) SE of Orroli **·** 9:30am–dusk daily **W** nuraghearrubiu.it

Torre Salinas

For excellent views of the valley, lagoons and rock pools around Muravera, climb one of the 17th-century Spanish towers along the coast, such as Torre Salinas, built to defend the area from Saracen pirate attacks.

 19

Muravera

A E6   **B** *i* www.comune. muravera.ca.it

Muravera lies at the mouth of the Flumendosa river, in the middle of an area dotted with fruit orchards. In ancient times it was the Phoenician city of Sarcapos. Today, the only building of historical interest here is the 15th-century church of San Nicola, located just off the main street.

However, Muravera is an ideal starting point for trips along the coast and into the valleys of the interior. To the east, the beach around Porto Corallo is long and sandy, interrupted by small rocky headlands. Near the port is another Spanish tower, which, in 1812, was used as a stronghold in one of the rare victories of the Sardinians over the North African pirates.

Northwards, 11 km (7 miles) along the SS125, also known as the Orientale Sarda road (*p108*), are the remains of the 12th-century Castello di Quirra and the small Romanesque church of San Nicola, the only church in Sardinia built of brick.

To the south, the coast around Capo Ferrato is quite beautiful, with basalt rocks, small white sandy coves and pine trees. Past the headland of Capo Ferrato is the Costa Rei, a stretch of straight coastline with beaches and tourist villages. The waters in the bay of Cala Sinzias further to the south are strikingly clear.

Inland, the route towards Cagliari along the SS125 offers spectacular scenery, with red rock among myrtle, juniper and strawberry trees. A trip down the Flumendosa river valley, beyond San Vito, is also extremely scenic.

A few kilometres inland from the Costa Rei is the charming hamlet of Castiadas, set around a 19th-century prison amid vineyards and citrus trees.

EAT

L'Aragosta
Start with the local salami and cheeses, then the tuna tartare, the grilled mixed seafood and a house tiramisu to finish at this relaxed, atmospheric seafood *ristorante*.

A E6 **A** Via Cristoforo Colombo 20, Costa Rei **w** laragostacostarei.it

€€€

SHOP

Tessart Cogoni
This showroom sells the latest Sardinian textiles and furniture, all hand-crafted in island motifs and colours by local artists – they make wonderful souvenirs to take home.

A E7 **A** Via del Mare 33, Villasimius **C** Mon-Fri **w** tessartcogoni.it

Crystal-clear water lapping the sandy shore near Muravera ↑

A DRIVING TOUR
THE ORIENTALE SARDA ROAD

Length 63 km (39 miles) **Stopping-off points**
Cala Gonone, Genna Silana Pass, Urzulei, San Pietro
Difficulty Mainly easy, but with some dirt tracks

Along the eastern peaks of the Gennargentu
National Park (p96), the SS125, or the "Orientale
Sarda" road, connects Olbia to Cagliari. The most
spectacular stretch is between Dorgali and Baunei:
63 km (39 miles) of winding road hewn out of the rock
by Piedmontese coal miners during the mid-1800s.
These "foreigners" carved a road through the remote
mountain valleys and felled trees that were sent to
the mainland. It is advisable to allow a full day for this
tour, to take into account the winding roads and the
opportunities to stop and admire the scenery.

Locator Map
See p94

The Orientale
Sarda Road

THE
EASTERN
COAST

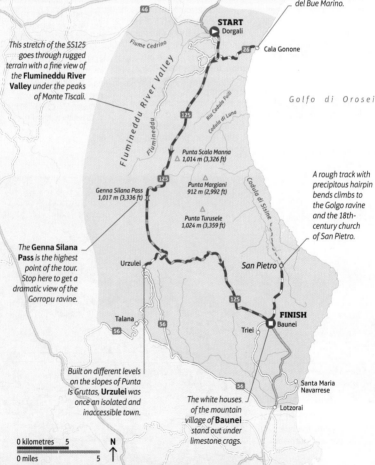

A 400-m (1,300-ft)
tunnel cut out of the
limestone rock leads
to the popular seaside
resort of **Cala Gonone**.
A winding road
continues to the Grotte
del Bue Marino.

This stretch of the SS125
goes through rugged
terrain with a fine view of
the **Flumineddu River
Valley** under the peaks
of Monte Tiscali.

START
Dorgali

Cala Gonone

Fiume Cedrino

Flumineddu River Valley

Flumineddu

Riu Codula Fuili

Codula di Luna

Golfo di Orosei

Punta Scala Manna
1,014 m (3,326 ft)

Punta Margiani
912 m (2,992 ft)

Punta Turusele
1,024 m (3,359 ft)

Genna Silana Pass
1,017 m (3,336 ft)

Codula di Sisine

A rough track with
precipitous hairpin
bends climbs to
the Golgo ravine
and the 18th-
century church
of San Pietro.

The **Genna Silana
Pass** is the highest
point of the tour.
Stop here to get a
dramatic view of the
Gorropu ravine.

Urzulei

San Pietro

Talana

56

56

FINISH
Baunei

Triei

Built on different levels
on the slopes of Punta
Is Gruttas, **Urzulei** was
once an isolated and
inaccessible town.

The white houses
of the mountain
village of **Baunei**
stand out under
limestone crags.

Santa Maria
Navarrese

Lotzorai

0 kilometres   5

0 miles   5

N ↑

↑ The town of Urzulei, nestled in the foothills of Punta Is Gruttas

A TRAIN TOUR
THE TRENINO VERDE

Stopping-off points Tortolì, Lanusei, Gairo Taquisara, Seui
Timetable www.treninoverde.com **Journey Time** 3 hours 30 minutes

A journey on the narrow-gauge Trenino Verde (little green train) from Arbatax to Mandas offers a trip back in time through some of the wildest landscapes in Sardinia. The line passes through softly rolling hills, carpeted with almond and olive trees, to the rugged mountains of Barbagia di Seui. This particular route – one of several across Sardinia – is especially scenic as it follows the craggy contours of the mountains; going towards Mandas, the best views can be appreciated from the left-hand side of the train (and vice versa).

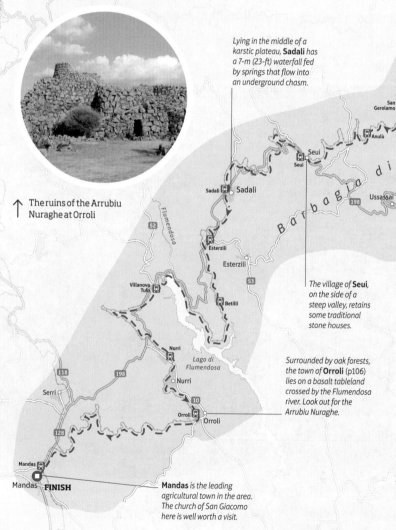

↑ The ruins of the Arrubiu Nuraghe at Orroli

*Lying in the middle of a karstic plateau, **Sadali** has a 7-m (23-ft) waterfall fed by springs that flow into an underground chasm.*

*The village of **Seui**, on the side of a steep valley, retains some traditional stone houses.*

*Surrounded by oak forests, the town of **Orroli** (p106) lies on a basalt tableland crossed by the Flumendosa river. Look out for the Arrubiu Nuraghe.*

*
Mandas is the leading agricultural town in the area. The church of San Giacomo here is well worth a visit.*

San Gerolamo
Anulù
Seui
Ussassai
198
Sadali
Flumendosa
52
Esterzili
Esterzili
53
Villanova Tulo
Betilli
Nurri
Lago di Flumendosa
Nurri
118
198
10
Serri
Orroli
Orroli
128
Mandas
Mandas
FINISH

Barbagia di

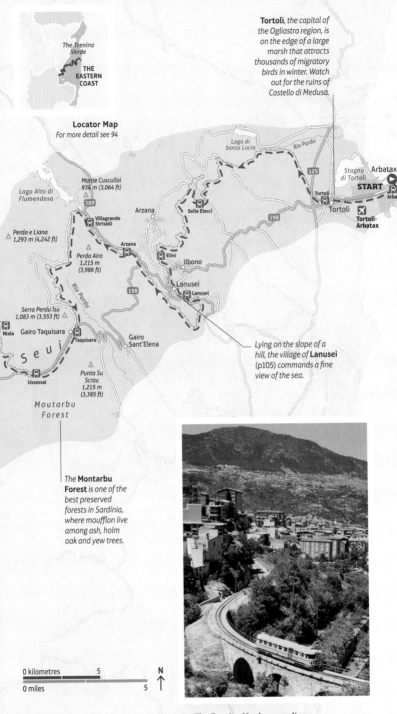

Tortolì, the capital of the Ogliastra region, is on the edge of a large marsh that attracts thousands of migratory birds in winter. Watch out for the ruins of Castello di Medusa.

Locator Map
For more detail see 94

The Trenino Verde

THE EASTERN COAST

Lago di Santa Lucia

Rio Pardu

125

Lago Alto di Flumendosa

Monte Cuscullai 934 m (3,064 ft)

389

Villagrande Strisaili

Perda e Liana 1,293 m (4,242 ft)

Arzana

Sella Elecci

Stagno di Tortolì

Arbatax
START

Arbatax

Tortolì

Tortolì

198

Tortolì-Arbatax

Perda Aira 1,215 m (3,986 ft)

Arzana

Elini

Ilbono

Lanusei

Rio Pardu

198

Serra Perdu Isu 1,083 m (3,553 ft)

Niala

Gairo Taquisara

Taquisara

Gairo Sant'Elena

Lanusei

Lying on the slope of a hill, the village of **Lanusei** *(p105) commands a fine view of the sea.*

Ussassai

Punta Su Scrau 1,215 m (3,385 ft)

S e u i

Moutarbu Forest

The **Montarbu Forest** is one of the best preserved forests in Sardinia, where moufflon live among ash, holm oak and yew trees.

0 kilometres   5

0 miles   5

N ↑

↑ The Trenino Verde ascending into the village of Lanusei

CENTRAL SARDINIA AND BARBAGIA

This rugged region was the ancient heart of the island, as attested by the wealth of archaeological sites found here, including the nuraghic village of Tiscali. The city of Nuoro – situated on an isolated plateau at the foot of the sacred Monte Ortobene – was also a centre of the nuraghic people; traces of their civilization have been found in 5,000-year-old ceramic fragments and tombs. The communities here put up a strong resistance to invasion attempts by the Romans from the 3rd century BC onwards, leading the region to be called Barbagia – the name derives from the Latin word *barbaria*, which was used by the Romans to refer to the remote areas here inhabited by "barbarians" (any culture that did not share the values and beliefs of the Roman civilization). Nuraghic religious rites were preserved right up to the advent of Christianity, and pagan cultures continued to thrive in Barbagia, enduring through several centuries of invasions. The region's isolated geography has limited its development, but Nuoro remains an important city, having spawned a number of great novelists, poets and sculptors during its cultural renaissance in the 19th and early 20th centuries. Today, tradition is still an essential part of local life, with numerous colourful folk festivals and religious festivities.

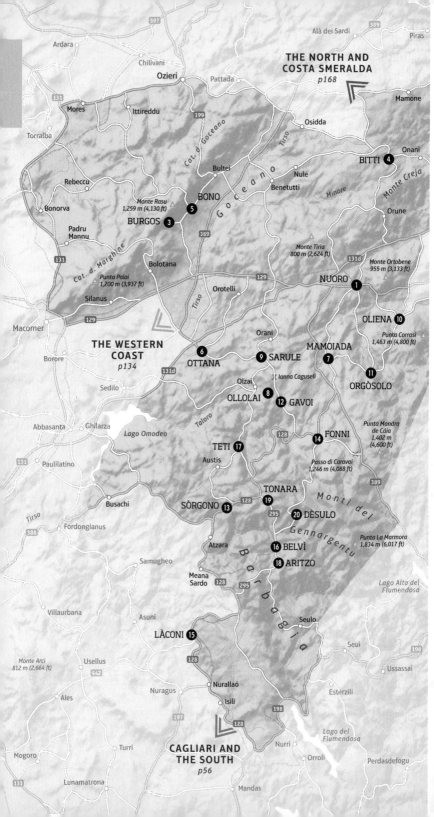

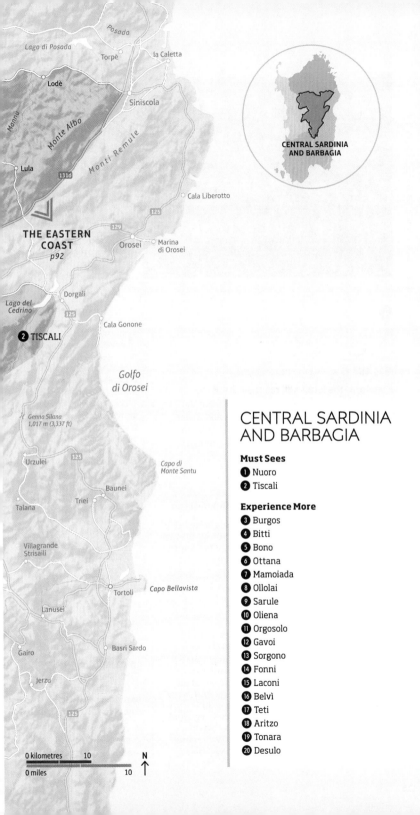

CENTRAL SARDINIA AND BARBAGIA

↑ A view over Nuoro, situated on the slopes of Monte Ortobene

NUORO

⚠E3 🚌🚂 **𝑓** www.provincia.nuoro.it

Nùgoro, as the locals still call their city, is the heart of the island's cultural life. It has been the birthplace of several renowned artists and writers, including Nobel Prize winner Grazia Deledda, and today houses a fine collection of museums in its pretty historic centre.

① 🖉

Museo Archeologico Nazionale di Nuoro

📍 Via Mannu 1 🕐 9am-1pm Tue-Sat (also 3-5pm Tue & Thu) 🌐 museoarcheologico nuoro.beniculturali.it

This museum combines the collections of fossils and fossil plants of the Nuoro Speleological Group with archaeological finds that have been excavated over many years in the area. Exhibits range from Neolithic to medieval objects, including the skeletons of an ancient hare, *Prolagus sardus*, and a collection of cave finds. Also of interest are nuraghic bronze statuettes. Finds from the Roman era include belt buckles and other everyday household objects.

② 🖉

Museo Deleddiano

📍 Via Grazia Deledda 28 📞 0784 25 80 88 🕐 10am-1pm, 3-8pm Tue-Sun (till 7pm in winter)

Born in Nuoro in 1871, writer Grazia Deledda was awarded the Nobel Prize for Literature

---

💬 INSIDER TIP
Local Art

For an insight into Sardinian fine art, check out the rotating exhibits at MAN *(www. museoman.it)*. This art museum displays works by local artists from the late 19th century to the present day.

---

in 1926 in recognition of her perceptive depiction of life in the colourful Barbagian communities around her. She has since become a symbol of Sardinian culture and an example of the island's prolific artistic production.

Now a museum, Deledda's birthplace retains the atmosphere of a mid-19th-century Sardinian home. The house has been arranged according to her own description, set out in her novel *Cosima*, with objects marking the stages of her career. The courtyard leads to what was the kitchen garden (now a venue for cultural events), while the upper floors are given over to displays of the covers of her books, programmes for her plays, and a copy of the diploma for her Nobel Prize.

---

③ 🖉

Museo del Costume

📍 Via Antonio Mereu 56 🕐 Mid-Mar-Sep: 10am-1pm, 3-8pm Tue-Sun; Oct-mid-Mar: 10am-1pm, 3-7pm Tue-Sun 🌐 isresardegna.it

Also known as the Museum of Sardinian Life and Folk Traditions, this museum was designed in the 1960s by architect Antonio Simon Mossa. The aim of the project was to recreate a typical Sardinian village as a setting for artifacts, objects and costumes representing Sardinian daily life.

On display are traditional pieces of furniture, such as a 19th-century chest and cover, and silver jewellery used to adorn aprons or handkerchiefs. Characteristic costumes worn daily or on special occasions by women are also on show, as are different types of traditional bread moulds, looms and hand-woven carpets. One room is dedicated to carnival masks and costumes. A collection of musical instruments is also on display alongside a multimedia system that enables visitors to hear the sounds of these instruments, which are used to perform traditional Sardinian folk music.

---

④

Monte Ortobene

🚗 6 km (4 miles) E of Nuoro

Nuoro was founded on the granite slopes of this mountain and the city's inhabitants have always held it in high regard. To reach its wooded areas, take the SS129 Orosei road east out of the city. On the outskirts of town you pass by the church of the Madonna

della Solitudine, where Grazia Deledda is buried.

At the summit is a statue of the Redentore (Christ the Redeemer) that overlooks the city below, and standing next to it is the church of **Nostra Signora di Montenero**. On the last Sunday in August this church is the focus of the festival known as the Sagra del Redentore, in which representatives from almost every town in Sardinia take part in a procession to Monte Ortobene.

⑤

Necropoli di Sas Concas

🚗 15 km (9 miles) W of Nuoro

Dating back to around 2700 BC, this ancient necropolis is one of the most extensive *domus de janas* complexes in the Barbagia region. To visit, take the SS131 west out of Nuoro

Christ the Redeemer by Vincenzo Jerace, on the top of Monte Ortobene

and then the SS128 south towards Oniferi. The site contains a total of 20 tombs, some of which are decorated with bas reliefs, such as the Tomba dell'Emiciclo (Tomb of the Hemicycle). The area is unattended, so a torch may be useful to view the details inside the tombs.

STAY

Agriturismo Testone
Just outside Nuoro, surrounded by thick forest and two little lakes, this working farm offers a traditional and authentic farmstay. Enjoy a warm welcome and hearty home-cooked meals.

🚗 Str. per Agriturismo Testone, off the SP41
🖥 agriturismo testone.com

€€€

2

TISCALI

⚑E3 ℹ Dorgali tourist office, Viale Umberto; www.enjoydorgali.it
🕒 9am-7pm (Oct-May: to 5pm)

Hidden in the depths of an enormous chasm in Monte Tiscali, this nuraghic village is Sardinia's most intriguing – and most spectacularly located – prehistoric site.

The remains of a nuraghic settlement were discovered here in the 19th century, by some woodcutters travelling over the mountain range that dominates the Lanaittu valley. Situated within a natural crater deep inside the 518-m (1,700-ft) high Monte di Tiscali, the village of Tiscali is virtually invisible from the outside. The site, which was inhabited up to the time of the Roman invasion in the 3rd century BC, consists of a number of round dwellings with juniper wood roofs and architraves around the doors. Years of neglect have led to the partial deterioration of the village, but it is still one of the most exciting nuraghic finds in Sardinia, in particular because of its unique position.

The only way to reach the village is on foot, along a path marked with red arrows. The climb can be hazardous and tiring, traversing over rocky ground, so it is highly advisable to go with a tour guide. The walk takes about 3–4 hours and is one of the most popular treks on the island.

> 💬 INSIDER TIP
> **Tiscali Tours**
>
> Guided hikes to Tiscali can be booked through Gennargentu Escursioni *(www.gennargentu. com)* and Cooperativa Ghivine *(www.ghivine. com)*. They can also arrange trips to other sights in the area, such as the ravine of Su Gorropu *(p101)* or the Codula di Luna *(p98)*.

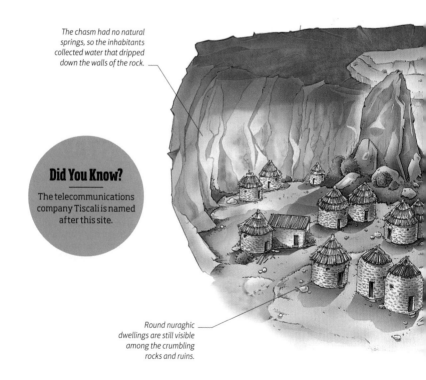

The chasm had no natural springs, so the inhabitants collected water that dripped down the walls of the rock.

Did You Know?

The telecommunications company Tiscali is named after this site.

Round nuraghic dwellings are still visible among the crumbling rocks and ruins.

↑ Exploring the remains of the nuraghic village inside the chasm

→ Hiking over the rocky mountain terrain towards the archaeological site

The difficult terrain and steep walls provided natural defences for the inhabitants of Tiscali.

The roofs were made of juniper wood.

← A reconstruction of the village, showing how the nuraghic settlement would once have looked

The walls of the dwellings were made of limestone blocks.

Medieval Burgos Castle
overlooking the town
from its conical peak ↑

EXPERIENCE MORE

❸
Burgos

D3 ☎ *i* www.comune
burgos.gov.it

The hamlet of Burgos lies
below a cone-shaped peak in
the Goceano mountains. The
town was founded in 1353
by Mariano d'Arborea and is
dominated by the ruins of
Burgos Castle, built in 1127.

GREAT VIEW
**Foresta di
Burgos**

From the Uccaidu pass,
northwest of Bono, there
are hiking trails up the
ridge to the summit of
Monte Rasu, at an
altitude of 1,258 m
(4,125 ft). From here
there are sweeping
views of the thickly
forested area of Foresta
di Burgos, as well as the
surrounding mountain
range and beyond.

The castle was the scene of
many battles between the
Sardinian principalities and
mainland colonists during the
Middle Ages. It was from here,
in 1478, that Artaldo di Alagon's
troops marched to the Battle
of Macomer, a decisive defeat
for the Sardinians, marking
the beginning of Aragonese
dominion. Within the outer
defensive walls, further fortifications surround a restored
tower. The entrance to the
tower was once through a
wooden stairway that could
be raised in case of a siege.

The Foresta di Burgos, 5 km
(3 miles) northwest of Burgos,
is a well-kept forested area with
holm oak and cork oak trees,
cedars, conifers and chestnut
trees. The area is also home to
a few of the small but sturdy
Sardinian horses known as
Giara, who graze in fenced-off
pastures. To save the species
from extinction, the Istituto di
Incremento Ippico di Orzieri
(the Orzieri Institute for Horse
Breeding) set up a breeding
centre here in 1971.

❹
Bitti

E3 ☎ *i* Town Hall,
Piazza G Asproni 47; www.
comune.bitti.nu.it

This picturesque pastoral
village has made a name for
itself thanks to the Tenores
di Bitti musical group, whose
interpretations of traditional
Sardinian close-harmony songs
have won them international
acclaim. Experts say the local
dialect is the one that most
resembles Latin.

The 19th-century church
of San Giorgio Martire stands
in the central Piazza Giorgio
Asproni. In the nearby parish
home you can see a small
collection of archaeological
finds from the area.

Not far from Bitti, on the
road to Orune (watch out for
the signs, which can be somewhat difficult to follow), is the
Su Tempiesu well-temple. This
consists of several chambers
made of large square basalt
stones, and houses a sacred

Arcangelo, which has been rebuilt several times over the years. Inside is a curious clock driven by the weight of four cannonballs, reportedly shot at the town during the 1796 siege, when the government troops were driven out by the city's inhabitants. This famous episode is re-enacted every year during the traditional festival held on 31 August. On this day the largest pumpkin from Bono's local kitchen gardens is awarded to the unfortunate person who comes last in the festival horse race, as a facetious sign of recognition of the "valour" of the routed army. Until recently, this pumpkin was later rolled down the mountain into the valley to symbolize the government troops escaping from the local inhabitants.

In early September Bono plays host to the colourful Fiera dei Prodotti Tipici Artigianali del Goceano, a fair featuring typical handicrafts from the Goceano region.

---

⑥

Ottana

Ⓐ D4 🚌 **ⓘ Town Hall, Via Libertà 66; www.comune. ottana.nu.it**

Ottana lies in the valley of the River Tirso, not far from the slopes of the Barbagia di Ollolai region. In the Middle Ages the town was an important religious centre. On the southern outskirts of town is the church of San Nicola, once the cathedral of the regional diocese. Built in 1150 in austere Romanesque style, its distinctive black and purple trachyte ashlars betray a strong Pisan influence. Inside is a 14th-century polyptych showing the Madonna flanked by the bishop of Ottana and Mariano d'Arborea, Count of Goceano. In the apse is a 16th-century wooden crucifix.

In the 1970s, Ottana became a site for the petrochemical and textile industries. Today,

it is dedicated to agriculture, artisanal foods and lumber, and its annual Carnival celebrations are deeply rooted in its pastoral traditions. Beginning with the Fuochi di Sant'Antonio Abate (Fires of St Anthony the Abbot) on 16 January, and ending on Shrove Tuesday, locals dress as *boes* (representations of farm animals with sheepskins, bells and horned masks) and *merdules* (masked men who drive the animals through town).

---

well. The well water was used in nuraghic rituals. A little way east of Bitti are five churches: Santo Stefano, Santa Maria, Santa Lucia, San Giorgio and Babbu Mannu (Holy Ghost), which become the hub of lively celebrations during religious festivals.

---

⑤

Bono

Ⓐ D3 🚌 **ⓘ Town Hall, Corso Angioy 2** 🌐 **comunebono. gov.it**

Set at the foot of the Goceano mountain range, the town of Bono is an ideal starting point for trips to the wooded Monte Rasu and the Foresta di Burgos. In the centre of town is the parish church of San Michele

> **The largest pumpkin from Bono's local kitchen gardens is awarded to the unfortunate person who comes last in the festival horse race.**

→ A typical carnival costume in Ottana

A group of Issohadores in full costume gather for the annual Carnival in Mamoiada

This typical rural church has a central structure surrounded by *cumbessias*, basic lodgings for monks and pilgrims to the sanctuary. The present-day church dates from the 17th century and its main feature is its single nave, at the end of which is an Aragonese niche with columns and an architrave made of volcanic rock, brought to light by restoration.

A further 6 km (4 miles) to the south, close to Gavoi, is the **Santuario della Madonna d'Itria**, an imposing church with *cumbessias*. Here, on the last Sunday of July, there is a horse race around the church, known as Sa Carrela.

❼ Mamoiada

⚠E4 🚌 **𝑖 Corso Vittorio Emanuele III 50; www. comune.mamoiada.nu.it**

Some old buildings, possibly of Aragonese origin, are still visible among the modern houses that line the main street of Mamoiada. In 1770 the town was referenced in the writings of the Savoyard viceroy Des Hayes as a place of some interest, with numerous vineyards and an exceptional number of sheep. Flocks are still taken every summer to the slopes of Barbagia di Ollolai to graze.

Mamoiada is best known for the forbidding masks of the Mamuthones and their counterparts, the Issohadores. These figures appear in the streets during the village's lively Carnival celebrations (*p33*), notably on the feast days of Sant'Antonio Abate (16 and 17 January) and on Shrove Tuesday.

Home to Mamoiada's eerie festival masks, the modest **Museo delle Maschere Mediterranee** showcases the rituals and costumes of the town's famous Carnival celebrations, as well as various other Carnival traditions of the Mediterranean. Get up close to mannequins dressed as black-masked Mamuthones, draped in thick sheepskins and heavy cow bells (*sa carriga*). More on Mamoiada's cultural heritage can be found just up the street at the Museo della Cultura e del Lavoro, and locally handcrafted masks can be purchased at shops throughout the town.

About 5 km (3 miles) southwest of Mamoiada, along a secondary road towards Gavoi, is the Santuario di San Cosimo.

🔍 HIDDEN GEM
Ancient Monolith

Standing inside the private garden of the B&B Perda Pintà in Mamoiada (*www. perdapinta.it*) is the freely accessible Sa Perda Pintà menhir – a large sculpted standing stone with 5,500-year-old circular carvings.

Museo delle Maschere Mediterranee

⊛⊛☺ 🏠 Piazza Europa 15 🕒 9am–1pm & 3–7pm daily (Oct–May: Tue–Sun) 🕸 museodellemaschere.it

Santuario della Madonna d'Itria

🏠 Off SP30, Gavoi 🕸 saitria.it

❽ Ollolai

⚠D4 🚌 **𝑖 Pro Loco, Piazza Marconi 1; www.proloco ollolai.it**

Ollolai was once the medieval administrative centre of the Barbagia di Ollolai region, an area that included the northern part of Barbagia, and retains the name today. The town's decline began in 1490 after a terrible fire and today it is a small hamlet.

Some original houses decorated with dark stone doorways are visible in the old centre and there are still a few craftsmen who weave traditional baskets out of asphodel in their courtyards.

A short distance west of Ollolai is the church of San Basilio, where a traditional religious festival is held on 1 September. A rough road climbs up to the S'Aschisorgiu peak at an altitude of 1,127 m (3,700 ft). From here there are fabulous views of the surrounding mountain range, earning the summit its nickname, "Sardinia's window".

9

Sarule

🅐D4 🚌 🛈 Town Hall, Via Emilio Lussu; www. comune sarule.gov.it

Sarule is a village of medieval origin which has preserved its tradition of carpet-weaving. Along the main street you can still see the workshops where vividly coloured carpets with stylized figures are woven on antique vertical looms and then sold on the premises.

Perched precariously on a spur overlooking the village is the isolated sanctuary of Nostra Signora di Gonare,

one of the most sacred shrines in Sardinia. The church was built in the 13th century for the then ruler of the principality, Gonario II di Torres, and by the 16th century it had become a famous pilgrimage site. The sanctuary was given a major overhaul in the 17th century with a dark stone exterior and austere buttresses.

To reach the sanctuary, you must take a rough road heading east from Sarule, climbing up Monte Gonare for 4 km (2.5 miles). This granite rock mountain is interspersed with the odd layer of limestone and outcrops of schist covered in vegetation. The slopes are populated by many species of birds, including partridges, turtle doves, woodpeckers, shrikes and various birds of prey. The forest is largely made up of holm oaks and maples, and in the spring the undergrowth is enlivened by brightly coloured cyclamen, peonies and morning glory. The road ends at an open space with *cumbessias* (pilgrims' houses), and a winding footpath up the

bluff through the holm oak forest leads to the sanctuary. From here there are marvellous views of Monte Ortobene towering over Nuoro, Monte Corrasi near Oliena, and the Gennargentu mountains in the distance.

From 1 to 8 September a lively festival takes place at the sanctuary in honour of the Madonna di Gonare, to which pilgrims travel on foot from all of the neighbouring villages. As well as religious festivities, a horse race is held, and the square resounds with poetry readings and sacred songs sung in the traditional dialect of the region.

> Along the main street of Sarule you can still see the workshops where vividly coloured carpets with stylized figures are woven on antique vertical looms.

The isolated sanctuary ↑ of Nostra Signora di Gonare near Sarule

STAY

Agriturismo Guthiddai

Beautiful working farm estate surrounded by mountain peaks, vineyards and olive groves.

E3 Località Guthiddai, Oliena
w agriturismo guthiddai.com

€€€

Su Gologone Experience Hotel

A country retreat set high in the mountains and decorated with local artwork.

E3 Località Su Gologone, Oliena
w sugologone.it

€€€

 10

Oliena

E3 Town Hall, Via Vittorio Emanuele 4; www.comune.oliena.nu.it

The approach to Oliena along the northern road from Nuoro is an unforgettable sight. In the evening, the lights of the town shine at the foot of the steep mass of Supramonte, which rises eastwards towards the Golfo di Orosei. The countryside is covered in vineyards, yielding the famous Sardinian wine Cannonau.

Some original houses, built around courtyards with external stairways and pergolas and brightly coloured rooms, are still visible along the narrow streets and alleyways. There are also several religious buildings, including the church of Santa Croce, said to be the oldest in the town. Rebuilt in the 17th century, its bell tower is decorated with an unusual trident motif.

The former Jesuit College on Corso Vittorio Emanuele II serves as a reminder of the arrival of this religious order in Oliena. From the beginning of the 17th century onwards, the Jesuits encouraged the town's economy by promoting wine-making and the breeding of silkworms. Next door to the Jesuit college, the church of Sant'Ignazio di Loyola has wooden statues of Sant'Ignazio and San Francesco Saverio, as well as an altarpiece depicting San Cristoforo.

In addition to its excellent wine, Oliena is famous for its jewellery, cakes and the traditional costumes (su hustumene) worn by the townswomen: a black shawl, interwoven with silk and gold, and a light-blue blouse. The most elaborate of these are saved for the impressive processions that take place during Oliena's two most important religious festivals : San Lussorio in August and S'Incontru on Easter morning.

South of Oliena, you'll find an array of hiking trails taking in the rugged and spectacular Supramonte di Oliena. Starting from the Monte Maccione refuge, you can cross the chain and descend into the Lanaittu valley floor.

The Su Gologone natural springs are 8 km (5 miles) east of Oliena. The waters are refreshingly cool in summer and turn into an extremely cold, rushing torrent in winter. Su Gologone, the largest spring in Sardinia, lies in a pleasant wooded area ideal for picnics.

For many years speleologists have been exploring the murky depths of the underground cave of Grotta Sa Oche, in the Supramonte mountains. Every year divers penetrate further

Did You Know?

Grotta Corbeddu, near Oliena, was the refuge of Giovanni Corbeddu Salis, the "Robin Hood of Sardinia".

Trekking over the rugged terrain of the Supramonte di Oliena mountains ↓

into the mountains to study the various aspects of this natural phenomenon.

Orgosolo

E4 **Town Hall, Via Sas Codinas; www.comune. orgosolo.nu.it**

This characteristic village in the interior of the island has been compared to an eagle's nest and a fortress, perched precariously on the mountainside. The villagers are known as rugged and hardy shepherds, proud of their lifestyle and traditions. Rampant banditry here in the 1960s was documented in Vittorio De Seta's film *Bandits at Orgosolo*, in which the hard life of the shepherds and their mistrust of the government is narrated with cool detachment. Locals' passion for social and political issues is also visible in the hundreds of murals painted on the walls of houses and on the rocks around Orgosolo. The images depict the harsh life of shepherds and their struggles to keep their land and traditions, as well as injustices committed elsewhere in the world.

Simple low stone houses line the steep and narrow streets of the town and some original features are still visible on a few isolated houses. The parish church of San Pietro on Corso Repubblica still has its 15th-century Gothic bell tower. Traditional dress – a brightly coloured apron embroidered with geometric patterns and a saffron-yellow headscarf – is still worn by a few local women.

In summer, two popular local festivals draw large crowds to the town: the Assumption Day Festival on 15 August and Sant'Anania's feast day on the first Sunday of June.

Just outside Orgosolo is the 17th-century church of Sant'Anania, built where the saint's relics are said to have been found. Orgosolo is an ideal starting point for excursions up to the surrounding Supramonte mountains, where open pastures are interspersed with dense forests of oak. A road leads to the Funtana Bona, 18 km (11 miles) south of Orgosolo. These natural springs emerge at an altitude of 1,082 m (3,550 ft), at the foot of the limestone peak of Monte Novo San Giovanni.

From here it is also possible to reach the shady Foresta di Montes, one of the largest holm oak forests in Europe, stretching out to the south. Although many trees were destroyed by fires – often started by shepherds in order to acquire more land for grazing – the vast forest is once again increasing in size thanks to replanting efforts, and today it attracts visitors from all over the island. Even in the heat of the summer, a walk through this area and the plateau around the River Olai is thoroughly enjoyable. The dense forest offers plenty of shade from the sun and you may well come across freely roaming sheep and pigs, as well as asphodels in bloom. The many footpaths around the Funtana Bona forest headquarters offer opportunities for hiking and mountain biking.

Gavoi

D4 **Town Hall, Via Dante 75; www.comune. gavoi.nu.it**

For many centuries this village was famous in Sardinia for the production of exceptional harnesses and bridles. Today its most characteristic product is cheese, including *fiore sardo* pecorino, made from sheep's milk. The centre of town is dominated by the conspicuously pink façade of the 15th-century church of San Gavino, which overlooks the square of the same name. Some of Gavoi's oldest and most characteristic streets begin here. A stroll down these narrow, windy cobbled alleys will reveal historic buildings with dark stone façades and wrought-iron balconies overflowing with flowers, such as the two-storey building on Via San Gavino.

In the little church of Sant' Antioco, in the upper part of town, dozens of ex votos in gold and silver filigree are pinned to the wall. There is also a fine statue of the saint, whose feast day is celebrated the second Sunday after Easter.

 13

Sorgono

🅐 D4 🚌 ℹ️ Pro Loco,
Corso IV Novembre 62;
www.prolocosorgono.com

Lying in a densely cultivated area of orchards and vineyards, famous for producing Cannonau wine, Sorgono has been an important town since Roman times.

Although rather dilapidated, the 17th-century Casa Carta, featuring a typical Aragonese window, and a 17th-century fountain of Pisan origin are both worth a visit.

Just west of town is one of the most fascinating and oldest rural sanctuaries in Sardinia, the Santuario di San Mauro.

DRINK

Cantina del Mandrolisai

In business since the 1950s, this well-known winery offers tastings and has a bottle shop.

🅐 D4 🅐 Corso IV
Novembre 20, Sorgono
🌐 cantinadel
mandrolisai.com

Surrounded by the traditional *cumbessias*, houses used by the pilgrims during their stay at the sanctuary, the building is a mixture of local architectural features and the characteristic Gothic-Aragonese style. A fine stairway flanked by two stone lions leads to the grey trachyte façade, which boasts a beautiful carved Gothic rose window. Numerous inscriptions are recorded on the stones of the church, some many centuries old and others more recent, carved by pilgrims to commemorate their visits to the sanctuary.

Various buildings were added to the original church to accommodate pilgrims and offer them adequate dining facilities, in particular during the San Mauro feast day. This lively celebration features a traditional *palio* horse race, performances on the piazza, street food and exhibitions on the sanctuary and the town.

Not far from the church are the ancient Tomba dei Giganti (Tomb of the Giants) di Funtana Morta and, on a hilltop overlooking the church, the Talei Nuraghe, built partly into the surrounding rock. A short walk northwest brings you to the Biru 'e Concas archaeological park, with an unusually high concentration of standing stones – some 200 menhirs dating back to between 3200 and 1800 BC.

↑ Prehistoric standing stones in Biru 'e Concas near Sorgono

 14

Fonni

🅐 E4 🚌 ℹ️ Via San Pietro 4;
www.comune.fonni.nu.it

Fonni is one of the highest towns in Sardinia, lying at an altitude of 1,000 m (3,280 ft). Its economy relies on tradition and tourism, with locally made sweets and expertly crafted fabrics and rugs among the items produced here. The town's major festival is held in mid-June to celebrate the return of the shepherds and their flocks from the winter pastures. Although some of the modern buildings have slightly diminished Fonni's charm, at first sight the town gives you the impression that it's sprouting from the Gennargentu mountainside.

On the edge of town is the Franciscan Madonna dei Martiri complex, which dates from the 17th century. Inside is a curious statue of the Virgin Mary made from pieces of ancient Roman sculptures.

On the road towards Gavoi, 4 km (2 miles) west of Fonni, is the Lago di Gusana. Its tranquil shores, surrounded by holm oaks, make it a popular spot for swimming and sunbathing.

Laconi

A D5 🚌 **i** Consorzio Perda Iddocca, Piazza Marconi; www.iddocca.it

The town of Laconi is built around a rocky spur of the Sarcidano mountain range and boasts beautiful panoramic views of the undulating scenery. Laconi also houses the ruins of Castello Aymerich in the park above the town. Only a single tower from the original fortress, built in 1053, remains. The rest of the castle includes later additions, such as the 15th-century hall and the 17th-century portico. The magnificent park around the castle is a popular destination for walks and picnics.

Near the 16th-century parish church is the birthplace and museum of Sant' Ignazio da Laconi, a miracle worker who lived here in the second half of the 18th century. You can also find a monument in his honour in the piazza.

Once the seat of the local noble overlords, Laconi has preserved the Neo-Classical Palazzo Aymerich, built in the first half of the 19th century by architect Gaetano Cima from Cagliari, who also built the Cathedral of Ozieri (p195). Within the palace is the **Menhir Museum**, a collection of prenuraghic megaliths. Among these are several anthropomorphic menhirs, single stones on which ancient sculptors carved human features.

The area around Laconi is dotted with well-preserved prehistoric remains, and further menhirs can be seen in situ at Perda Iddocca and Genna 'e Aidu. It is advisable to be accompanied by a local guide to make the most out of a visit to these sites.

Menhir Museum
🖈🖈 **A** Via Amsicora 12 **O** Summer: 10am-1pm & 3:30-7pm Tue-Sun; winter: 10am-1pm & 3:30-6:30pm Tue-Sun **w** menhirmuseum.it

 PICTURE PERFECT
Picturesque Park

Parco Aymerich, the large urban park in Laconi where the ruins of Castello Aymerich can be seen, has a multitude of photogenic spots to choose from, including the castle, waterfall and orchid-filled garden.

Belvì

A D4 🚌 **i** Via Roma 17; www.comune.belvi.nu.it

The village of Belvì, once the most important economic and trading centre in the region, lies in a dominating position overlooking the Iscara river valley, which is full of fields of hazelnut trees and orchards.

The railway connecting Mandas and Sorgono runs along a stretch of road near the village, rattling through magnificent scenery as well as tackling a thousand tortuous bends and lofty viaducts (p133).

Several historic houses are still visible in the village. One of these, on the main street, Via Roma, houses the private **Museo di Scienze Naturali** (Natural Science Museum). Founded in 1980 by a group of enthusiasts (including a German naturalist who lived in Belvì for almost 10 years), the museum is divided into two main departments – palaeontology and mineralogy – and also hosts occasional exhibitions of its collection of typical Sardinian fauna and insects.

Museo di Scienze Naturali
🖈🖈 **A** Via San Sebastiano 56 **C** 339 753 10 25 **O** 10:30am-1:30pm & 3:30-7:30pm daily

→

Statuette of a warrior god in the Museo Archeologico Comprensoriale, Teti

Teti

A D4 🚌 **i** Corso Italia 63; www.comune.teti.nu.it

Perched on the rocky mountains that dominate Lago di Cucchinadorza, the village of Teti distinguishes itself by its small museum, the **Museo Archeologico Comprensoriale**. Run by a team of enterprising young locals, the museum illustrates the history of the area's ancient nuraghic settlements (in particular the village of S'Urbale and the sacred precinct of Abini). Displays include pieces found during excavations and a reconstruction of a dwelling from 1000 BC. The halls of the lower floor are used for temporary exhibitions on local culture.

About 1 km (half a mile) southwest of Teti is the archaeological site of S'Urbale, inhabited from 1200 to 900 BC. The remains of many prehistoric dwellings are still visible here. The ancient nuraghic village of Abini lies 10 km (6 miles) to the north of Teti.

Museo Archeologico Comprensoriale
🖈🖈 **A** Via Roma 6 **C** 0784 681 20 **O** Summer: 9:30am-1pm & 3:30-6pm Tue-Sun; winter: 9:30am-12:30pm & 3-5:30pm Tue-Sun

↑ Wrought-iron gate and pointed arch at the entrance to Castello Arangino in Aritzo

18

Aritzo

D4 🚌 **ℹ Town Hall, Corso Umberto I; www.comune. aritzo.nu.it**

Situated amid the cooler hills at the foot of the Gennargentu mountains, the small town of Aritzo was once famous for selling snow. This icy ware was packed in straw-lined boxes and kept in deep snow pits, then transported throughout the rest of the island during the hot summer months.

There are still many traces of the old town. Some houses retain typical stone façades and long, wooden balconies. Among the most impressive buildings are the Neo-Gothic Castello Arangino on Corso Umberto and the 17th-century Aritzo prison on Via Maggiore.

The market for snow has long dwindled, but the town has continued its tradition of making wooden furniture, which can be bought from craftsmen's

workshops. Another industry here is chestnuts: visit during the autumn harvest to indulge in an array of seasonal specialities and nutty desserts.

The balmy climate, high altitude and panoramic views make Aritzo a pleasant tourist destination in the summer. Rodeos are a popular attraction outside town, and walking and horseback tours can be taken to the Gennargentu massif and the upper Flumendosa

river valley. Just north of Aritzo is the distinctive Tacco di Texile, a mushroom-shaped limestone pinnacle, 975 m (3,200 ft) high. From here there are spectacular views of the mountains of the Barbagia region.

During the Middle Ages, the humble Sant'Efisio (Saint Ephysias) made his home in the area. For many years he preached to the local inhabitants and eventually converted them to Christianity.

19

Tonara

D4 🚌 **ℹ Town Hall, Viale della Regione 12-14; www. comunetonara.it**

In the past, the economy of Tonara was based largely on the chestnut and hazelnut groves that surround the town, and on other products typical of a mountain environment. Since tourism discovered this side of the mountain, the town's production of cow bells, *torrone* (nougat) and handwoven rugs has become famous. During the local festivals in the town square, blacksmiths forge the celebrated Tonara bells by hammering the metal on specially shaped stone moulds. The inhabitants are more than willing to tell you how to arrange to see craftsmen at work and purchase

---

SARDINIAN NOUGAT

Nougat (*torrone* in Italian) is one of the most common sweets in central Sardinia. Every local fair or festival will have stalls selling nougat made in Tonara, Desulo or one of the other mountain villages. The main ingredients are almonds, walnuts, hazelnuts, honey and egg whites (in some cases the yolk is also used). The different styles of nougat are created by variations in the type of honey, the flavour of the nuts or number of eggs used. There are many nougat confectioners and visitors are welcome to watch the preparation - blocks of nougat are cut for you while you wait. Torronificio Marotto in Tonara *(Via Roma 6)* makes particularly delicious and fragrant nougat.

their wares. The atmosphere of this typical mountain village is reflected in the shepherds' houses, which have changed very little in over a century.

Tonara is another popular starting point for excursions to the Gennargentu massif. One of the most appealing goes to Punta Muggianeddu (1,467 m/4,800 ft). The road climbs through holm oak and chestnut woods to reach the summit, from which there are magnificent views.

Desulo

E4 🚌 **ℹ Town Hall, Via Lamarmora 73 www. comune.desulo.nu.it**

Perched on the slopes of Gennargentu at an altitude of 895 m (2,900 ft), Desulo (Dèsulu in Sardinian) was

A shepherd guiding his flock over the rolling landscape of Desulo ↓

not converted to Christianity or ruled by outsiders until well into the 7th century. Unfortunately, unregulated building development has had a devastating impact on the village and has almost eliminated the traditional schist houses. It is still quite common, however, to see villagers in traditional dress – made up of bright red, yellow and blue embroidered fabrics – on special occasions, such as the Autumn in Barbagia festival *(p46)* held in the first week of November.

The local economy is based on sheep-raising and on the ancient tradition of cultivating chestnut groves and mountain pastures. In the past, the skilled woodcarvers who lived here would travel to the various markets and fairs throughout Sardinia to sell their handmade spoons, cutting boards and other wooden objects, as well as locally grown chestnuts.

The parish church of Sant' Antonio Abate, and others such as the Madonna del Carmelo and San Sebastiano, are worth a visit to admire their colourful

EAT

Panificio Chessa Basilia

Head to this bakery to pick up traditional Sardinian pastries and breads, both sweet and savoury, before a hike up Punta La Marmora.

E4 🏠 **Via Lai 12, Desulo** 📞 **078 461 9325** 🕐 **Sun**

€€€

wooden statues sculpted in the mid-1600s. But the main reason to visit this village is its natural scenery and the splendid views of the highest peak on the island. There are plans to give the area National Park status, incorporating it into the Gennargentu National Park. Desulo is a favourite destination for hikers keen to climb up Gennargentu and Punta La Marmora *(p96)*, and a growing number of hotels and hostels are being constructed in the area to cater for groups of walkers.

A DRIVING TOUR
MONTE ALBO

Length 87 km (54 miles) **Stopping-off points** Bitti, Lodè, Lula **Difficulty** Easy

The massive white limestone ridge that gave this mountain its name (*albo* means white) extends like a bastion between the Barbagia and Baronia regions. Part of this tour follows a narrow road along the base of the limestone cliffs, giving you a close-up of this majestic formation, while atop the maquis-covered slopes of the mountain you can enjoy magnificent panoramic views. The area is destined to become a reserve to protect 650 plant species as well as moufflon, wild boar and raptors.

Locator Map
For more detail see p114

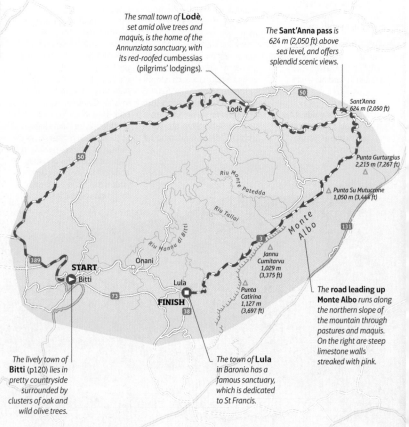

The small town of **Lodè**, set amid olive trees and maquis, is the home of the Annunziata sanctuary, with its red-roofed *cumbessias* (pilgrims' lodgings).

The **Sant'Anna pass** is 624 m (2,050 ft) above sea level, and offers splendid scenic views.

Sant'Anna 624 m (2,050 ft)

Punta Gurturgius 2,215 m (7,267 ft)

Punta Su Mutucrone 1,050 m (3,444 ft)

Jannu Cumitarvu 1,029 m (3,375 ft)

Punta Catirina 1,127 m (3,697 ft)

The **road leading up Monte Albo** runs along the northern slope of the mountain through pastures and maquis. On the right are steep limestone walls streaked with pink.

START Bitti

FINISH Lula

The lively town of **Bitti** (p120) lies in pretty countryside surrounded by clusters of oak and wild olive trees.

The town of **Lula** in Baronia has a famous sanctuary, which is dedicated to St Francis.

0 kilometres 5
0 miles 5

N

↑ The town of Bitti, with the slopes of Monte Albo in the background

The town of Laconi, on ↑
side of the Sarcidano
mountain range

A TRAIN TOUR
THE CAGLIARI–SORGONO RAILWAY

Stopping-off points Dolianova, Senorbì, Mandas, Laconi, Belvì
Timetable www.trenitalia.com; www.treninoverde.com
Journey Time 4 hours 15 minutes

Compared to travelling by car, the train line between Cagliari and Sorgono offers a slow but picturesque approach to the foothills of the Gennargentu mountain range. In the first stretch, up to Mandas, the train goes over the rolling hills of Trexenta. At Mandas, you will need to break your journey to pick up the Trenino Verde service *(p110)* up to Sorgono *(p126)*. This part of the rail route climbs up to the road house at Ortuabis, an area of thick vegetation with a backdrop of mountain peaks, and on beyond Belvì through a wood of dense tree heathers. It offers both spectacular scenery and an insight into travel from another age.

CENTRAL SARDINIA AND BARBAGIA

The Cagliari–Sorgono Railway

Locator Map
For more detail see p114

Near the station at **Belvì** *(p127) you can visit the Museo di Scienze Naturali (Natural Science Museum).*

Laconi (p127) is a popular tourist destination in the Sarcidano region.

Lush scenery and waterfalls characterize the stretch **between Laconi and Meana.**

Did You Know?

Writer D H Lawrence described this journey in his book *Sea and Sardinia* (1921).

The Romanesque **San Pantaleo Cathedral** *at Dolianova was built by the Pisans. Inside is a 5th–6th-century christening font.*

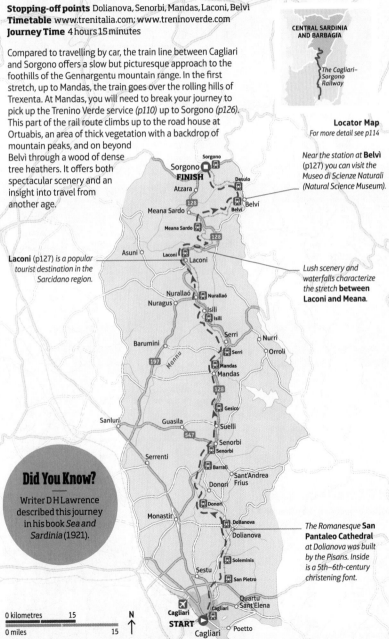

Sorgono
Sorgono FINISH
Desulo
Atzara
Belvì
Meana Sardo — Belvì
128
Meana Sardo
128
Asuni — Laconi — Laconi
Nurallaó — Nurallaó
Nuragus
Isili — Isili
Serri — Nurri
Barumini — Serri — Orroli
197 — Mandas — Mandas
128
Gesico
Sanluri — Guasila — Suelli
547 — Senorbì — Senorbì
Serrenti — Barrali
Sant'Andrea Frius
Donori — Donori
Monastir — Dolianova — Dolianova
Soleminis
Sestu — San Pietro
Quartu Sant'Elena
Cagliari — Cagliari
START — Cagliari — Poetto

0 kilometres — 15
0 miles — 15
N ↑

THE WESTERN COAST

The natural harbours and fertile land in this part of Sardinia have attracted foreign ships for centuries. The first to arrive were the Phoenicians, who established cities around the safe harbours of Sulki (later Sulci), on the island of Sant'Antioco, and Tharros around 1000 BC. The Phoenicians often settled close to the existing nuraghic populations, as was the case at Tharros, and for a time the two communities lived peacefully side by side; both realized the commercial potential of obsidian from the slopes of nearby Monte Arci. After the slow decline of Tharros due to frequent Saracen pirate raids, power was transferred inland to Oristano in 1070. Bosa, originally founded by the Phoenicians, was transformed by the Romans and then the Spanish, who granted the town the status of a royal city. The Spanish also had a major influence on Alghero, which they remodelled into a Catalonian town in the 14th century. Largely neglected under subsequent rulers, the region was revived in the 20th century with land reclamation projects and the establishment of tourist resorts along the coast.

See inset right

PORTO TORRES

Marina di Sorso

Pozzo San Nicola

Sorso

Rosário

Platamona Lido

Palmadula

Marina di Sorso

Osilo

ARGENTIERA 9

Sassari

Ossi

Osini

Usini

Ittiri

Ossi

Florinas

Alghero AirPort ✈

Olmedo

Uri

Tramariglio

Fertilia

Lido S. Giovanni

CAPO CACCIA 2

ALGHERO 1

Villanova Monteleone

MONTELEONE ROCCA DORIA 12

Romana

Pozzomaggiore

Montresta

Padria

Capo Marargiu

Temo

BOSA 3

Sindia

Bosa Marina

Suni

Tresnuraghes

Scano di Montiferro

San Leonardo de Siete Fuentes

M e d i t e r r a n e a n S e a

CUGLIERI 14

Monte Ferru 1,050 m (3,445 ft)

SANTU LUSSURGIU 16

Bonarcado

Santa Caterina di Pittinuri

Seneghe

Capo Mannu

Milis

Putzu Idu

Bauladu

SALE PORCUS RESERVE 21

Riola Sardo

Stagno di Cabras

Solarussa

SAN SALVATORE 20

19

CABRAS

Simaxis

Marina di Torre Grande

SAN GIOVANNI DI SINIS 22

5 **ORISTANO**

THARROS 4

24 **SANTA GIUSTA**

Capo San Marco

Golfo di Oristano

Capo della Frasca

ARBOREA 23

Sant'Antonio di Santadi

Terralba

Uras

San Nicolò d'Arcidano

THE WESTERN COAST

| 0 kilometres | 15 |
| 0 miles | 15 |

N
↑

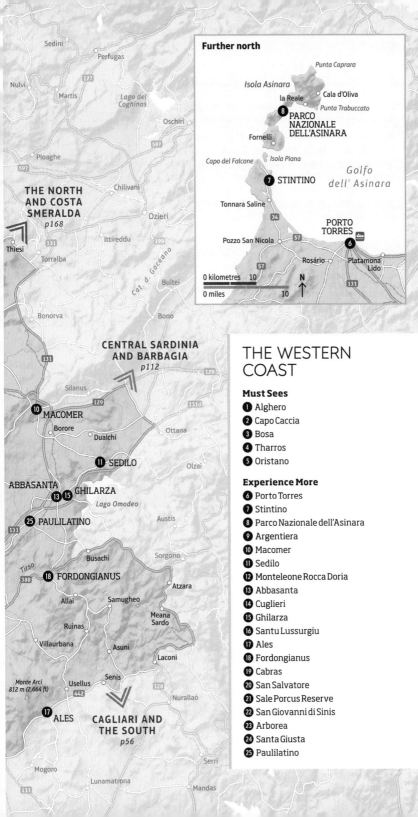

Further north

Punta Caprara

Isola Asinara

la Reale
Cala d'Oliva
8 Punta Trabuccato
PARCO
NAZIONALE
DELL'ASINARA

Fornelli

Isola Piana

Capo del Falcone

Golfo dell' Asinara

7 STINTINO

Tonnara Saline

34

PORTO
TORRES

Pozzo San Nicola
57
6

Rosário
Platamona
Lido

0 kilometres   10

0 miles   10

131

N

Sedini

Perfugas

Nulvi

Martis

127

Lago del Coghinas

Oschiri

597

Ploaghe

597

Chilivani

THE NORTH
AND COSTA
SMERALDA
p168

Thiesi

131

Torralba

Ozieri

Ittireddu

199

Cat. d. Goceano

Bultei

Bono

Bonorva

CENTRAL SARDINIA
AND BARBAGIA
p112

Silanus

131

129

131d

10 MACOMER

Borore

Dualchi

Ottana

129

11 SEDILO

Olzai

ABBASANTA

13 15 GHILARZA

Lago Omodeo

Austis

25 PAULILATINO

131

Busachi

Sorgono

Tirso

388

18 FORDONGIANUS

Atzara

Allai

Samugheo

Meana
Sardo

Ruinas

Villaurbana

Asuni

Laconi

*Monte Arci
812 m (2,664 ft)*

Usellus

Senis

128

442

Nuralláo

17 ALES

CAGLIARI AND
THE SOUTH
p56

Mogoro

Serri

131

Lunamatrona

Mandas

THE WESTERN COAST

Must Sees

1 Alghero
2 Capo Caccia
3 Bosa
4 Tharros
5 Oristano

Experience More

6 Porto Torres
7 Stintino
8 Parco Nazionale dell'Asinara
9 Argentiera
10 Macomer
11 Sedilo
12 Monteleone Rocca Doria
13 Abbasanta
14 Cuglieri
15 Ghilarza
16 Santu Lussurgiu
17 Ales
18 Fordongianus
19 Cabras
20 San Salvatore
21 Sale Porcus Reserve
22 San Giovanni di Sinis
23 Arborea
24 Santa Giusta
25 Paulilatino

❶

ALGHERO

🗺 C3 ✈ Alghero Fertilia, 10 km (6 miles) N 🚉🚌 ℹ Ex Casa del Caffè, Via Cagliari 2; www.alghero-turismo.it

Alghero was established in the early 12th century by the aristocratic Doria family from Genoa. The city was conquered by the Aragonese in 1353, and has retained a strong Spanish influence ever since. The old centre lies within the ancient fortified quarter and the local economy is based on tourism and handicrafts – particularly jewellery and coral items.

① Porta a Terra

📍 Piazza Porta a Terra

This 14th-century city gate now has a rather stranded air, as most of the associated fortifications were demolished to make room for present-day Via Sassari. The gate was once known as Torre degli Ebrei (dels Hebreus in Catalan), or Tower of the Jews, because of the contribution made by the Jewish community to Catalan king Pietro III's conquest of the city. The tower was originally one of two gates, and was linked by a drawbridge to the large Gothic arch (now a war memorial). The tower contains a tourist information centre and an exhibition space, and has views of the city and the harbour from its terrace.

② Bastioni and Forte della Maddalena

Lining the seafront, the city's well-preserved ramparts are a popular place for a stroll with locals and tourists alike – particularly at sunset. Starting from the south on Lungomare Dante, the route passes along a series of bastions named after famous explorers including Christopher Colombus and Marco Polo. Several towers – the Torre di San Giacomo, the Mirador rampart, the Torre de Castilla and the Torre de la Polvorera – overlook the path, which eventually leads to the port. Not far from the steps that run from the seafront

> 💬 INSIDER TIP
> **Perfect Picnic**
>
> The Alghero daily market near the Porta a Terra is a great place to buy picnic supplies – pick up some fresh pecorino cheese, carasau bread, a bottle of Vermentino and some seasonal fruit for a Sardinian feast.

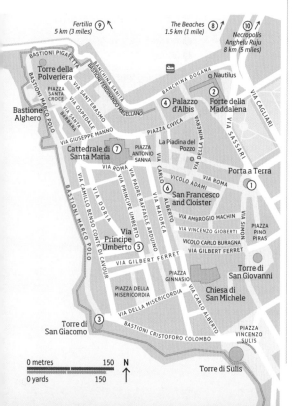

Fertilia
5 km (3 miles) ⑨ ↖

The Beaches ⑧ ↗
1.5 km (1 mile)

⑩ ↗
Necropolis
Anghelu Ruju
8 km (5 miles)

BASTIONI PIGARETA

Torre della
Polveriera

BANCHINA SANTA

BASTIONI MARCO POLO

BASTIONI SANTA CROCE

PIAZZA
SANTA
CROCE

VIA SANT'ERASMO

BASTIONI FERDINANDO MAGELLANO

BANCHINA DOGANA

🚢 ○ Nautilus

Bastione
Alghero

VIA OSPEDALE

VIA SANTA
BARBARA

VIA GIUSEPPE MANNO

PIAZZA CIVICA

④ Palazzo
d'Albis

② Forte della
Maddalena

VIA CAGLIARI

Cattedrale di ⑦
Santa Maria

PIAZZA
ANTONIO
SANNA

VIA DELLA MINERVA

La Piadina del
Pozzo

VIA SASSARI

VIA ROMA

VIA ROMA

Porta a Terra

VICOLO ADAMI

⑥ San Francesco
and Cloister

①

VIA CAMILLO BENSO CONTE DI CAVOUR

VIA DORIA

VIA PRINCIPE UMBERTO

VIA PADRE RAFFAELE ARDUINO

VIA CARLO ALBERTO

VIA MAIORCA

VIA AMBROGIO MACHIN

VIA VINCENZO GIOBERTI

PIAZZA
PINO
PIRAS

VIA SIMON

Via
Principe
Umberto ⑤

VICOLO CARLO BURAGNA

VIA GILBERT FERRET

VIA GILBERT FERRET

Torre di
San Giovanni

PIAZZA
GINNASIO

PIAZZA DELLA
MISERICORDIA

VIA DELLA MISERICORDIA

VIA CARLO ALBERTO

Chiesa di
San Michele

Torre di ③
San Giacomo

BASTIONI CRISTOFORO COLOMBO

PIAZZA
VINCENZO
SULIS

0 metres   150   N ↑
0 yards   150

Torre di Sulis

↑ Alghero's attractive waterfront, lined by the old city walls

to the old Porta a Mare city gate is Forte della Maddalena, the city's most important Spanish fortification. It is also known as Garibaldi's Tower, after Italian revolutionary and hero Giuseppe Garibaldi, who landed here on 14 August 1855; a plaque on the wall commemorates this event.

 ③

Torre di San Giacomo

🏛 Cnr Bastioni Cristoforo Colombo and Bastioni Marco Polo

Standing on the waterfront, opposite the 17th-century church of Carmen, is the Torre di San Giacomo. This restored fortification differs from the other towers in Alghero with its unique octagonal form. It is also known as the Torre dei Cani (the Dogs' Tower) reflecting its earlier use as an enclosure for the stray dogs of the town.

 ④

Palazzo d'Albis

🏛 Piazza Civica (Plaça de la Dressana)

This 16th-century palace with twin lancet windows is also known as Palazzo de Ferrera. It is a rare example of Catalan civic architecture, and is famous for having hosted Holy Roman Emperor (and king of Spain) Charles V in October 1541. The emperor stopped at Alghero with his fleet on the way to Algiers, and was very flattering in his reactions to the city. According to tradition, the emperor spoke to the populace from the balcony of Palazzo d'Albis, and had the following to say about the city: "*Bonita, por mi fé, y bien assentada*" ("Beautiful, by my faith, and quite solid"), and told the inhabitants "*Estade todos caballeros*" ("You are all gentlemen"). The monarch's sojourn ended with a massive requisition of cattle, which he needed for the Spanish troops. The animals were then slaughtered after an impromptu bullfight, held by the palazzo in Piazza Civica.

EAT

La Piadina del Pozzo
Casual eatery serving fresh and fast *piadinas* (flatbread sandwiches).

🏛 Via Minerva 25
📞 079 492 12 39

 €€€

Azienda Agrituristica Sa Mandra
A rustic agriturismo serving delicious local food and drink.

🏛 Strada Provinciale 44,
🌐 aziendasamandra.it

€€€

Nautilus
Dine on Catalan-style lobster, seafood risotto and the catch-of-the-day by the port.

🏛 Via Maddalenetta 4
🌐 nautilusalghero.it

 €€€

⑤ Via Principe Umberto

This narrow street, which begins at the cathedral, was one of the main arteries in the old walled city. Of interest are the Gothic Casa Doria, also known as the Palazzo Machin after the family that lived here in the 17th century and, in Piazza del Teatro, the 19th-century Neo-Classical Teatro Civico. The latter still hosts a variety of performances in its restored auditorium.

 ⑥

San Francesco and Cloister

🏠 Via Carlo Alberto ⏰ Jul-Sep: 9:30am-1pm & 4:30-8pm; Oct-Jan: 9:30am-12:30pm & 4:30-8pm 🌐 complessosanfrancesco alghero.com

San Francesco may very well be the most important Catalan monument in the whole of Sardinia. Built at the end of the 1300s and then partially rebuilt in the 16th century when some of the structure collapsed, the church displays different stylistic influences. The slim

Did You Know?

Alghero was originally named Alquerium for the abundant algae off its coast.

bell tower was added in the 17th century, and features a Gothic hexagonal body set on a square base.

The church's two-aisle, white sandstone interior still has Baroque altars made of carved wood and, under the star-spangled Gothic vault of the presbytery, there is an 18th-century altar. The sculptures include a *Dead Christ* and *Christ at the Column*.

The cloister, accessible from the sacristy, is well worth a visit. It is an eclectic sandstone construction, built in different periods. The lower part dates from the 14th century, while the upper part was added in the 1700s. The 22 columns are in two sections, with round or polygonal bases and sculpted capitals. During the summer music season, the Estate Musicale Internazionale di Alghero, concerts and other

cultural events are held in these lovely surroundings. In other seasons of the year events and art exhibitions are held in the old refectory.

Just south of San Francesco is the church of San Michele, with a brightly coloured tiled cupola that has become a symbol of Alghero.

⑦ Cattedrale di Santa Maria

🏠 Piazza Duomo 📞 079 97 92 22 ⏰ Jul-Aug: 10am-1pm, 7-9:30pm Mon, Tue & Thu-Sat; Apr-May & Sep-Oct: 10:30am-1pm, 4-6:30pm Mon, Tue & Thu-Sat

The doorway of Alghero's Neo-Classical cathedral opens out onto the small Piazzetta Duomo. The cathedral, dedicated to Santa Maria, was first built in the 14th century. In the mid-16th century the building was restructured in the Catalan-inspired late Gothic style. The unusual octagonal bell tower dates from the same period.

In the interior there is a striking difference between the layout of the central part,

↑ The white sands and turquoise sea at Le Bombarde beach

domus de janas. Many of the tombs have been decorated with architectural details such as steps, pillars, false doors and false windows. Among the most interesting *domus de janas* are tomb A and tomb 28, which feature carvings of bull heads (a symbol of divinity). Grave goods found here are on display in Cagliari's Museo Archeologico Nazionale *(p62)*.

which is late Renaissance, and that of the 16th-century Gothic presbytery. Items of Catalan jewellery are on display in the sacristy.

 8

The Beaches

The port of Alghero has never been an important trading place, partly because of its remote location and marshy coast. There is no heavy industry in the area and, as a result, the sea is particularly clean here. A series of appealing resorts can be found just outside the old town.

The best-known beach is Le Bombarde, a heavenly strip of pure white sand bordered by crystal-clear sea and fringed by forest, 8 km (5 miles) northwest of the city. Another good beach nearby is the Lazzaretto, which owes its name to the hospital for the poor that existed there during the period of the black plague. When the weather is clear, the impressive vertical profile of Capo Caccia *(p146)* stands out on the horizon.

 ←

Walking through the shady cloister of the church of San Francesco

 9

Fertilia

⌂ 7 km (4 miles) NW of Alghero

To the north of Alghero is the coastal town of Fertilia, a small yacht harbour built during the Fascist era as the centre of the land reclamation programme. Nearby you can still see the 13 arches of the Roman bridge at the ancient city of Carbia. At one time the bridge connected Carbia to Portus Nympharum, now Porto Conte bay. A few minutes away stands the site of Palmavera Nuraghe. This prehistoric complex contains two towers and a courtyard surrounded by a barbican.

10

Necropolis Anghelu Ruju

⌂ SP42 🕐 Apr-Oct: 9am–6pm daily (May-Sep: to 7pm); Nov-Mar: 10am–2pm daily 🌐 necropolianghelu ruju.com

East of Alghero is the intriguing Necropolis Anghelu Ruju, the largest pre-nuraghic burial place of its kind in Sardinia. Discovered by chance in 1903, the site contains almost 40

STAY

B&B La Mia Isola
Centrally located near the old town, this B&B offers a selection of simple but colourful family-friendly rooms with modern amenities.

⌂ Via Brigata Sassari 8 🌐 lamiaisolaalghero.it

€€€

Alghero Resort Country Hotel
Set on a former 18th-century equestrian estate, this modern hotel has tennis courts and a swimming pool, and offers personalized excursions in the area.

⌂ Via Carrabuffas 🌐 algheroresort.it

€€€

El Faro Hotel
Set on a rocky promontory surrounded by the sea, this hotel is perfect for a romantic getaway full of panoramic views. Rooms are fresh and modern, and breakfast is complimentary.

⌂ Via Porto Conte 52 🌐 elfarohotel.it

€€€

Sunset over Alghero's atmospheric waterfront

A SHORT WALK
ALGHERO

Distance 1 km (half a mile) **Nearest bus stop** Mercato Civico **Time** 15 minutes

Despite the considerable damage wrought by Allied bombardments in World War II, the heart of the old city is, for the most part, intact and can easily be explored on foot. The main roads from Bosa (to the south) and Sassari (to the northwest) lead to the city walls, from where you can embark on a walk around the narrow, high-sided streets of the old town. Strongly influenced by Spanish culture, Alghero remains the most Spanish city in Sardinia. You'll find ample evidence of this legacy as you stroll through the medieval streets, lined with Spanish-style churches and restaurants serving classic Catalan dishes.

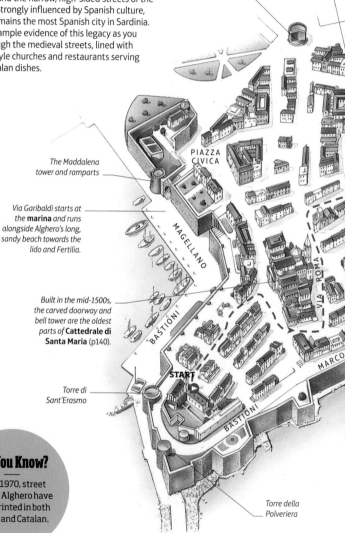

San Francesco is a jewel of Catalan architecture, with parts dating back to the 14th century. The lovely cloister becomes an open-air concert venue in summer (p140).

Porta Terra tower

PIAZZA CIVICA

The Maddalena tower and ramparts

MAGELLANO

*Via Garibaldi starts at the **marina** and runs alongside Alghero's long, sandy beach towards the lido and Fertilia.*

VIA ROMA

*Built in the mid-1500s, the carved doorway and bell tower are the oldest parts of **Cattedrale di Santa Maria** (p140).*

BASTIONI

START

MARCO

Torre di Sant'Erasmo

BASTIONI

Did You Know?

Since 1970, street signs in Alghero have been printed in both Italian and Catalan.

Torre della Polveriera

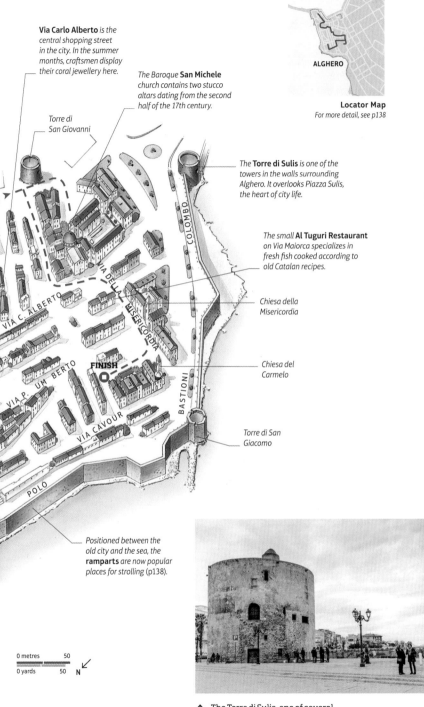

Via Carlo Alberto is the central shopping street in the city. In the summer months, craftsmen display their coral jewellery here.

The Baroque **San Michele** church contains two stucco altars dating from the second half of the 17th century.

Torre di San Giovanni

The **Torre di Sulis** is one of the towers in the walls surrounding Alghero. It overlooks Piazza Sulis, the heart of city life.

The small **Al Tuguri Restaurant** on Via Maiorca specializes in fresh fish cooked according to old Catalan recipes.

Chiesa della Misericordia

Chiesa del Carmelo

VIA C. ALBERTO

VIA DELLA MISERICORDIA

COLOMBO

BASTIONI

FINISH

VIA P. UM BERTO

VIA CAVOUR

POLO

Torre di San Giacomo

Positioned between the old city and the sea, the **ramparts** are now popular places for strolling (p138).

ALGHERO

Locator Map
For more detail, see p138

0 metres   50
0 yards   50   N

↑ The Torre di Sulis, one of several towers that punctuate the ramparts

CAPO CACCIA

Ⓐ B3 🕐 Grotta di Nettuno: 8am-7pm daily
🌐 ampcapocaccia.it/grottanettuno.asp

Towering above the sea, with a lighthouse perched on its outermost point, the Capo Caccia promontory is a natural haven rich in wildlife and offers fantastic views of Alghero and the coast.

EXPERIENCE **The Western Coast**

The name Capo Caccia derives from the *caccia*, or wild pigeon hunting, that was once popular on this promontory. Naturalists have also long been drawn here, not only by the wild pigeons, but also by the swifts, peregrine falcons and herring gulls that nest in the crevices and gullies of the precipitous cliffs. On the western side of the headland, 656 steep steps (known as the Escala del Cabirol, or Roe Deer's Staircase) take you down the cliff to the fascinating Grotta di Nettuno (Neptune's Grotto). The cave can also be reached in about 20 minutes by boat from Alghero; trips run from April to October.

🔍 HIDDEN GEM
Le Prigionette

Among Capo Caccia's many points of interest, one of the least explored attractions is Le Prigionette - a wild pocket of forest and coastline with hiking and biking trails, plus the chance to spot albino donkeys, deer and wild horses.

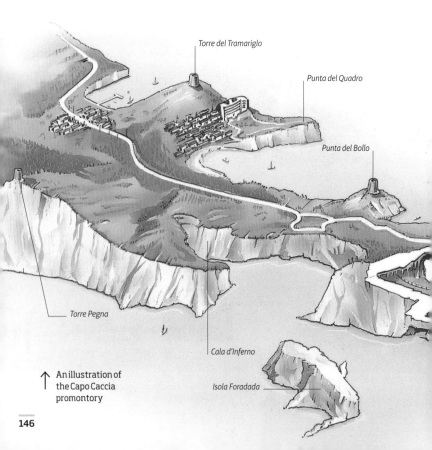

Torre del Tramariglo

Punta del Quadro

Punta del Bollo

Torre Pegna

Cala d'Inferno

↑ An illustration of the Capo Caccia promontory

Isola Foradada

1 The protected reserve at Capo Caccia extends into the sea to cover the marine area surrounding the promontory.

2 The Grotta di Nettuno extends for 2,500 m (8,200 ft); around 580 m (1,900 ft) can be explored on a guided tour.

3 Despite its barren appearance, Isola Foradada – a small island opposite Capo Caccia – is home to an endemic species of brassica.

The name of Grotta Verde (Green Grotto) derives from the colour of the moss and other plants that cover the cave's stalagmites and stalactites.

From the ridge of land separating the headland from the lighthouse point, the Escala del Cabirol steps wind down to the entrance of the Grotta di Nettuno.

Lago La Marmora

Grotta di Nettuno, one of the most picturesque caves in Sardinia, was first explored in the 1700s.

TOP 3   TOUR OPERATORS

Progetto Natura
w progettonatura
sardegna.com
Ecologically sensitive
dolphin-spotting
and snorkelling tours
led by professional
marine biologists.

Poseidon Diving Center
w poseidondivingcenter.com
Scuba diving lessons
and tours of the cliffs
and caves of Parco
Naturale Regionale
di Porto Conte.

Sea Kayak Sardinia
w seakayaksardinia.com
Kayak rentals, lessons
and tours of secluded
coves, suitable for all
ability levels.

3

BOSA

 C3 🚗🚌 *i* bosaonline.com.

The pastel-coloured houses of Bosa lie on the bank of the Temo river, the only navigable river in Sardinia. The town was originally founded by the Phoenicians, and later maintained a close relationship with the Iberian peninsula under Spanish rule. Bosa is famous for its artisan traditions of gold-filigree jewellery and lace-making. In the Sa Costa medieval quarter, a labyrinth of cobblestone alleys and steps, you can still see women sitting outside their homes making lace.

① 🅜

Casa Deriu

🏠 Corso Vittorio Emanuele II 59 🕐 Hours vary; check website 🌐 museidibosa.it

Casa Deriu is a typical 19th-century Bosa building, which has been transformed into an exhibition centre. The ground floor features traditional local products such as cakes, wine and bread, as well as a display of old black-and-white photographs. On the first floor is a fine reconstruction of the elegant Deriu apartment, with its olive wood parquet, frescoed vaulted ceiling, majolica tiles from Ravenna and locally made lace curtains.

The top floor houses the Pinacoteca di Antonio Atza municipal art gallery, featuring the collection of Melkiorre Melis, a local artist and one of the leading promoters of 20th-century applied arts in Sardinia. The eclectic works on display span a 70-year period of graphic art, oil painting, ceramics and posters. There are also a number of Arab-influenced works, which Melis executed while he was director of the Muslim School of Arts and Crafts in Tripoli.

②

Cattedrale

🏠 Piazza Duomo 📞 0785 37 32 86 🕐 9-11:30am & 3-5pm daily (3:30-6:30pm in summer)

Dedicated to the Virgin Mary, Bosa's majestic cathedral was rebuilt in the 19th century in the late Baroque Piedmontese style. Its relatively plain exterior features two cupolas decorated with colourful majolica tiles, and a red sandstone bell tower. Inside the cathedral are several notable artorks, including a statue of the *Madonna and Child* from the Catalan school, sculpted in the 16th century. On either side of the main altar are two marble lions killing dragons. The elegant side altars are made of multi-coloured marble.

↑ The picturesque town of Bosa, situated on the banks of the Temo river

③
Corso Vittorio Emanuele II

Named after the last king of Sardinia and first king of Italy, the main street in Bosa runs parallel to the river. It is lined with aristocratic buildings from the 18th and 19th centuries, many of which feature wrought-iron balconies festooned with plants. A number of the residences now house goldsmiths' workshops where filigree and coral jewellery are made; some have displays of their works outside. There are also cafés and restaurants dotted along the length of the cobbled street, with pleasant outdoor tables from which to watch the world go by.

> Corso Vittorio Emanuele II is lined with aristocractic buildings from the 18th and 19th centuries, many of which feature wrought-iron balconies festooned with plants.

Did You Know?

Environmentalists say that the seaside near Bosa is the cleanest in Italy.

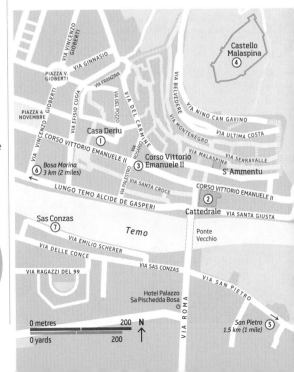

Castello Malaspina

🏠 Via Ultima Costa 14
🕐 Hours vary; check website 🌐 castellodibosa.it

Built in 1112 by the Malaspina dello Spino Secco family, this castle is also known as the Castello di Serravalle, after the hill on which it stands. Only the towers and outer walls have survived to the present day, but it is still an impressive structure nonetheless. The original castle complex was enlarged in the 14th century, when the main tower, built of light ochre trachyte, was added.

Inside the walls, the only complete building is the church of Nostra Signora di Regnos Altos. Restoration carried out in 1974–5 brought to light a cycle of Catalan School frescoes, one of the few that are left in Sardinia.

From the ramparts there are magnificent views of the church of San Pietro, the lower Temo river valley and the red roofs of the Sa Costa quarter. You can walk down to the centre of town by following the steps skirting the walls that once defended Bosa to the east.

Castello Malaspina atop the Serravalle hill and *(inset)* visitors walking along its ramparts ↓

San Pietro

🏠 Via S. Pietro 📞 340 395 50 48 🕐 Apr–Jun: 9:30am–12:30pm & 3:30–5:30pm daily; Jul–Aug: 9:30am–12:30pm & 4–6pm daily; Sep: 9:30am–12:30pm & 3–5pm daily; Oct 9:30am–12:30pm, daily; Nov–Mar: by appointment only

About 1.5 km (1 mile) east of the left bank of the Temo stands the church of San Pietro, built in red trachyte stone, one of the oldest and most interesting of Sardinia's Romanesque churches. It was constructed in different stages, beginning in the second half of the 11th century; the bell tower, apse and side walls were added the following century. The façade combines elements of Romanesque with touches of French Gothic, imported by the Cistercian monks. On the architrave of the doorway is a notable *Madonna and Child with Saints Peter, Paul and Constantine.*

The area around the church has been inhabited since Phoenician times and was once the main heart of Bosa. This changed at the end of the 16th century, when the village's population moved to the newly constructed Sa Costa district.

Bosa Marina

Bosa Marina, just over 3 km (2 miles) west from the centre of town, has a lovely wide, sandy beach that stretches for around 1 km (half a mile).

→ Tanning equipment on display in the Museo delle Conce, housed in a former tannery in Sas Conzas

Lapped by crystal-clear sea, the beach is well equipped for water sports such as kite-surfing, windsurfing, and scuba diving, and there are plenty of cafés and restaurants where you can buy refreshments. A long jetty at the western end of the beach leads to the tiny Isola Rossa, overlooked by the Aragonese tower on the mainland. Temporary exhibitions are held in the tower in summer.

Further beaches can be found along the adjacent coastline – the stretch that runs north up to Alghero is particularly spectacular.

Bosa Marina is also the starting point for the **Trenino Verde** route that winds inland to Macomer (p158). The little green train skirts the Pedras Nieddas (black stones) beach before going up the Rio Abba Mala valley to Modolo, Tres-nuraghes and Sindia.

Trenino Verde
 treninoverde.com

⑦
Sas Conzas

This area on the left bank of the Temo river was once the home of the town's tannery district – it was far enough removed from the centre to keep the unpleasant smells at bay. Evidence of tanning in Bosa can be traced back to the Roman era, but it was during the late 19th and early 20th century that the industry reached its peak. A series of distinctive pink buildings were constructed to house the growing businesses; abandoned in the late 20th century after a crisis in the leather goods market, the structures have today been preserved. One of them now houses the **Museo delle Conce**, a museum devoted to the local tanning industry, with displays of tools and other equipment.

The Sas Conzas quarter can best be admired from the palm-lined street on the other side of the river, Lungo Temo De Gasperi, where the fishermen of Bosa moor their boats. At the eastern end of Sas Conzas is the pretty Ponte Vecchio (Old Bridge), built of red trachyte.

Museo delle Conce
⊛ ⌂ Via Sas Conzas 62
☎ 0785 37 62 20 ⌂ 9:30am-12:30pm & 3:30pm-5:30pm Tue-Sun

 GREAT VIEW
Cala Managu

Capo Marargiu, 17 km (11 miles) north of Bosa Marina, offers beautiful views along the coastline towards the gorgeous Cala Managu beach - and if you're lucky, you may also spot a rare griffon vulture soaring through the blue skies above.

STAY

S' Ammentu

This charming guest house, in a 17th-century building in the historic part of Bosa, offers rooms with antique furnishings, exposed stone walls and modern amenities.

⌂ Via del Carmine 55
 samentu.com

€€€

Hotel Palazzo Sa Pischedda Bosa

Overlooking the bank of the Temo river, this elegant and finely restored Art Nouveau hotel has lovely views and provides a generous breakfast buffet.

⌂ Via Roma 8 hotel sapischedda.com

€€€

4

THARROS

C5 San Giovanni di Sinis Summer: 9am-7pm daily; winter: 9am-5pm Tue-Sun tharros.sardegna.it

Bordered by sea on two sides, this ancient city is one of the most intriguing archaeological sites in the Mediterranean, with a history that spans more than 2,000 years.

The city of Tharros was founded by the Phoenicians around the end of the 8th century BC, on a spit of land called Capo San Marco, which offered safe anchorage for cargo-laden ships. By the 6th and 5th centuries BC, Tharros had become a flourishing port and its prosperity continued under the Romans, from 238 BC onwards. This lasted until the 11th century, when the diocese of the bishop moved to Oristano and the city was abandoned. Only a third of the area has been excavated so far. Most of the visible remains date to the 3rd and 2nd centuries BC, but there is also evidence of previous civilizations: the nuraghic village and the Phoenician Tophet (sanctuary) located on the hill, Su Murru Mannu.

The remains of the ancient city of Tharros and *(inset)* an original Corinthian capital ↓

> **INSIDER TIP**
> **Protection from the Elements**
>
> Tharros is an exposed, outdoor site with little shade, so be sure to wear a hat, use sunscreen, and bring mosquito repellent, too.

1️⃣ The Torre di San Giovanni was built in the 16th-17th century to defend the Sinis peninsula from pirates.

2️⃣ A sophisticated drainage system ran along the middle of the paved road.

3️⃣ The cistern is made of large blocks of sandstone.

DRINK

Vento Maestro Lido
Refresh after a day exploring the ancient wonders of the Sinis peninsula with an alfresco aperitif at this beachside bar just north of the Tharros site.

🏠 Via Lungomare, San Giovanni di Sinis
🌐 ventomaestro.it

↑ A statue of celebrated ruler Eleonora d'Arborea, in the piazza named after her

⑤

ORISTANO

▲C4 🚌🚏 *ⓘ*EPT, Piazza Eleonora 18; www.gooristano.com

On the northern border of the Campidano region, in the middle of a fertile plain with a network of pools, Oristano is the largest town in western Sardinia. It was founded in 1070 after Tharros was abandoned, and prospered between 1100 and 1400 under enlightened rulers such as Mariano IV and his daughter Eleonora. Today, its small historic centre is mostly a pedestrian-only zone, with a tranquil air amid the elegant streets.

①

Cattedrale

Piazza Manno 🄲0783 76 70 97 🄾8am-8pm daily

Dedicated to the Virgin Mary, the cathedral was built in 1228 by Lombard architects. It was renovated in the 17th century in the Baroque style and now displays a mixture of influences. Original features include the octagonal bell tower with its onion dome and brightly coloured majolica tiles, the bronze doors and the Cappella del Rimedio, which has a fine marble balustrade decorated with Pisan bas relief sculpture depicting Daniel in the lions' den. The rich and varied Tesoro del Duomo (Cathedral Treasury) is housed in the chapterhouse, and silverwork, vestments and illuminated manuscripts can be seen upon request.

②

Torre di Mariano II

Piazza Roma

Also called Porta Manna or Torre di San Cristoforo, this sandstone tower at the northern end of the former city walls was built in 1291 by the ruler of the Arborea principality, Mariano II. Together with the Portixedda tower opposite, it is all that remains of the old city walls. The tower is open on its inner façades and looks over Piazza Roma, the heart of city life, with its fashionable shops and outdoor cafés.

③

Corso Umberto

This pedestrian street, also known as Via Dritta, is the most elegant in Oristano. Lined with smart shops and impressive buildings – such as Palazzo Siviero and Palazzo Falchi – it is the most popular street in town for the traditional evening stroll.

THE KNIGHTS OF THE STAR

The Sa Sartiglia festival is held on the last Sunday of Carnival and on Shrove Tuesday. It was probably introduced in 1350 by Mariano II to celebrate his wedding. On 2 February the procession leader, *su Componidori,* is chosen. On the day of the event he is dressed by a group of girls in a white shirt and a woman's mask, with a bride's veil and black hat on his head. He then leads a procession of knights and musicians to the tournament grounds by the cathedral, where he has to run his sword into the hole in the middle of a star hanging from a string, and pick it up. If he succeeds, this signals a prosperous year.

San Francesco

🏛 Via Duomo 10 📞 0783 782 75 🕐 9:30–noon & 4–6:30pm daily

This Neo-Classical church was built over a Gothic church that was destroyed in the early 19th century. In the interior is one of the most interesting statues in Sardinia: a crucifix executed by an unknown late 14th-century Catalan artist. Another important work, by Pietro Cavaro, depicts *The Stigmata of San Francesco.*

Piazza Eleonora d'Arborea

This long, tree-lined square is named after the ruler who established the famous *Carta de Logu* body of laws in 1392 *(p50).* A 19th-century statue of Eleonora stands in the middle of the square, surrounded by noble buildings such as the Palazzo Corrias and Palazzo Comunale, the town hall.

Antiquarium Arborense

🏛 Piazza Corrias 🕐 9am–8pm Mon–Fri, 9am–2pm & 3–8pm Sat–Sun 🌐 antiquarium arborense.it

Housed in the Neo-Classical Palazzo Parpaglia, this fascinating museum features

archaeological finds from Tharros, an art gallery and an exhibit on medieval Oristano. The gallery has interesting altarpieces in Catalan style: the San Martino *retablo* (15th century) attributed to the workshop of the Catalan artist Ramon de Mur; the *Retablo di Santo Cristo* (1533), by followers of Pietro Cavaro, of which only nine panels remain; and the *Retablo della Madonna dei Consiglieri* (1565) by the Cagliari artist Antioco Mainas, depicting the councillors of Oristano and the Virgin Mary.

The archaeological collection has grown out of various private collections, most notably that of local lawyer Efisio Pischedda. Today it contains over 2,000 Neolithic obsidian scrapers, bone hair slides, small amphorae from Greece and Etruria, and Roman glass objects and oil lamps. Among the most notable objects to look out for are a terracotta mask used to ward off evil spirits, scarabs made out of green jasper, and carved gemstones dating from the Roman period.

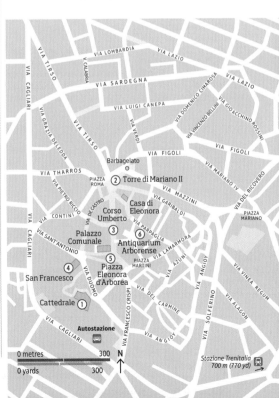

EXPERIENCE MORE

Porto Torres

⚑ C2 🚉 ℹ️ www.comune.
porto-torres.ss.it

The chief port in northern Sardinia, Porto Torres lies in the Golfo dell'Asinara. It was once a prosperous colony known to the Romans as Turris Libisonis. Trade with the city of Karalis (modern-day Cagliari) was carried out along the main road on the island. The city enjoyed a close relationship with Rome, as evidenced by the ancient mosaics at the Foro delle Corporazioni (Forum of Corporations), at the Ostia Antica archaeological site just outside the Italian capital.

After a lengthy period of decline beginning in the Middle Ages, Porto Torres recovered in the 19th century, when it became the port for Sassari. It continued to grow in the 20th century with the development of local industries.

The **Basilica di San Gavino**, built in the Pisan style in the 11th century, is the largest Romanesque monument in Sardinia. Noteworthy design features include the portal in the northern façade, with its 15th-century bas relief, and the other Gothic doorway, which betrays some Catalan influences. Inside the crypt you'll find an area of late Roman–early Christian ruins, as well as 18th-century statues of the martyrs Gavino, Proto and Gianuario, and a medieval inscription celebrating Emperor Constantine I.

By the port, the Turris Libisonis archaeological area presents a faithful picture of an ancient Roman quarter, and the **Antiquarium Turritano** contains finds from the excavations here. Not far away is the seven-arched Ponte Romano (Roman bridge).

A short distance from here lies one of the most fascinating sites of ancient Sardinia, the pre-nuraghic **Santuario di Monte d'Accoddi**. From Porto Torres, head towards Sassari along the SS131; shortly after the Sorso junction (kilometre marker 222.3) a signposted road leads to the archaeological site. The sanctuary dates from the Copper Age (2450–1850 BC) and provides the only example of a megalithic altar in the entire western Mediterranean. The shape is that of a truncated pyramid with a trapezoid base, held up by walls of stone blocks. On the southern side, a ramp leads up to the top, about 10 m (33 ft) high, while the base is about 30 m by 38 m (98 ft by 124 ft).

Around the altar you can see foundations for houses, some sacrificial stone slabs and fallen menhirs. A group of *domus de janas* (rock-cut tombs) was once part of this complex. Items found here are on display at the Museo Archeologico Nazionale in Sassari (p184).

Basilica di San Gavino

♿ 🚫 🏠 Vicolo M Angellu 5
🕐 Apr–Oct: 9am–1pm & 3–6pm daily; Nov–Mar: by appt only
🌐 basilicasangavino.it

Antiquarium Turritano

♿ 🚫 🏠 Via Ponte Romano 99
🕐 9am–6pm Tue–Sun
🌐 antiquariumturritano.it

Santuario di Monte d'Accoddi

♿ 🚫 🏠 🚗 7.5 km (4.5 miles) SE of Porto Torres 📞 334 807 44 49 🕐 Apr–Oct: 9am–6pm Tue–Sat (Jun–Aug: to 7pm), 9am–2pm Sun; Nov–Mar: 9am–2pm Tue–Sun

Colourful houses reflected in the still waters of Porto Torres ↓

Medieval Aragonese
tower at La Pelosa,
north of Stintino

7

Stintino

 B2 🚌 🛈 Town Hall, Via
Torre Falcone 26; www.
comune.stintino.ss.it

The road to Capo Falcone, at
the very northwestern tip of
Sardinia, passes by the enor-
mous wind turbines at the Alta
Nurra ecological energy plant.
Beyond this is the pleasant

🔺 GREAT VIEW
Varied Vista

The spectacular Capo
Falcone promontory
near Stintino offers a
dramatic contrast of
coastal views, with
windswept cliffs to
the west and tranquil
beaches to the east.

fishing village of Stintino,
whose name stems from the
Sardinian word *s'isthintinu*
(narrow passageway), the
traditional name for the inlet
where the village lies. Now
a holiday town, Stintino was
once famed for its tuna fishing
grounds, just off the island of
Asinara. In the summer the
two ports, Portu Mannu and
Portu Minori, have facilities for
aquatic sports. The long, sandy
beach is the most accessible in
the area and very popular.

North of Stintino, the road
skirts the coastline as far as
Capo Falcone. The place is still
"defended" by a tower on its
highest point and by the two
Aragonese forts at La Pelosa
and Isola Piana, in the inlet of
Fornelli, opposite the island
of Asinara.

Parco Nazionale
dell'Asinara

🔺 B1 🚌 🛈 www.parco
asinara.org

The rugged island of Asinara,
once home to the Fornelli
maximum-security prison,
became a national park in 1997.
The island is less than 18 km
(11 miles) long and barely 7 km
(4 miles) wide, ending at the
headland of Scomunica. The
island's ecosystem is unique in
the entire western Mediterranean and includes rare and
endangered animal species.

The pristine coastline and
lack of traffic make Asinara
an ideal refuge for raptors,

EAT

Biscottificio
Demelas

Traditional bakery
specializing in *dolci Sardi*
(Sardinian sweets),
such as the sweet and
savoury *seadas*
pastries, as well as
fresh pastas, including
delicious pockets of
ricotta ravioli.

🔺 B2 🏠 Via Guglielmo
Marconi 3, Stintino
🌐 biscottificio
demelas.com

---

various species of sea bird,
moufflon and wild boar. There
is also a rare species of small
endemic albino donkey, from
which the island took its name
(*asino* meaning donkey). The
rocky, volcanic terrain sup-
ports a holm oak forest, and
the typical low-level brush
shields numbers of rare plants.

As a protected area, the
island cannot be visited without an official tour guide. Day
boat trips start at Stintino and
Porto Torres. Tours are by bus,
on foot or, for a comprehensive look, by offroad vehicle.

↑ A pair of rare albino
donkeys in Parco
Nazionale dell'Asinara

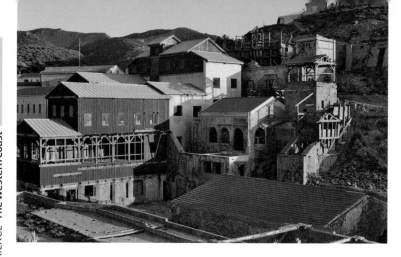

Argentiera

 B2 ⛽ ⛰ **40 km (25 miles) E of Sassari via SP18** *i* www.comune.sassari.it

Many places in Sardinia still carry reminders of the island's former booming mineral industries. At the village of Argentiera, not far from the modern town of Palmadula, the ancient Romans, and the Pisans in the Middle Ages, dedicated themselves to mining the precious metal that gave its name to the area (*argento* meaning silver). In the second half of the 19th century, mining complexes with wooden and masonry buildings were constructed along the coast, so that the mined silver could then be transported by sea to other destinations, where it would be processed and sold.

An entire community grew up around the mine, but it all came to an end in 1963 when the mine closed. For years Argentiera lay quiet as a ghost town, but recently some of the buildings have begun to be restored and the whole area has been developed into an open air museum: **MAR-Miniera Argentiera**. Volunteers guide visitors around, retelling the stories of the old miners, and an exhibit space is set up with mining tools and

photographs. In the summer, the tranquil bay at Argentiera, with its crystal-clear water sparkling with silver dust, is a perfect spot for a swim.

MAR-Miniera Argentiera

 La Miniera de l'Argentiera, Via Carbonia 🕘 **9am-noon & 2-5pm daily** 🌐 landworks. site/mar-argentiera

---

 ⑩

Macomer

D3 ⛽ *i* **Town Hall, Corso Umberto I; www.comune. macomer.nu.it**

Built on a platform of volcanic rock, Macomer is one of the most important commercial centres in the Sardinian interior. The town developed around key communication routes – the Carlo Felice road (the SS131 that runs through most of the

> 🔍 HIDDEN GEM
> ### Living History
> Step back in time at the Museo Etnografico "Le Arti Antiche" (*www. esedraescursioni.it*) in Macomer. Housed in a traditional Sardinian stone house from the 19th century, it features displays of authentic period furnishings.

↑ Abandoned buildings in the old mining town of Argentiera, now open-air museum

island) and the railway – and owes its prosperity to agriculture, livestock raising, dairy products and light industry. It still retains traces of its past in features such as the 17th-century parish church of San Pantaleo, built in the Spanish Gothic style. On the evening of 16 January the traditional Sa Tuva celebration is held in the square in front of Santa Croce in honour of Sant'Antonio Abate. A huge bonfire lights up the entire quarter.

Not far from the town centre, near the Carlo Felice road, a short walk will take you to the impressive Santa Barbara Nuraghe. Its sheer size means that it dominates a series of smaller towers and ramparts.

---

⑪

Sedilo

D4 ⛽ *i* **Town Hall, Piazza San Giovanni Battista; www. comunesedilo.gov.it**

The rocky terrain in the Abbasanta plateau gave the people of Sedilo the raw material to build their houses. There are still a few originals remaining, representing a style that has all but disappeared from local architecture.

The main sight of interest here is the church of San Giovanni Battista in the centre of town. However, Sedilo's most notable claim to fame is the Sanctuary of Santu Antine, otherwise known as San Costantino (Constantine), after the early champion of Christianity – much revered in Sardinia. The church, with the typical *cumbessias* (basic accommodations for pilgrims), stands on a cliff overlooking Lake Omodeo. Within the precinct there are numerous nuraghic sculptures on display, including the so-called *Perda Fitta*, thought to be an icon of female divinity. According to some legends, this impressive monolith is actually the body of a woman who was turned to stone because she was disrespectful to the patron saint.

Artificial Lake Temo and the expansive Nurra plain, seen from Monteleone Rocca Doria ↓

The open space opposite the sanctuary is the setting for the annual S'Ardia competition. This horse race ends the July festivities commemorating Constantine the Great's victory over Maxentius in the Battle of the Milvian Bridge in AD 312. The inside walls of Santu Antine are covered with dozens of ex voto offerings.

 12

Monteleone Rocca Doria

⚿C3 🚌 🛈 Town Hall, Via S. Antonio 1; www.comune.monteleoneroccadoria.ss.it

Situated on the top of the Su Monte cliff (420 m/1,380 ft), the little village of Monteleone Rocca Doria has a sweeping view of Lake Temo and the Nurra plain. Today it is a tranquil, enchanting parcel of land although its inhabitants look back proudly on its noble, militaristic past. In the 13th century the Doria family from Genoa built a fortress here, which was totally destroyed

in 1436 after a three-year siege by troops from Aragon, Sassari, Bosa and Alghero. All that can be seen of it now are the crumbled walls and towers.

Many inhabitants departed to found the town of Villanova Monteleone, but a few people remained behind. The atmosphere today is one of peace and quiet. In the centre of the village stands the 13th-century Romanesque parish church of Santo Stefano.

13

Abbasanta

⚑D4 🚌 ⓘ Town Hall; www.comune.abbasanta.or.it

This picturesque village, whose historical centre still has many traditional houses made of dark local basalt, revolves around the parish church of Santa Cristina, with its impressive Renaissance-inspired architecture. Situated in the middle of a highly developed agricultural region, Abbasanta owes much of its importance to its strategic position near main artery routes, both ancient and modern.

Not far from the village are the Santa Cristina sanctuary near Paulilatino (*p167*) and one of the most significant archaeological sites in the whole of Sardinia: the **Nuraghe Losa**. In order to reach the latter, take the SS131 Carlo Felice road towards Cagliari until you reach kilometre marker 123 (indicated on a road sign). Here, a turning to the right leads to the entrance to the

archaeological site, which is fenced off. Together with the monuments at Su Nuraxi (*p68*) and Nuraghe Santu Antine in Torralba, this well-preserved nuraghic complex is one of the most important remaining from the immediate pre-Punic period (c 510 BC).

In the middle of this vast structure is a keep thousands of years old, dating from the second millennium BC, while the ramparts were likely built several centuries later. The outer defensive walls were the last to be built, and date from the 7th century BC.

Inside the nuraghe there are three roofed chambers with a great many niches, which are thought to have been used for storage. A spiral staircase leads to the upper floor and a terrace with a panoramic view over the landscape.

All around the main structure are the foundations of a series of later buildings, dating from the Bronze Age to the Middle Ages.

A small Antiquarium stands about 100 m (328 ft) from the nuraghi themselves. It houses an interesting exhibition of plans and illustrations of a number of nuraghic monuments in this part of Sardinia.

Nuraghe Losa

🚫🚫😊🚻 ⚑SS131 Carlo Felice 123.5 km
🕐 8:30am-dusk daily
🌐 nuraghelosa.net

14

Cuglieri

⚑C4 🚌 ⓘ Via Carlo Alberto 33; www.comune.cuglieri.or.it

The agricultural town of Cuglieri lies on the western slopes of Mount Montiferru, with a panoramic view of the sea. It is dominated by the striking silver-domed Basilica di Santa Maria della Neve, which has an 18th-century façade and twin bell towers. The barrel-vaulted interior of the church is adorned with stucco and features eight chapels – four on each side of the nave – and there is also an impressive Baroque-style altar made from marble and stone. The walk up to the church makes a delightful stroll, winding through alleyways and stepped streets lined with tall stone houses. The square in front of Santa Maria offers a fine view of the town and the coast between Santa Caterina di Pittinuri and Porto Alabe.

The coast is 15 km (9 miles) away on main road SS292. There you'll find the seaside town of Santa Caterina di Pittinuri, which is set around

↑ The Nuraghe Losa tower near Abbasanta, dating from the 2nd millennium BC

← Kayaking through the natural limestone bridge of S'Archittu near Cuglieri

a white-stone inlet enclosed by a limestone cliff, where the Spanish Torre del Pozzo tower stands. This scenic stretch of coast abounds with rocky headlands and white sand and pebble beaches, as well as caves and beautiful ravines. The most recognizable sight is S'Archittu, a large natural bridge created by erosion.

A dirt road off main road SS292, between Santa Caterina di Pittinuri and S'Archittu, leads to the ruins of the Punic-Roman city of Cornus, the setting for the last battle between the Romans and Carthaginians headed by Amsicora (215 BC). In the 9th century the city was abandoned after repeated Saracen raids, and the inhabitants founded Gurulis Nova, present-day Cuglieri, on the nearby mountainside. The dirt road peters out just before the early Christian town of Columbaris, but the acropolis of Cornus is visible on the hill to the southwest. Although the archaeological site may seem abandoned, it still has some sarcophagi and the remains of a three-nave basilica, all of which are thought to date back to the 6th century.

Ghilarza

🅰 D4 🚌 ℹ Town Hall; www.comune.ghilarza.or.it

An unfinished Aragonese tower stands in the centre of town, but Ghilarza is known principally as the place in which the famous Italian political theorist, writer and activist Antonio Gramsci spent his childhood years. A small door on Corso Umberto leads to the **Casa Museo di Antonio Gramsci**, a research and study centre as well as a museum of historical material, including everyday work and personal items relating to the Communist leader. On the second floor is the small bedroom that was Gramsci's from 1898 to 1908.

A short distance away, on the road to Nuoro, is the beautiful church of San Pietro di Zuri, which was relocated, along with the village of the same name, after the artificial Lake Omodeo was created in 1923.

Casa Museo di Antonio Gramsci

🏠 Corso Umberto 1 🕐 Apr-Sep: 10am-1pm & 3:30-7:30pm Wed-Mon; Oct-Mar: 10am-1pm & 3:30-6:30pm Wed-Mon 🌐 casamuseogramsci.it

> Ghilarza is known principally as the place in which the famous Italian political theorist, writer and activist Antonio Gramsci spent his childhood years.

16

Santu Lussurgiu

△C4 ⊞⊟ **🚹 Town Hall, Viale Azuni 62; www. comunesantulussurgiu.it**

The village of Santu Lussurgiu lies 500 m (1,640 ft) above sea level on the eastern slope of Mount Montiferru, an extinct volcanic mountain. The historic centre is fascinating, with its steep, narrow streets and tiny squares surrounded by beautiful tall stone houses painted in bright colours. Some of

EAT

Sas Benas

Served under beautiful stone arches and on crisp white linens, set menus here include stuffed zucchini, beef carpaccio, aubergine ravioli and wild asparagus spaghetti.

△C4 🏠 **Via Cambosu 6, Santu Lussurgiu** 🕒 **Mon** **sasbenas.com**

€€€

Stone Art Café

Arty and modern eatery for creative waffles, tarts, salads, veggie wraps and burgers.

△D4 🏠 **Via Oristano 56, Abbasanta** 📞 **347 097 48 59** 🕒 **Sun**

€€€

L'Oliveto

Surrounded by an olive grove, this pizzeria has a romantic atmosphere and serves wonderful seafood dishes as well as pizzas.

△C4 🏠 **Via Tirso 23, Cabras** 📞 **078 39 26 16** 🕒 **Tue**

€€€

the buildings also feature decorated architraves and wrought-iron balconies.

On Via Roma, an elegant 18th-century structure houses the **Museo della Tecnologia Contadina** (Museum of Rural Culture), founded by the local Centro di Cultura Popolare. The "Su Mastru Salis" collection is the work of Maestro Salis, the museum curator, who has collected more than 2,000 objects related to the culture of Santu Lussurgiu.

A guided visit to the museum is like taking a trip into the past. Room after room contains fascinating displays of everyday objects used by farmers, shepherds and coal merchants. Equipment includes a fulling mill, an implement used to soften and felt fabric. Over 40 of them were once in use in the Santu Lussurgiu area.

There are still several craftsmen in the village who specialize in making knives and fittings for horse-riding such as bridles. At Carnival time the street in front of the museum is turned into a track for a horse race between pairs of riders dressed as knights.

A few kilometres from Santu Lussurgiu there is a forest of pine, holm oak and oak near the village of San Leonardo de Siete Fuentes, which is famous for its springs of diuretic mineral water that flows out of seven fountains at a constant temperature of 11°C (52°F). The streams meander through a wood that is popular with families.

In the centre of town is the small church of San Leonardo, which once belonged to the Knights of Malta. It was built with dark trachyte stone in the 12th century, but acquired its present Romanesque-Gothic appearance later. The single-nave interior bears the insignias of the Knights of Malta.

In early June, San Leonardo plays host to the annual Fiera Regionale del Cavallo, the most important horse fair on the island, packed with equestrian races and other events.

💬 **INSIDER TIP**
Olive Oil

Not far south of Santu Lussurgiu is the farming town of Seneghe, the capital of olive oil. During the Prentzas Apertas festival (late November) you can taste award-winning olive oils and visit the mills that produce it.

Museo della Tecnologia Contadina

⊛⊛ 🏠 **Via D Meloni 1** 🕗 **By appt only** **museo tecnologiacontadina.it**

17

Ales

△D5 ⊟ **🚹 Town Hall, Corso Cattedrale 53; www.comune.ales.or.it**

Ales, the main village in the Marmilla area, lies on the eastern slope of Monte Arci. In its upper part stands the cathedral of San Pietro, built

Casa Aragonese in Fordongianus, featuring *(inset)* a Catalan-style doorway ↓

> **Santu Lussurgiu's historic centre is fascinating, with its steep, narrow streets and tiny squares surrounded by beautiful tall stone houses painted in bright colours.**

in 1686 by Genoan architect Domenico Spotorno, who used the ruins of the 12th-century church on this site as material for his construction. Twin bell towers with ceramic domes rise above the elegant façade, while in the Baroque interior, the sacristy is graced with delightful carved furniture and a rare 14th-century crucifix. The Archivio Capitolare contains elegant jewellery.

In the same square stand the Palazzo Vescovile (Bishop's Palace), the ground floor of which now houses the "Palazzo delle Muse" modern art collection, and the Oratorio della Madonna del Rosario.

Ales is also the birthplace of Marxist writer and founder of the Italian Communist Party Antonio Gramsci (1891–1937) (p161). His former home on Corso Cattedrale is marked with a plaque.

Ales is a good starting point for a hike to the top of Trebina Longa and Trebina Lada, the highest peaks on Monte Arci. Along the way you are likely to spot pieces of obsidian, the hard black volcanic glass that was historically used to make spears, scrapers and arrowheads. The obsidian of Monte Arci was in great demand, and not only supplied the whole of Sardinia, but was also sold throughout the Mediterranean in the 4th–3rd millennia BC.

18

Fordongianus

 D4 ✉ ℹ **Via Traiano 7; 0783 601 23**

Located in the Tirso river valley, Fordongianus was once known as Forum Traiani and was the largest Roman city in the interior. Today the centre still boasts many old red- and grey-stone houses. One of the best preserved is Casa Aragonese, a typical house of the early 1600s with Catalan-style doorways and windows. Nearby is the 16th-century parish church of San Pietro Apostolo, largely rebuilt in red trachyte. The **Roman Baths** lie on the banks of the river, with a fine portico and rooms with mosaic pavements. The rectangular pool is still fed by hot spring water.

A short distance south of Fordongianus is the church of San Lussorio, built by Victorine monks around AD 1100, over an early Christian crypt.

Roman Baths
◈ ▢ Via Terme
🕐 9:30am–8:30pm daily
🌐 forumtraiani.it

Cabras

🅐C4 🚌 🅘 **Town Hall, Piazza Eleonora d'Arborea 1; www.comune.cabras.or.it**

This town, 7 km (4 miles) west of Oristano, is characterized by its traditional one-storey houses. It stands on the edge of the Stagno di Cabras, the largest freshwater lake and marsh in Sardinia (21 sq km/ 8 sq miles), which is connected to the sea via a series of canals. The presence of both fresh and salt water attracts coots, marsh harriers, peregrine falcons and purple gallinules.

Evidence of the area's Phoenician past can be seen in the long, pointed fishing boats known as *is fassonis*, made of dried rushes and other marsh plants. Another Phoenician technique still in use is the marinading process known as *sa merca*, in which fresh fish is wrapped in plant leaves from the lake and left to soak in salt water.

In a modern complex by the lagoon, the **Museo Civico Giovanni Marongiu di Cabras**

↓ Giants of Mont'e Prama, Museo Civico Giovanni Marongiu di Cabras

displays finds from Tharros (*p152*) and other local archaeological sites, and also explores the ethnographic and ecological make-up of the area. Perhaps the most fascinating of all the exhibits here are the ancient nuraghic sculptures known as the Giants of Mont'e Prama – 3,000-year-old archers, boxers and warriors carved out of sandstone and standing up to 2.5 m (8 ft) tall, the only known statues from the nuraghic period.

A few kilometres west of Cabras is the Laguna di Mistras. Separated from the sea by sandbars, in wetlands of international scientific importance, this lagoon is home to grey herons, flamingos, cormorants, and ospreys.

Museo Civico Giovanni Marongiu di Cabras

♿ 🏛 Via Tharros 121
🕙 10am–6pm daily
🌐 museocabras.it

San Salvatore

🅐C4 🅘 **www.corsadegli scalzi.eu**

Typical white houses for pilgrims, or *cumbessias*, surround the country church

THE VERNACCIA WINE OF SARDINIA

The white Vernaccia made in the fertile countryside north of Oristano is perhaps Sardinia's most famous sweet dessert wine. It is produced in the towns of Cabras, San Vero Milis, Zeddiani, Narbolia, Riola and Baratili. Full-bodied and strong (15% vol.), it is aged for at least three years in large oak barrels. You can take tours of the vineyards and pause for a wine-tasting session at many of the local wineries in Cabras.

of San Salvatore. These small lodgings are occupied for nine days each year in late August and early September, for the novena of the saint's feast day, on the first Saturday in September. The event is marked with a barefoot *(scalzi)* race in memory of local youths, who, in the Middle Ages, left the village to escape from the Saracens but returned to save the statue of the saint.

San Salvatore was built in the 17th century on the site of a nuraghic sanctuary for the worship of sacred waters. In the 6th century the site was transformed into an underground church. In the left-hand nave stairs lead to the hypogeum or burial chamber, which has six compartments: two rectangular ones flanking a corridor leading to a circular atrium with a well, around which three further chambers lie. The hypogeum was partly hewn out of the rock; the vaulted ceilings are made of

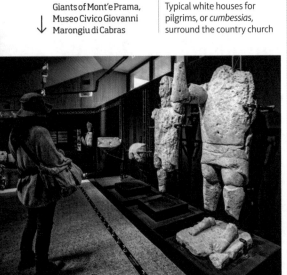

Flamingos wading in the shallow waters of the Sale Porcus Reserve ↑

sandstone and brick. The walls here are decorated with 4th–5th-century Roman graffiti depicting animals (elephants, panthers and peacocks) and heroes and gods (Hercules fighting the Nemean lion, Mars and Venus with a small winged cupid). There are even a few Arabic inscriptions referring to Allah and Mohammed, and numerous depictions of ships, which experts believe are ex voto offerings. The Latin letters "RVF", interlaced as in a monogram and repeated several times, seem to derive from the Phoenician language and are said to stand for "cure, save, give health".

In the 1950s and 1960s the church's central square was used as a location for so-called "spaghetti westerns", temporarily transforming this tiny village into a Wild West town for the screen.

Just east of the sanctuary are the ruins of the Domu 'e Cubas Roman baths, with a polychrome mosaic floor.

㉑

Sale Porcus Reserve

▲ C4 🚗 23 km (14 miles) NW of Cabras via SP6 & SP7

The Sale Porcus marsh is one of the largest reserves on the Sinis peninsula, its many white sand dunes covered with thick scrubby maquis vegetation. In winter and spring, over 10,000 greater flamingos and thousands of cranes, wild geese, cormorants and mallards make their home here. The oasis also attracts several rare and endangered species such as the vulpoca, the rosy gull and the purple sultan chicken.

In summer, evaporation transforms the lake into a white plain with a thick, hard salty crust that you can walk across. Historically, the salt from this expansive plain was harvested to season meat, hence the name Sale Porcus, which roughly translates as "pork salt".

In 1982, Sale Porcus was granted "Riserva Naturale Orientata" status and is now protected by **LIPU** (Lega Italiana Protezione Uccelli,

or the Italian League for Bird Protection), who are the point of contact for bird-watching and conservation in the area. One of the least intrusive ways to explore this natural oasis is on horseback. For more details on environmentally friendly visits to the reserve, contact **Engea Sardegna**, the regional chapter of the Ente Nazionale Guide Equestri Ambientali (National Body for Equestrian Environmental Guides).

LIPU

🛈 Sezione LIPU Oristano, Strada 16 E 2, Arborea; www.lipu.it

Engea Sardegna

🛈 Via Umberto I 37, Silvano Pietra; www.cavalloe cavalli.it

Did You Know?

Flamingos get their pink colour from plant pigments in their food.

The Torre 'e Seu Spanish tower overlooking the sea near San Giovanni di Sinis

22

San Giovanni di Sinis

C4 **i** www.tharros. sardegna.it

At the edge of the Sinis peninsula, this bathing resort was once famous for its fishermen's huts made of wood and reeds. Today only a few survive; the largest group lies east of the main road, not far from the ancient site of Tharros (p152).

As you enter the tiny village of San Giovanni di Sinis, you will see the early Christian church of San Giovanni, which, together with San Saturnino in Cagliari (p65), is the oldest in Sardinia. It was built in the 5th century, though much of the present-day church was the result of 9th- and 10th-century rebuilding.

Near San Giovanni di Sinis is the WWF Torre del Sevo reserve, where some of the last dwarf palms in the area survive. A dirt road at the northern end of San Giovanni di Sinis leads to the reserve; at the gate there is a path to the sea and the Torre 'e Seu Spanish tower.

23

Arborea

C5 **i** Viale A Omodeo 5 **w** comune.arborea.or.it

Arborea was built in the first half of the 20th century on a regular grid plan typical of modern cities. All the civic buildings (school, parish church, hotel and town hall) are found in Piazza Maria Ausiliatrice, from which the main streets radiate. The broad avenues are lined with trees and the two-storey Neo-Gothic houses are surrounded by gardens.

HIDDEN GEM
Marceddì

South of Arborea is the small fishing village of Marceddì, known for its delicious clams and guarded by a Spanish defence tower. The village is at the site of a former Phoenician settlement, Neapolis. The lagoon here is great for bird-watching.

The **Museo della Bonifica** is dedicated to the land reclamation scheme of the 1920s and 1930s, and also contains finds from excavations in the area, including the Roman necropolis of S'Ungroni, north of Arborea, discovered during the land reclamation in 1932.

Museo della Bonifica

 Corso Italia 44 3–6pm Fri, 9:30am–12:30pm & 3–6pm Sat, 9:30am–12:30pm Sun (by appt only all other days) w museoarborea.it

---

24

Santa Giusta

C5 **i** Via Garibaldi 84 ; www.comune.santa giusta.or.it

This agricultural town, built on the banks of the Santa Giusta lake and marsh, was built over the ruins of the Roman city of Ottona. The **Basilica di Santa Giusta**, a jewel of Pisan Romanesque architecture blended with striking Arab and Lombard elements, stands on the rise as you enter the town.

The cathedral was built in the early 12th century and has a narrow façade with a triple-lancet window. The interior columns are in various styles, and originally came from the nearby Roman cities of Tharros, Neapolis and Othoca. From the sacristy there is a stunning view of the lake, one of the best fishing areas in Sardinia, where you can still see the long *is fassonis* boats of Phoenician derivation. During the festival of Santa Giusta in May, a lively regatta is held here. The local gastronomic speciality is *bottarga* (salted mullet roe).

Basilica di Santa Giusta
◈◈ ⬧ Via Manzoni 2
☎ 0783 35 92 05 ⬥ 8am-5:30pm daily

25
Paulilatino

⬧ D4 ▦ ⓘ Viale della Libertà 33; www.comune.paulilatino.or.it

This village at the edge of the Abbasanta basalt plateau is surrounded by olive groves and cork oak woods. The houses are built of dark stone with Aragonese doorways and wrought-iron balconies. The same stone was used for the 17th-century church of San Teodoro, an Aragonese Gothic structure with a stained-glass rose window and a bell tower with an onion dome. Other notable sights include the **Museo Etnografico Palazzo Atzori**, which has exhibits on local folk culture.

About 4 km (3 miles) away, off the SS131, is the nuraghic **Sanctuary of Santa Cristina**. Within its stone walls is a well temple dedicated to the local mother-goddess dating from the 1st millennium BC. The sacred nature of this site has been maintained over the centuries with the construction of a church dedicated to Santa Cristina. Worshippers still continue to flock to the church, which is surrounded by *muristenes* (houses for pilgrims). To its right is another archaeological zone, which includes a nuraghe and two nuraghic-age stone dwellings.

Museo Etnografico Palazzo Atzori
◈◈ ⬧ Via Nazionale 127
⬥ Hours vary, check website
🌐 museopalazzoatzori.com

Sanctuary of Santa Cristina
◈◈◉ ⬧ Km 114,300, SS131 Cagliari-Sassari
⬥ 8:30am-dusk daily
🌐 pozzosantacristina.com

> At the edge of the Sinis peninsula, San Giovani di Sinis was once famous for its fishermen's huts made of wood and reeds. Today only a few survive.

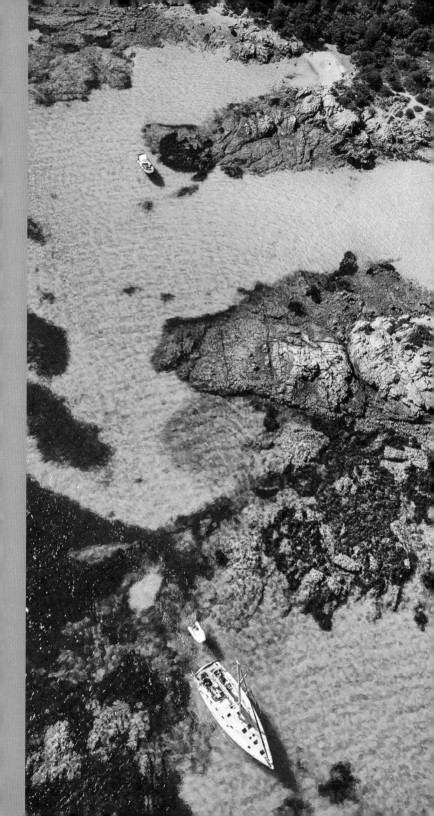

THE NORTH AND THE COSTA SMERALDA

It was here, in the rocky Gallura region, that the island's very first inhabitants are thought to have arrived some 450,000 to 150,000 years ago, after crossing the strait between Tuscany and Sardinia. During the early Neolithic era, a unique culture was established in Arzachena, leaving behind a series of megalithic tombs. Later, in the Bronze Age, the volcanic Logudoro region – one of the most fertile areas on the island – was settled by the nuraghic civilization. The city of Olbia was founded by the Phoenicians in the 8th century BC, and went on to become an important port under the Romans. By the Middle Ages, however, pirate raids had forced most of the population of Olbia and other settlements to move inland. This gave rise to towns such as Tempio Pausania and Sassari, which prospered over the following centuries while the coast was left deserted. Little changed until the 1960s, when the Costa Smeralda was developed by a consortium of financiers led by the Aga Khan. The resulting influx of tourists has altered the coastline beyond recognition, bringing with it the construction of countless villas, hotels and marinas.

THE NORTH AND THE COSTA SMERALDA

Monacia-d'Aullène
Sotta
Figari
Chera
Pianottoli-Caldarello
Chiova-d'Asino

CORSICA (FRANCE)

Bonifacio

Strait of Bonifacio

Punta Falcone
Capo Testa
SANTA TERESA GALLURA **8**
Porto Pozzo
Campovaglio

Punta di li Francesi
Portobello di Gallura
Vignola Mare
Bassacutena
133

Golfo dell' Asinara

Costa Paradiso
Aglientu

LUOGOSANTO **13**

Lago del Liscia

ISOLA ROSSA **24**
90
Trinità d'Agultu e Vignola

G a l l u r a

CASTELSARDO
22
Codaruina
133
Luras
AGGIUS **14**
TEMPIO PAUSANIA **17**
CALANGIANUS **12**

200
Lago di Casteldoria
Terme di Casteldoria

Platamona Lido
Marina di Sorso
Sedini
134
672
La Variante
Monte Limbara 1,362 m (4,468 ft)

Sorso
Sennori
Laerru
Perfugas

Sills

Nulvi
Martis
127

BERCHIDDA **16**

S Elente

Osilo
Chiaramonti
Monte Sassu 640 m (2,100 ft)
Lago del Coghinas
Oschiri

Coghinas

Oschiri

Punta di Senalonga 1,076 m (3,530 ft)

3 SASSARI
Tula

131 **291**

Ossi
SANTISSIMA TRINITÀ DI SACCARGIA **2**
672
132
597
199

Usini
Ploaghe

Uri
Florinas

Monteleone Rocca Doria

Ittiri
131
Ardara
Chilivani
Monte Lerno 1,094 m (3,589 ft)

L o g u d o r o
Mores
128b
OZIERI **20**
PATTADA **23**
BUDDUSÒ **15**

Borutta
389

Thiesi
Torralba
CENTRAL SARDINIA AND BARBAGIA p112
Osidda

THE WESTERN COAST p134

Nule

Bultei
Benetutti

199

THE NORTH AND THE COSTA SMERALDA

Must Sees

1. The Maddalena Archipelago
2. Santissima Trinità di Saccargia
3. Sassari

Experience More

4. Porto Rotondo
5. Golfo Aranci
6. Olbia
7. Palau
8. Santa Teresa Gallura
9. Porto Cervo
10. Arzachena
11. Sant'Antonio di Gallura
12. Calangianus
13. Luogosanto
14. Aggius
15. Buddusò
16. Berchidda
17. Tempio Pausania
18. San Teodoro
19. Alà dei Sardi
20. Ozieri
21. Tavolara
22. Castelsardo
23. Pattada
24. Isola Rossa

Isola Razzoli
Isola Budelli
Isola Spargi

THE MADDALENA ARCHIPELAGO 1

Isola Maddalena

La Maddalena
Casa di Garibaldi
Isola Caprera

PALAU 7
125
Baia Sardinia
Capo Ferro
PORTO CERVO 9
Cannigione
Capo Capaccia
ARZACHENA
10
Capriccioli
Costa Smeralda
San Pantaleo
125
PORTO ROTONDO 4
GOLFO ARANCI 5
Liscia
Capo Figari
11 **SANT'ANTONIO DI GALLURA**
Golfo di Olbia

OLBIA 6
Telti
Punta Timone
21 **TAVOLARA**
Olbia Costa Smeralda Airport
Porto S. Paolo
Isola Molara
729
Loiri
125
Capo Coda Cavallo
24
131d
Monti
389
Padru
18 **SAN TEODORO**
Monte Nieddu
971 m (3,186 ft)
24
Budoni
Punta la Batteria
19 **ALÀ DEI SARDI**
95
Piras
67
Posada
Lago di Posada
Posada
Torpè
la Caletta
Mamone
Lodè
Santa Lucia
THE EASTERN COAST
p92
Siniscola
Bitti
Lula
131d
Monti Remule

THE EASTERN COAST p92

0 kilometres 15
0 miles 15

N

❶

THE MADDALENA ARCHIPELAGO

 E1 🚢 From Palau 🛈 www.lamaddalenapark.it

Seven islands make up the Arcipelago della Maddalena, which became a marine reserve of international status at the beginning of 1997. Rugged, jagged coasts, rocks hewn by wind and water erosion, and tenacious maquis vegetation characterize this group of islands. Used as a military base in the 18th century, the archipelago today is a favourite with sailing fanatics, fans of underwater fishing and those in search of a tranquil beach break amid unspoilt surroundings.

EAT

Zi Anto
Relax at this casual seaside restaurant and bar, soaking up the panoramic views of the surrounding turquoise sea. Dishes on offer include locally caught fish, paninis and pizzas.

🏠 Località Punta Tegge, La Maddalena
📞 0789 72 21 50

€€€

①
La Maddalena

🚢 From Palau 🛈 0789 73 63 21

Located on the island of the same name, La Maddalena is the only town in the whole archipelago. It was founded in 1770 and replaced a small village built on the shores of the Cala Gavetta bay. Following an unsuccessful invasion on the part of the French in 1793, British admiral Horatio Nelson used La Maddalena as an operational base for his fleet between October 1803 and January 1805. The island's strategic position was later capitalized upon by the Savoy rulers in 1887, when the entire Maddalena Archipelago was turned into a naval base. The town developed rapidly in this period, as attested by a series of 19th-century buildings running along the seafront on Via Amendola. Evidence of the island's military past can also be found in Piazza Garibaldi, where the Municipio

The harbour of the archipelago's only town, La Maddalena ↓

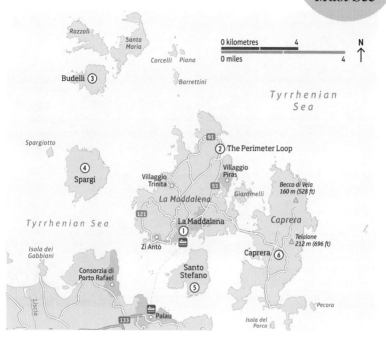

Razzoli

Santa Maria

Corcelli   Piana

Budelli ③

Barrettini

Tyrrhenian Sea

Spargiotto

② The Perimeter Loop

Villaggio Piras

Spargi ④

Villaggio Trinità

Becco di Vela 160 m (528 ft) △

La Maddalena   Giardinelli

Tyrrhenian Sea

La Maddalena

Caprera

Isola dei Gabbiani

La Maddalena ①

Zi Antò

Teialone 212 m (696 ft) △

Caprera ⑥

Consorzia di Porto Rafael

Santo Stefano ⑤

Pecora

Liscia

Palau

Isola del Porco

Did You Know?

New York's Statue of Liberty was reputedly built with granite from the Maddalena Archipelago.

(town hall) has on display a French bomb dating from France's attempt to conquer Sardinia in 1793. A few streets north, the elegant church of Santa Maria Maddalena has two candelabra and a silver crucifix given by Admiral Nelson to the island.

Today, town life centres around Piazza Umberto I and Piazza Garibaldi. The latter branches off into Via Garibaldi, which is a favourite spot with local residents for a leisurely evening stroll, particularly in summer. A wide variety of boat trips are offered from the harbour, which lies a 20-minute ferry ride away from Palau (*p188*) on the mainland.

②
The Perimeter Loop

A scenic route of about 45 km (28 miles) loops around the perimeter of La Maddalena island, providing magnificent views of the archipelago, Corsica and the four Corsican islands of Lavezzi.

Picturesque highlights on La Maddalena itself include the beautiful bays of Cala Spalmatore, Stagno Torto and Baia Trínità; Monte Guardia Vecchia, the island's highest mountain, with the Savoyard fort of San Vittorio at its summit; and the rocky island of Giardinelli, which is connected to La Maddalena by a narrow strip of land. Further north are Porto Massimo, the inlets of Abbatoggia and Cala d'Inferno, and the other large fortification on the island, Forte dei Colmi.

→

Baia Trinità, one of many appealing stops on a tour round La Maddalena island

This tour also passes by the **Museo Archeologico Navale "Nino Lamboglia"**, on the northwestern outskirts of La Maddalena town. This interesting maritime museum contains finds from the "ship of Spargi", an ancient Roman cargo vessel that was shipwrecked in the 2nd century AD and rediscovered in the 1950s.

Museo Archeologico Navale "Nino Lamboglia"
⊗ 🏛Località Mongiardino
🕐10am–1pm Mon–Sat
🌐sardegnacultura.it

Did You Know?

The Romans referred to the archipelago as *Cuniculariae*, or "rabbit islands".

→

The glittering turquoise waters of Cala Corsara, on the island of Spargi

③

Budelli

🚢 From La Maddalena, Palau

This beautiful uninhabited island is remarkable for the unique Spiaggia Rosa, a stunning beach of rose-coloured sand. Taking its colour from the shells of micro-organisms that inhabit the seashore, the beach is today off-limits to visitors for conservation reasons, but can still be viewed from afar in the company of national park guides.

Otherwise, the main attraction here is the island's beautifully unspoiled natural setting. The clear, unpolluted water makes Budelli popular for scuba diving, either to observe marine life or for underwater fishing.

④

Spargi

🚢 From La Maddalena
ℹ 0789 73 63 21

Spargi is little more than 2 km (1 mile) in diameter and is completely uninhabited. The terrain is fairly barren and the coast steep and inaccessible, but there is a lovely beach for bathing – although keep in mind that it has no facilities. An ancient Roman ship was found near the Cala Corsara cove on the southern coast; its cargo is now in the Museo Archeologico Navale "Nino Lamboglia" at La Maddalena (p173). Tourist boats make regular stops at Cala Corsara.

⑤

Santo Stefano

🚢 From La Maddalena

The small island of Santo Stefano lies about halfway between Palau and the island of Maddalena. Dominating the landscape is the Santo Stefano (or San Giorgio) fortress, also known as Napoleon's fort, built at the end of the 18th century. It was from here that Napoleon launched his 1793 invasion of La Maddalena.

There is a tourist village on the beach of Pesce, on the western coast.

TOP 3 ARCHIPELAGO BOAT TOURS

Fil Rouge Sail
🌐 giteavelafilrouge.it
Tour around the turquoise seas and white sandy beaches in a comfortable and quiet sailboat.

Leone di Caprera
🌐 leonedicaprera.com
Cruise the islands by day or evening in a small vintage motor boat from the 1950s.

Elena Tour Navigazioni
🌐 esclusiveinbarca.com
Rent your own boat complete with skipper and beach equipment.

↑ Sailing around the tranquil coast of Budelli at dusk

Caprera

 From Palau 📓 **0789 79 02 11**

The second-biggest island in the archipelago, Caprera has 45 km (28 miles) of coastline, and is connected to the island of La Maddalena by the 600-m (1,968-ft) Passo della Moneta bridge. Surrounded by azure seas, the rugged landscape is composed of pink granite rocks and fragrant maquis vegetation. Walkers will particularly enjoy the climb up the steps to the top of Monte Teialone (212 m/695 ft), the highest point on Caprera, with breathtaking views.

The island became the property of Giuseppe Garibaldi, one of the founding fathers of modern Italy, in 1856. His former estate is now part of the **Compendio Garibaldino** museum area. A visit here includes a fascinating tour of the stables, moorings and the Casa Bianca (white house) where Garibaldi lived. The stable still has a period steam engine used for threshing, while the Casa Bianca contains mementos of Garibaldi's life, including weapons, flags, portraits, clothes (including his famous red shirt) and a model of the Battle of Solferino. Garibaldi's favourite room was the salon, and he asked to be taken there before he died. The calendar and clocks in the room have not been changed since that day, and still show the exact time of his death: 6:20pm on 2 June 1882.

Also on Caprera, at the southwestern tip of the island, is the Centro Velico Caprera, one of the oldest and most famous sailing schools in Italy.

Compendio Garibaldino

🖼️ 🔞 😊 🕐 Summer: 8:30am-1:20pm & 1:40-7:30pm Tue-Sat, 8:30am-2pm Sun; winter: hours vary, check website 🚫 1 Jan, 25 Dec 🌐 compendio garibaldino.it

→

Statue of Giuseppe Garibaldi at the Compendio Garibaldino

A beach on Caprera, an island in the Maddalena Archipelago

2

SANTISSIMA TRINITÀ DI SACCARGIA

🅰C2 🏠From Sassari, follow the SS131 for 10 km (6 miles), then turn off on the SS597 to Olbia 📞347 000 78 82 or 079 43 50 19 ⏱9am–6pm daily (winter: call in advance)

Standing resplendently in a windswept valley, this Romanesque church is the most famous in Sardinia. Both simple and impressive, it exudes an aura of serene spirituality.

Beautifully preserved, Santissima Trinità di Saccargia is the island's most important Romanesque church. Around the year 1112, the ruler of the region, Constantine, is said to have donated the building to the Camaldolesi monks, who decided to enlarge it with the help of Tuscan craftsmen. The portico is the only one of its kind on the island, and the apse frescoes inside – attributed to Pisan artists – are a rare example of Romanesque wall painting in Sardinia.

 HIDDEN GEM
Mesu'e Montes

Just south of the church is the Necropolis of Mesu'e Montes, a large archaeological site that's full of interesting carvings and offers extensive views of the valley below.

↑ The atmospheric nave, lit by small openings in the side walls

← The eye-catching exterior of the church and *(inset)* the colourful Romanesque frescoes in the apse

→ A cross-section of Santissima Trinità di Saccargia

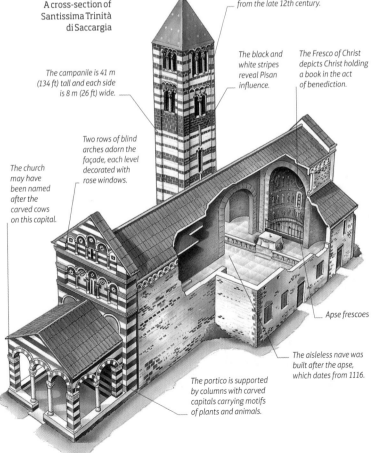

The double-lancet windows date from the late 12th century.

The black and white stripes reveal Pisan influence.

The Fresco of Christ depicts Christ holding a book in the act of benediction.

The campanile is 41 m (134 ft) tall and each side is 8 m (26 ft) wide.

Two rows of blind arches adorn the façade, each level decorated with rose windows.

The church may have been named after the carved cows on this capital.

Apse frescoes

The aisleless nave was built after the apse, which dates from 1116.

The portico is supported by columns with carved capitals carrying motifs of plants and animals.

SASSARI

⚠C2 🚌🚉 ℹPalazzo di Città, Via Sebastiano; www.turismosassari.it

Sardinia's second most important city commercially, politically and culturally, Sassari lies on a tableland that slopes down to the sea among olive groves and well-cultivated valleys. The city has a long history of invasions, conquests and raids, but also boasts a tradition of stubborn rebellion and uprisings and has always succeeded in asserting its independence.

① Duomo

🏛Piazza Duomo ℂ079 23 25 74 ⏰8:45am-noon & 4:30-7pm Mon-Sat, 9-11:30am & 5-7pm Sun

Sassari cathedral is dedicated to San Nicola (St Nicholas). Its impressive Baroque façade is in rather striking contrast to its size and to its setting in the small, simple and elegant 18th-century Piazza Duomo, with its characteristic semicircular shape. Built on the site of a Romanesque church, the Duomo that can be seen today is the result of successive alterations carried out over the centuries. Traces of the original church are still visible on the base of the façade and bell tower.

At the end of the 15th century, the structure underwent a radical transformation that not only changed its shape but created today's unusual proportions. The side walls were propped up by stone buttresses decorated with gargoyles of mythical and monstrous animals, while the interior was rebuilt in the Gothic style.

In the late 18th century, grand decorations were added to the façade: volutes, flowers, cherubs and fantastic figures. In the middle, a statue of

↓ The Duomo *(right)*, standing opposite San Giacomo church

San Nicola is surmounted by the figures of the three martyr saints, Gavino, Proto and Gianuario, set in three niches. At a later stage, an octagonal section decorated with multicoloured majolica tiles was superimposed on the original Lombard-style lower part of the campanile. The interior, which has been totally restored, has retained its simple Gothic lines despite the presence of lavishly decorated Baroque altars. The ornate choir – the work of 18th-century Sardinian artists – is particularly striking.

The Museo del Duomo, reached through the Cappella Aragonese (Aragonese chapel) on the right, houses the

 INSIDER TIP
Exploring Sassari

Allow yourself at least a morning to walk around the old town, which has preserved its original layout with winding alleyways branching off from the main streets. Look out for part of the old city walls at the beginning of Corso Trinità.

EXPERIENCE The North and the Costa Smeralda

↑ Looking along Corso Vittorio Emanuele II, at the heart of the old town

processional standard, a 15th-century panel painting. Other treasures include a silver statue of San Gavino, embossed using a Mexican technique that was in fashion in the late 17th century.

②
Santa Maria di Betlem

🏛 Piazza Santa Maria
📞 079 23 57 40 🕐 7am-noon, 5-8pm daily (winter: to 7pm daily)

The church of Santa Maria di Betlem is situated in the square of the same name, at the northwestern entrance to the city. Built by Benedictine monks in 1106, it was later donated to the Franciscans. The elegant original structure was the subject of frequent rebuilding in the 18th and 19th centuries, and the church has consequently lost its early qualities of lightness and purity of form. The only intact part of the earlier church is the 13th-century façade, decorated with small columns and capitals and pierced by a lovely 15th-century rose window. The once-austere Gothic interior is now adorned with heavy-handed Baroque

decoration and altars, but the side chapels have retained their Late Gothic style. Each is dedicated to a craftsmen's guild as a reminder of the social role the church played in the community. This link is still celebrated annually, on 14 August, during the Di li Candareri festivities, when votive candles donated by the

various guilds are carried here in procession from the Chiesa del Rosario (Church of the Holy Rosary) to the west.

The cloister is partly walled in but can still be visited. It contains the 14th-century granite stone Brigliadore fountain, which was once the source of most of Sassari's water supply.

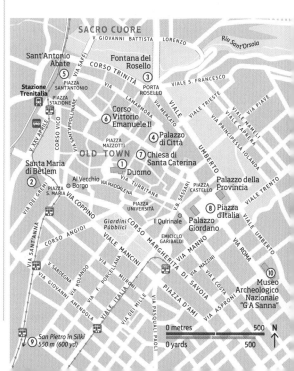

③ ⑧ Fontana del Rosello

⌂ Via Col di Lana ☎ 079 20 08 07 ⏱ 10am-1pm Tue & Sun, 10am-1pm & 3-6pm Wed-Sat

On the right-hand side of the church of Santissima Trinità, in Piazza Mercato, is a small stone stairway known as the Col di Lana. This leads to the Fontana del Rosello, an ornate fountain standing outside the old city walls, at the lower end of the Valverde gorge.

A water source has existed here since at least the 13th century, but this fountain was executed in the early 1600s by Genoese artists, who still had a preference for the classical styles of the Renaissance. The base consists of two superimposed white and green marble boxes, around the bottom of

which are eight sculpted lions' mouths that function as water spouts. On each corner of the base is a statue of a figure symbolizing one of the four seasons. The original statues were destroyed during uprisings against the Savoyard government in 1795–6, and were replaced in 1828.

Reclining across the middle of the fountain is a bearded divinity known as Giogli, surrounded by small towers that symbolize the city. Crowning the structure are two arches, atop which is a small equestrian statue of San Gavino.

Unfortunately, very little remains of the steep valley and woods that were once the natural backdrop for this little jewel of late Renaissance art. However, this has not diminished the locals' love for their fountain, which has become a symbol of the city.

> **Reclining across the middle of the Fontana del Rosello is a bearded divinity known as Giogli, surrounded by small towers that symbolize the city.**

④ Palazzo di Città

⌂ Corso Vittorio Emanuele II 35 ☎ 079 201 51 22 ⏱ 10am-1pm & 3-6pm Tue-Sat, 10am-1pm Sun

This Neo-Classical palazzo was built between 1826 and 1829, after the demolition of the pre-existing Municipal House. It was designed by the Piedmontese architect Giuseppe Cominotti, who divided the space between offices for the city council and a new theatre, with a horse-shoe shape inspired by the Carignano theatre of Turin. The council moved to its current location in the Palazzo Ducale in the 20th century, but the theatre still functions as performance space. The building also now houses the Tourist Board and a small museum of local history and culture. The latter features an interesting display of local costumes and 19th-century

EXPERIENCE The North and the Costa Smeralda

STAY

Piazza Azuni 18
Centrally located
guest house with
modern rooms and
city views.

 Piazza Domenico
Alberto Azuni 18
📞 340 312 59 72

€€€

La Perla
A welcoming B&B
offering airy rooms and
a delicious breakfast.

 Via Monte Grappa 78
🌐 chicaccommodation.it

€€€

Stella del Golfo
Outside town, this B&B
has sea views from its
rooms and terraces.

 Str. Vicinale
Marchetto 10
📞 079 390 000

€€€

 The Baroque façade of Sant'Antonio
Abate, built in the 18th century

paintings and watercolours illustrating everyday rural and town life, as well as religious and civil events. Among the most notable works are local artist Eugenio Tavolara's depictions of Carnival and Holy Week.

Tradition holds that during the Di li Candareri festivities on 14 August *(p179)*, the mayor toasts the procession from the palazzo balcony, wishing the crowd *"a zent'anni"* (may you live a hundred years). The participants then cheer or boo in judgment of the mayor's work over the last year.

The marble Fontana del Rosello, topped *(inset)* by a statue of San Gavino

⑤ Sant'Antonio Abate

 Piazza Sant'Antonio
🕐 7–10am daily, also 4:30–7:30pm Sat

Dating from the early 1700s, the stately Baroque façade of this church dominates the tree-lined square at the end of Corso Trinità.

The upper part of the portal still bears the emblem of the brotherhood responsible for building the church. The Latin cross interior has one of the most elegant high altars in Sassari, which bears a carved and gilded wooden altarpiece. The panels were executed in the late 1700s by the Genoese painter Bartolomeo Augusto.

The church stands in Piazza Sant'Antonio, once the site of the old northern gate of the same name, and formerly the hub of the city's commercial and political life. The only vestiges of this past are a part of the medieval city walls, and a fortified tower.

⑥ Corso Vittorio Emanuele II

The city's main street crosses the heart of the old town and connects Piazza Sant'Antonio

and Piazza Cavallino. The Corso is lined with 16th-century Aragonese buildings and 19th-century houses, and you can often catch a glimpse of court-yards and interiors that testify to their former splendour. This is Sassari's main shopping street, with shops of all kinds, from clothing to ironmongery.

⑦ Chiesa di Santa Caterina

 Via Santa Caterina
📞 079 231 6 92 🕐 5–9pm
Sat, 10am–1pm Sun

This church was built at the end of the 16th century for the Jesuits, and combines Sardinian Gothic style with Renaissance elements. In the interior there are paintings by the artist Giovanni Bilevelt.

> 🔍 HIDDEN GEM
> **Peaceful Park**
> In the southwestern suburbs of the city is the lovely Parco di Monserrato, a revital-ized green space with a wealth of tree-lined avenues and numerous historic buildings and pools to explore.

Did You Know?

Sassari is the birthplace of two Italian presidents: Francesco Cossiga and Antonio Segni.

Piazza d'Italia

This large square is laid out at the edge of the 19th-century quarter of Sassari. It is a well-proportioned public space, with tall palm trees and well-kept flower beds, guarded by a statue of Vittorio Emanuele II and surrounded by elegant Neo-Classical structures.

One of the finest buildings is the Palazzo della Provincia (provincial government building), built in pure Neo-Classical style. The council chamber on the first floor is open to the public. On the walls are 19th-century paintings depicting important events in the city's political history, such as *The Proclamation of the Sassari Statutes* and *Giovanni Maria Angioj Entering Sassari*. You can also see the adjacent royal apartments, built in 1884 on the occasion of a visit by the

king and queen of Sardinia. In summer the palazzo's court-yard is the venue for concerts and plays.

The lovely 19th-century Bargone and Crispi arcades on the northwestern side of Piazza d'Italia shelter the city's oldest bars and pastry shops and lead to the palm-tree-lined Piazza Castello.

San Pietro in Silki

📍 Via delle Croci 📞 079 21 60 67 🕐 6:15am–noon & 4–7pm daily

The Romanesque church of San Pietro in Silki faces a lovely tree-lined square and was most probably named after the medieval quarter built here in the 1100s. Behind the church's simple 17th-century façade is a large atrium leading to a Gothic nave with four side chapels. The first of these was dedicated to the Madonna delle Grazie in the second half of the 15th century. It is named after a statue of the Virgin Mary that was found inside a column from the square in front of the church. The statue is one of the best examples of Catalan Gothic sculpture in Sardinia.

Opposite San Pietro, on the other side of the square, is the Frati Minori monastery, which houses one of the island's richest libraries. The collections consist of over 14,000 volumes, removed from Franciscan monasteries after their closure.

Museo Archeologico Nazionale "G A Sanna"

📍 Via Roma 64 🔒 Currently closed for renovation; check website for details of reopening 🌐 musei. sardegna.beniculturali.it

The Sassari archaeological museum was donated to the Italian state by the Sanna

---

 HIDDEN GEM
Roman Reconstruction

Historians of all ages will be fascinated by a visit to the Castrum Romano La Crucca (www.facebook.com/ castrumromano.la crucca), a recreated wooden Roman fort situated west of Sassari in La Crucca.

The elegant Palazzo della Provincia, standing on the side of the Piazza d'Italia

family, who built these premises in 1931 to house finds collected by Giovanni Antonio Sanna, an important figure in the island's history and director of the local mine.

Two entire storeys are given over to various periods of Sardinian civilizations, from the Neolithic to the Middle Ages. Arrowheads, nuraghic bronze statuettes, amphoras, furnishings, weapons, tools, ceramics and jewels are on display in chronological order. On the ground floor, panels illustrate the evolution of Sardinia, and every room has time charts on display.

There are also architectural reconstructions of prehistoric buildings such as dwellings, *domus de janas* (rock-cut tombs) and giants' tombs. In the last hall, among floor plans, sarcophagi and statues, is a reconstructed mosaic floor from a patrician Roman villa in nearby Turris Libisonis (present-day Porto Torres). The mosaic shows lobsters, sea horses and seals chasing one another in an eternal circle. The next room contains a small art gallery with works by Sardinian artists from the 14th to the 20th centuries.

There is also a traditional crafts section with displays of jewels, costumes, musical instruments and craftsmen's tools, almost all of which are still used in central-northern Sardinia today.

EAT

Al Vecchio Borgo
Serves locally sourced and authentically prepared dishes – such as fried zucchini flowers, freshly caught fish, and pasta – in an intimate setting.

⌂ Largo Porta Utzeri 2
🕓 Sun 📞 079 201 50 52

――――――――――

Il Quirinale
Close to the Piazza d'Italia, this spacious and modern restaurant offers a variety of seafood and meat dishes as well as excellent pizzas and a well-curated local wine list.

⌂ Via Camillo Benso Conte di Cavour 3 🕓 Mon
🌐 ilquirinale.it

The interior and *(inset)* façade of the Museo Archeologico Nazionale

Pleasure boats and
luxury villas lining the
marina in Porto Rotondo ↑

EXPERIENCE MORE

4

Porto Rotondo

🅰 E1 🚌 ⓘ Via Rudargia 8;
www.portorotondo.eu

Porto Rotondo is not so much
a town as a large, meticulously
planned tourist village that
grew from nothing during the
Costa Smeralda boom. The
buildings, placed around the
inevitable yacht marina, were
designed to blend in as much
as possible with the natural
surroundings. The result is
certainly pleasant, and Porto
Rotondo has been a great
success as a tourist resort,
despite its perhaps slightly
artificial air.

The Porto Rotondo quay and
Piazzetta San Marco are lined
with famous designer shops,
and throughout the summer
the cafés and restaurants are
crowded with visitors, drinking, dining, meeting friends,
or just watching the world go
by. Out of season the town
suddenly becomes rather
quiet – deserted even.

The church of San Lorenzo,
whose façade was designed by
noted Italian sculptor Andrea
Cascella, holds several extraordinary wooden statues by
Mario Ceroli depicting various
biblical scenes and figures.

Just outside Porto Rotondo
is the attractive headland of
Punta della Volpe, which separates the Golfo di Marinella
from the Golfo di Cugnana.

5

Golfo Aranci

🅰 E1 🏠🚻🚌 ⓘ Via Libertà
74; www.golfoaranci.
sardegna.it

The name "Aranci" refers to
oranges, but you won't see any
orange groves here. Rather,
Golfo Aranci owes its name to
a mistaken interpretation of
the local name Golfu di li Ranci,
meaning "Gulf of the Crabs".
Formerly a part of Olbia, the
village became independent
in 1979. A number of ferries
from the mainland use Golfo

Aranci as a stopping place,
and Corsica Sardinia Ferries
(*p204*) has a direct service
from here to Livorno.

The waters here are home
to one of the island's more
unusual attractions: **MuMart**.
This underwater museum of
contemporary sculptures is

↑ The view from Golfo
Aranci towards the
island of Figarolo

The building of the airport just outside Olbia, specifically to serve the Costa Smeralda, has cemented this role.

Olbia is a modern city and usually considered a stop-off on the way to the coast. Of special interest in the town are a Roman cistern in Piazza Margherita, proof of ancient Roman occupation, and the Romanesque San Simplicio. This church was first built in the 11th century and enlarged in the 13th century.

On Via Milano in the historic centre of Olbia, the Mercato Porto Romano street market sets up on Tuesday mornings, (8am–2pm), and is loaded with organic produce, baked goods, meats and hand-made crafts.

Two prehistoric sites near Olbia are well worth a visit: the Cabu Abbas nuraghic complex (4 km/2 miles to the northeast) and the Sa Testa holy well.

To reach Cabu Abbas from the old port of Olbia, head along Corso Umberto and then Via d'Annunzio. Once past the railway you will see the country church of Santa Maria Cabu

GREAT VIEW
Romantic Ruins

The stone fortress ruins of the 13th-century Castello di Pedres, outside Olbia, sit high on a hill with magnificent views of the countryside and sea beyond. Below the ruins lies the Tomba dei Giganti Su Mont'e s'Abe (Giants' Tomb of Mont'e s'Abe).

Abbas. From here a dirt path winds up towards the top of the mountain, another 15 minutes on foot. The site offers a great view of the island of Tavolara. There is a central well with a tower where the remains of sacrifices – burnt bones and pieces of pottery – were found in 1937.

To reach the Sa Testa holy well, take road SP82 to Golfo Aranci as far as the Pozzo Sacro hotel. This site consists of a wide paved courtyard, from which 17 covered steps lead down to a well chamber.

accessed by a yellow submarine that holds up to 30 guests at a time. There are over a dozen artworks on display, mostly humanoid forms, which have been created by a group of Italian and international artists and represent subjects related to the sea. Fish and jellyfish swim freely around, and occasionally you can even see a mermaid. It is also possible to dive or snorkel to the site as it's not far from Terza Spiaggia (Third Beach) and is well marked by buoys.

MuMart

⊛ ⊗ ☺ 🅰 Porto di Golfo Aranci 🅾 Submarine tours: 10am & 3pm daily 🅦 museo marinoartistico.com

---

Olbia

🅰 E2 ⊠ 🚌 🚊 🍴 *i* www. olbiaturismo.it

Olbia is only 200 km (125 miles) from the port of Civitavecchia on the mainland of Italy, and has always been the principal drop-off point on the island, rather than the capital, Cagliari.

TRANSFORMATION OF THE COSTA SMERALDA

In the early 1960s, a stretch of coastline in northeastern Sardinia was transformed into the most exclusive tourist resort in the Mediterranean: the Costa Smeralda (Emerald Coast). The beaches were the preserve of grazing cattle until 1962, when the Consorzio Costa Smeralda was formed to transform the area. An architectural committee was founded to supervise new building, with architects Luigi Vietti, Jacques Couëlle, Giancarlo and Michele Busiri Vici, Antonio Simon Mossa, Raimond Martin and Leopoldo Mastrella appointed to design the resorts. The area has since changed beyond recognition, with luxury hotels, sumptuous villas and huge holiday villages, as well as the famous yacht club and a prestigious golf course.

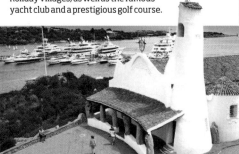

⑦
Palau

🅰E1 🚌🚢 ℹ️0789 70 70
25; www.palauturismo.com

The logical departure point for a trip to the Maddalena archipelago (p172), Palau also owes its success to the appeal of the narrow-gauge Sassari-Tempio-Palau railway, part of the Trenino Verde (p205). Life here can be rather frenetic in the summer and revolves around the ferry boat wharf and the yacht harbour. From Palau you can travel to some of the most fascinating and famous places on the coast, such as the jagged Capo d'Orso (Bear Cape) promontory, which ends in a large, bear-shaped rock, sculpted by the wind.

For some extraordinary views of the coast and of the islands, head north to Punta Sardegna, taking the road that goes up to Monte Altura, and then go on foot to the beach of Cala di Trana, on the tip of the headland. The landscape is particularly lovely in the early morning and at sunset, despite the fact that ongoing 21st-century construction work is slowly but surely spoiling the unique beauty of this part of Sardinia.

---

⑧
Santa Teresa Gallura

🅰D1 🚌 ℹ️Piazza Vittorio Emanuele 24; www.santa teresagalluraturismo.com

The area around Santa Teresa was inhabited in Roman times and was vital to the Pisans, who used the local granite for building. The present-day town was built from scratch during the Savoyard period on a grid plan with streets intersecting at right angles, in the middle of which is a small square and the church of San Vittorio. The local economy is based on fishing as well as tourism.

High up on the rocky headland stands Torre Longosardo, a tower built in the 16th

> **The beating heart of the Costa Smeralda and a paradise for European VIPs, Porto Cervo is centred around its two yacht harbours.**

century during the Aragonese period; it affords a magnificent view of Porto Longone bay and, in the distance, the white cliffs circling the city of Bonifacio in Corsica, located only 12 km (7.5 miles) away.

To the left the coast falls away to the beach of Rena Bianca, which ends not far from Isola Municca, a tiny island where you can find the remains of an abandoned Roman quarry.

About 5 km (3 miles) away is Capo Testa, a rocky promontory connected to the mainland by a thin sandbar. The headland can be reached by taking a scenic drive around the bays of Colba and Santa Reparata. A walk through the quarries – which supplied the Romans with granite for the Pantheon –

Bear rock at Capo d'Orso, and (inset) looking towards Palau town from Punta Sardegna

A summer evening at the Porto Cervo quay amid spectacular luxury yachts ↑

accompanied by the fragrance of the maquis, will take you to the Capo Testa lighthouse.

Porto Cervo

⚑E1   🚌   🛈 0789 89 20 19; www.marinadiporto cervo.com

The beating heart of the Costa Smeralda and a paradise for European VIPs, Porto Cervo is centred around its two yacht harbours, abounding with some of the most luxurious private craft in the world. In summer there is a series of prestigious sporting events, including regattas and golf tournaments. The traditional evening stroll along Via della Marina – lined with designer shops on one side and plush yachts on the other – is almost obligatory. Cultural attractions include the Church of Stella Maris, which has a painting attributed to El Greco.

There are plenty of good beaches nearby, such as Liscia Ruja, 10 km (6 miles) south, framed by the sheltered Cala di Volpe.

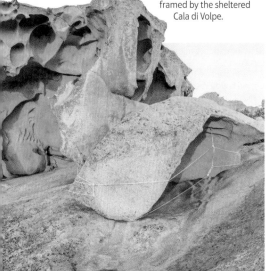

EAT

Gelateria 15 SottoZero

The best ice cream in Santa Teresa Gallura by popular consensus - grab a pistachio oil-flavoured gelato to enjoy while strolling around town.

⚑D1   🏠 Via XX Settembre 15, Santa Teresa Gallura
☎ 0789 75 40 82

€€€

DRINK

Baretto

Sip pina coladas from fresh pineapples and nibble on bar snacks at this tourist-heavy but immensely appealing cocktail bar on the busy main square in the heart of Santa Teresa Gallura.

⚑D1   🏠 Piazza V Emanuele 23, Santa Teresa Gallura
🌐 ilbarettosanta teresa.com

STAY

Tenuta Pilastru

Nestled in the Galluran countryside, this romantic resort has some wonderful rock features.

Località Pilastru km 5, Arzachena
tenutapilastru.it.

€€€

Stazzo Lu Ciaccaru

Rural and restful, this elegant stone-built hotel has beautiful rooms, a sparkling swimming pool and lush walking trails.

Località Lu Ciaccaru, Arzachena
stazzoluciaccaru.it

€€€

Hotel Relais ValKarana

Family-friendly former farmhouse on the shores of Lago del Liscia. The luxurious rooms all have stunning views of the lake and mountains.

E1 Località Lu Lioni, Sant'Antonio di Gallura
valkarana.com

€€€

The mushroom-shaped "Fungo" rock towering above Arzachena ↑

---

⑩ Arzachena

E1 Piazza Risorgimento 8; www.arzachenaturismo.com

As recently as the 1960s, this small town was a peaceful shepherds' village. Today it is the thriving centre of the glitzy Costa Smeralda, and has undergone considerable change. Towering above the houses is a curious rock formed by wind erosion, known as "the Fungo" (mushroom), and there are many traces of prehistoric settlements in the vicinity. These have been incorporated as the **Arzachena Archaeological Park**, which includes the Nuraghe Albucciu, the Tomba dei Giganti Coddu Vecchju and the Necropolis of Li Muri.

Lying 2 km (1 mile) east of Arzachena, just past the edge of town, the well-preserved Nuraghe Albucciu is unusual for the way that it incorporates a natural outcrop of granite rock into its structure. Other notable features include a corridor and a false dome. Inside, there is a ladder to the upper level, which is where daily domestic activities were carried out.

The impressive Tomba dei Giganti Coddu Vecchju (Giants' Tomb of Coddu Vecchju), lying 5 km (3 miles) to the south-west of town, is a collective tomb that dates back to the Bronze Age. In the middle of the funerary monument there is a stele 4 m (13 ft) high, surrounded by a semi-circular wall of stone slabs set into the earth.

The Neolithic Necropolis of Li Muri is situated 8 km (5 miles) west of Arzachena. The site includes a number of ancient burial chambers surrounded by concentric circles of stones. These funerary circles share similar characteristics with megalithic burials in Corsica and the French and Spanish Pyrenees, and are an important artifact of the Arzachena Culture that once flourished in this area.

Arzachena Archaeological Park

Viale Costa Smeralda 56; www.gesecoarzachena.it Sites: 10am–4pm Tue–Sun (Li Muri: by appt only)

---

⑪ Sant'Antonio di Gallura

E1 Town Hall, Piazza Matteo Ruzittu 1; www.comunesantantoniodigallura.ot.it

This village has always been an important farming and sheep-raising centre. In September, the feast days of Sant'Antonio, San Michele and Sant'Isidoro are celebrated with a procession in which decorated oxen and tractors follow the statues of the saints through the streets.

In the heart of town is a small archaeological park,

known for its landscape of intricate wind-sculpted rocks. This site was inhabited as far back as prehistoric times.

⑫
Calangianus

🅐D2   🚌   🛈 Town Hall, Via Sant'Antonio 2; www. comune.calangianus.ot.it

Everywhere you look in the forests around Calangianus you'll find evidence of cork harvesting: the barked cork oaks have a characteristic reddish colour that will remain until the bark grows again, while the cork strips themselves are heaped up in large piles to dry.

Calangianus is the centre of cork production in the Gallura region, and there are a number of workshops and factories in town that process the material. There is also a highly regarded trade school whose curriculum focuses on the cultivation of cork oaks and making the maximum use of cork bark.

→

Cycling past the Basilica di Nostra Signora on the quiet streets of Luogosanto

HIDDEN GEM
Wild Olives

Surround yourself with ancient olive trees, some nearly 4,000 years old, at the Olivastri Millenari di Santo Baltolu reserve *(www.facebook.com/ olivastrimillenariluras)*, north of Calangianus.

An old monastery in the centre of town has been transformed into the **Museo del Sughero**, dedicated to the art and history of cork-making.

Also of interest in the old town – in a small, isolated square – is the small parish church of Santa Giusta, which was built in the 17th century.

Near the village of Luras (12 km/7 miles northwest of Calangianus), a series of prehistoric tombs is open to visitors. To reach the site, go through the village in the direction of Luogosanto and then turn right just before the end of town. At the point where the paved road ends, take the dirt road on the right, which takes you to the Ladas Dolmen, the most impressive of them all.

Museo del Sughero

⊗   🏠 Via San Francesco 3 🕐 10am–1pm & 3–6pm Mon–Sat   🌐 museodel sughero.com

⑬
Luogosanto

🅐D2   🚌   🛈 Town Hall, Piazza della Basilica 2; www. comune luogosanto.gov.it

The small village of Luogosanto is surrounded by maquis, and is well known for the production of bitter honey, often served with *seadas* (cheese pastries). The village is typical of the Gallura region, backed by greenery and wind-eroded pinkish-grey rocks. Every seven years a solemn but colourful ceremony celebrates the opening of the Porta Santa (holy door) of the Basilica di Nostra Signora di Luogosanto. San Quirico's feast day ends with a huge dinner for all of the villagers, featuring the traditional dish *carr'e cogghju*, made with pork and cabbage.

About 2 km (1 mile) to the south of Luogosanto is the San Trano hermitage, perched at 410 m (1,345 ft), dominating the landscape towards the north of the town. This small church was built in the early 13th century in memory of the two hermit saints Nicola and Trano, who, according to legend, lived in the small cave to the rear of the altar.

In a nearby park, surrounded by small squares, steps and street lamps, is the Filetta spring, renowned for its fresh drinking water.

EAT

Punto di Ristoro Nuraghe Majori

Rustic spot for pizzas and pastas, perfect after a day at the nearby nuraghic site. You can also purchase local preserves, honey, sausages and cheeses.

 D2 Strada Palau km 2, Tempio Pausania

📞 320 306 06 34

€ € €

 14

Aggius

 D2 🚌 *i* Town Hall, Via Pasquale Paoli 39; www. comune aggius.gov.it

Natural features have shaped this village and its surroundings. A granite outcrop dominates the landscape of Aggius, both in the Parco Capitza, which towers over the town, and in the amazing labyrinth of rock formations in the nearby Valle della Luna.

Once the dominion of the Doria family from Genoa, and then ruled by the Aragonese, Aggius owes

its prosperity to the quarrying and processing of granite. Local handicrafts are also important to the economy – especially rug-making, every stage of which is carried out using traditional techniques.

The centre of Aggius is the perfect place for a stroll; the lovingly preserved old stone houses are among the most attractive in the Gallura region. On the first Sunday in October the town comes to life with the traditional Festa di li 'Agghiani (Bachelor's Feast) – ostensibly an opportunity for young couples to meet – at which the Gallurese *suppa cuata* (bread and cheese soup) is served.

From Aggius, the road to Isola Rossa leads to to the Valle della Luna, with its weird rock formations. Nearby is the large Izzana Nuraghe, which is accessed via a dirt road that veers off from the main road, towards the right.

15

Buddusò

 E3 🚌 *i* Town Hall, Piazza Fumu 1; www. comunebudduso.ss.it

In the Roman era, Buddusò – then known as Caput Thirsi – was the site of a station on the main road from Karalis (Cagliari) to Olbia. More recently, however, this unassuming little town has

enjoyed a period of prosperity thanks to demand for its quality granite and cork.

The local dark stone can be seen in the buildings that line the cobbled streets of the old town. Also found here is the church of Santa Anastasia, which is worth a visit to view the paintings in the sacristy.

A tour through the Monti di Alà mountain range makes a good day trip. Also nearby are the Iselle Nuraghe (on the road to Pattada) and Loelle Nuraghe, towards Mamone.

 16

Berchidda

 D2 🚌 *i* Town Hall, Piazza del Popolo 5; www. comune.berchidda.ot.it

Built on the southern slopes of Monte Limbara, in a hilly landscape that stretches as far as Monte Azzarina, Berchidda is a large village whose economy is based on sheep-raising, dairy products, cork processing and viticulture. If you're passing through, pick up a bottle or two of the local Vermentino (one of the best known Sardinian white wines) and a generous hunk of pecorino cheese.

About 4 km (2 miles) from the centre of Berchidda, a steep climb will take you to the ruins of the Castello di Montacuto, which was the fortress of local ruler Adelasia

↑ Al fresco dining in the colourful old town of Tempio Pausania

INSIDER TIP
Wonderful Wine

Learn about - and taste - Vermentino and other locally produced wines at the Museo del Vino *(www.muvisardegna.it)* in Berchidda.

di Torres and her husband Ubaldo Visconti before becoming the domain of the Doria and Malaspina families from the mainland. Monte Limbara, the geographical heart of the Gallura region, towers in the background.

17

Tempio Pausania

 D2 🚌 ℹ Town Hall, Piazza Gallura 3; www.comune. tempiopausania.ot.it

The capital of Gallura, Tempio Pausania consists of a large number of modern buildings that tend to obscure the charming old town. However,

←

A mountain goat standing in the solitude of the rocky Valle della Luna near Aggius

investigate further and you'll discover the town's true heart, filled with two- and three-storey buildings with granite stone walls and characteristic balconies. A short walk from the town hall and the central Piazza Gallura is the cathedral – founded in the 15th century but rebuilt in the 1800s. Also nearby are the Oratorio del Rosario and the small church of Santa Croce.

Not far from the centre of town, a short walk down Viale San Lorenzo, are the Rinaggiu springs, whose mineral water is famous for its curative qualities. As well as the traditional festivals, the International Festival of Folklore is held here in July.

A short distance away, on the SS133, is the turning for the Maiori Nuraghe, one of the best preserved megalithic structures in the area. Head south from the town on the SS392 for 17 km (10 miles) and you will pass close to the summit of Monte Limbara, which can be reached in a few minutes on foot from the paved road. Along the way you will find the Giardino Botanico di Curadoreddu (about 6 km/ 4 miles from Tempio Pausania), where you can admire an impressive view of mountain rock pools and waterfalls. Water flows from one great mass of rocks to the other, creating cascades and hollows. The spectacle is at its most striking during winter.

CORK AND GALLURA

Cork is obtained from the stripped bark of cork oak trees and has always been a key part of the Gallura regional economy. Today, the Tempio Pausania region produces 90 per cent of the bottle stoppers used in Italy, although the cork is also used for local handicrafts and as a building and insulating material. Cork cannot be stripped from the tree before it is at least 25-30 years old. The first layer stripped is porous and elastic and of scant commercial use. Only nine to ten years after this first barking process is the true - and profitable - new layer of cork obtained.

 18

San Teodoro

F2 **Piazza Mediterraneo 1; www. santeodoroturismo.it**

To the south of the Capo Coda Cavallo headland, just opposite the rocky island of Tavolara, is the village of San Teodoro. It makes an excellent starting point for excursions to the Cinta beach, a long strip of sandy terrain that separates the Stagno di San Teodoro from the sea. Fairly close to the Orientale Sarda road, this lake and marsh is one of the few remaining coastal marshes that once lay south of the Bay of Olbia. Mallards and coots are a common sight on the water. When the birds feel in danger, they gather in large groups and make a loud noise to defend themselves. Other species that are frequently

> Rocks and maquis, and forests of enormous cork oaks with the characteristic marks of stripping, make up the landscape of Alà dei Sardi.

spotted here include grey and red heron, Kentish plovers and the hovering kestrel, one of Italy's smallest raptors.

 19

Alà dei Sardi

E2 **Town Hall, Via Roma 74; www.comune. aladeisardi.ot.it**

Rocks and maquis, and forests of enormous cork oaks with the characteristic marks of stripping, make up the landscape of Alà dei Sardi and its plateau, the last tract of the rocky interior overlooking the Bay of Olbia.

Alà dei Sardi may not have much to offer tourists, but the charming main street is lined with the small granite stone houses characteristic of this region, and the village is renowned for its beef and honey products. Considerable development is also underway, following the construction of Italy's biggest wind farm just outside the village.

The environs of Alà dei Sardi are a treasure trove of ancient monuments. Roughly 3 km (2 miles) southeast, just off the road to Sos Sonorcolos, is the well-preserved Nuraghe Boddò.

↑ The Church of San Teodoro and its piazza at night

North from Alà dei Sardi, following signs to the town of Monti, the route crosses a sizeable plateau studded with astonishing rock formations. The road forks off to the Sanctuary of San Pietro l'Eremita, and passes through some stunning scenery, with gaps allowing occasional views of the sea and the unmistakable profile of the island of Tavolara in the distance.

 20

Ozieri

D3 **Pro Loco, Via Regina Margherita 1; www.welcometozieri.it**

Ozieri lies in a natural hollow and its situation is one of the most attractive sights in the northeast of Sardinia. The town has a rich history that goes back millennia and has added invaluably to our knowledge of the remote pre-nuraghic cultures that developed here. The traditions and architecture of Ozieri are fascinating to delve into.

The layout of the town is quite varied, seemingly blending in with the slopes of the hills, and among the tall houses you can glimpse the occasional covered roof terrace filled with flowers. The major sights in the old town are Piazza Carlo Alberto and Piazza Don Pietro Satta, centred around the 19th-century Fontana Grixoni. On the edge of the historic quarter is the Neo-Classical cathedral, which contains a splendid 16th-century Sardinian polyptych by an artist known only as the Maestro di Ozieri. The painting depicts the famous miracle of the Sanctuary of the Madonna of Loreto, and reveals Spanish influences as well as traces of Flemish mannerisms. The 17th-century San Francesco monastery houses the **Museo Archeologico**, with finds from archaeological digs in the local area. Most of this material is from the era of the Ozieri civilization, the predominant culture here from around 3500 to 2700 BC.

The territory surrounding Ozieri is also rich in historic and archaeological sites and ruins, such as the *domus de janas* at Butule, the San Pantaleo necropolis and the dolmen at Montiju Coronas.

The **Grotta di San Michele** is a cave that lies behind the Ozieri hospital, near the track-and-field stadium (during the construction of the latter, part of the cave was destroyed). Large quantities of decorated ceramics were found here, as well as human bones, a mother-goddess statuette and pieces of obsidian from Monte Arci. All these finds support the theory that there was some continuity from the earlier Bonu Ighinu culture to the time of the Ozieri.

Museo Archeologico di Ozieri

 ⌂ Piazza Pietro Micca ⏱ 9am–1pm & 3–7pm Tue-Sun (to 6pm Sun) 🌐 museo comune.ozieri.ss.it

Grotta di San Michele

⌖ ⌂ Ozieri Hospital 📞 079 78 76 38 ⏱ 10am–1pm & 2–5pm (3–6pm in summer) Tue-Sun

㉑
Tavolara

🅰F2 🚌 🚹 www.olbia turismo.it

This island is a mountain of limestone rising from the sea to a height of 500 m (1,640 ft). The eastern side is an inaccessible military zone, but the low sandy area called Spalmatore di Terra has beaches, a small harbour, restaurants and a few houses. Together with the neighbouring islands of Molara and Molarotto, Tavolara is a marine reserve. The granite cliffs are pierced by caves and crevices, while sea lilies grow in Spalmatore di Terra and the rock is covered with juniper, helichrysum, rosemary and lentiscus. The island is also home to over 150 moufflon, According to tradition, Carlo Alberto, the king of Piedmont and Sardinia, landed on the island to find the legendary "goats with golden teeth" (a phenomenon caused by a grass they eat), and was so fascinated by the island that he officially dubbed his guide and island inhabitant, Paolo Bertoleoni, "King of Tavolara". In summer there are regular boat services from Olbia *(p187)* and Porto San Paolo.

↑ The jagged cliffs of Tavolara island rising up over Spalmatore di Terra beach

22

Castelsardo

⚑ C2 🚌 🚹 Town Hall, Via Vittorio Emanuele 2; www.castelsardoturismo.it

Perched on a volcanic headland, Castelsardo has known a number of name changes in its history. The town was founded in 1102 by the aristocratic Doria family from Genoa, and was originally known as Castelgenovese, a name it kept until 1448, when it became Castell-aragonese, after the town's new conquerors. The present name dates from 1767.

The town is dominated by the Castello dei Doria. Built in the 13th and 14th centuries, this castle is now occupied by the **Museo dell'Intreccio** (Museum of Wickerwork), which displays local baskets made from traditional materials such as palm, asphodel and cane. From the castle terraces there are fantastic views; on clear days you can see Corsica.

Overlooking the sea is the **cathedral of Sant'Antonio Abate**. Constructed in the 17th century on the site of an existing Romanesque church, the cathedral has a bell tower roofed with majolica tiles. From here there is a splendid view of the water below. Inside the cathedral are fine 16th-century carved wooden furnishings.

On Easter Monday, the traditional Lunissanti procession is held in Castelsardo. The streets are lit by flaming torches, and traditional hooded figures form a slow, solemn procession, accompanied by the sounds of age-old chants. The procession ends in the heart of the old town in the upper part of Castelsardo, at the **church of Santa Maria delle Grazie**. The building does not have a traditional façade, and entry is gained through the side door. In the interior is a 14th-century crucifix known as the Cristo Nero (Black Christ).

To one side of the SS134 near Multeddu, not far from Castelsardo, is the impressive Roccia dell'Elefante (Elephant Rock) or Sa Pedra Pertunta (The Perforated Rock). This massive block of dark trachyte has been gradually sculpted by the wind into the uncanny likeness of an elephant with its trunk raised. In ancient times the rock was used as a burial place, and at the base you can still see two small carved openings for *domus de janas* (rock-cut tombs).

Did You Know?

The total length of Sardinia's coastline is equivalent to a quarter of the coast of mainland Italy.

DRINK

Cantina Ligios
Beautiful winery outside Castelsardo with tours of the vineyard and tastings of its products, including a Cannonau and other bold reds blended from Cabernet Sauvignon and Syrah grapes.

⚑ C2 🏠 Via G Mazzini 68, La Muddizza
🌐 cantinaligios.it

The vibrant town of Castelsardo and its pristine beach ↑

Museo dell'Intreccio

 ⏱ 🅰 Via Marconi
🕐 Hours vary, check website
🌐 mimcastelsardo.it

Cattedrale di Sant'Antonio Abate

🅰 Piazza Duomo 📞 339 245 43 87 🕐 Hours vary; call for details

Church of Santa Maria delle Grazie

🅰 Piazza della Misericordia 📞 331 802 95 07 🕐 Ask priest for keys

---

㉓
Pattada

🅰 D3 🚌 ℹ Town Hall; www.comune.pattada.ss.it

Situated in the middle of a territory rich in prehistoric nuraghi, Pattada is world-famous for the production of steel knives. The industry originated here because of a rich vein of iron ore, which has been worked for centuries. The village blacksmiths still carry on the tradition of making steel blades, and handles from animal horn or wood.

In the vicinity of Pattada is the Fiorentini – an area of greenery resulting from reforestation – and the ruins of the medieval castle of Olomene.

㉔
Isola Rossa

🅰 D1 🚌

As the hills of Gallura slope down towards the sea, they form a landscape characterized by rose-coloured crags, sculpted into strange shapes by wind erosion. Here, the small fishing village of Isola Rossa lies on a headland, at the foot of an impressive 16th-century sentinel tower. The village is not an island (isola), but was given its name ("Red Island") after the small, red-coloured rock island out in the bay. Fishing boats are drawn up on the beach below the village after each day's catch is brought in.

The coastline either side of Isola Rossa is worth visiting, especially towards the east, where Monte

🔍 HIDDEN GEM
Architectural Marvel

Just north of Isola Rossa is La Cupola, a domed house designed in 1969 for Italian filmmaker Michelangelo Antonioni. To build it, a giant balloon was inflated and covered in concrete. The house is not open to the public but can be seen from outside.

Tinnari overlooks the sea. To the west, the coast gently slopes to meet the mouth of the Rio Coghinas, a short distance from Castelsardo.

Not far from Isola Rossa is the small agricultural town of Trinità d'Agultu, which developed in the late 19th century around the church of the same name. As is so often the case in Sardinia, the simple country church became a sanctuary and pilgrimage site. Consequently, it is also an important trade and commercial centre during the associated festivities and pilgrimages.

A DRIVING TOUR
THE LOGUDORO

Length 115 km (70 miles) **Stopping-off points** Ozieri, Martis **Difficulty** Easy

The impressive Romanesque churches in the north of Sardinia are the result of encounters between different cultures that have inhabited the region. Following the fall of the Roman Empire, Sardinia did not hold a central role in the Mediterranean until after AD 1000, when Pisan and Genoese merchants, soldiers and preachers came to the island. It is difficult to assess how much of each church was created by local artists and artisans and how much by those from Pisa and Genoa. Whatever the facts, the structures have few equals in the rest of mainland Italy and make a fascinating day tour by car.

The traditional name of **San Pietro di Simbranos** (or delle Immagini) derives from the bas-relief on the façade depicting an abbot and two monks (the immagini or "images").

Nostra Signora di Tergu was built over the remains of a monastery founded by Tuscan monks.

Outside Martis lies the **Foresta Fossile di Carrucana**, a petrified forest formed by volcanic activity millions of years ago.

Built in the 12th century by the monks of Vallombrosa, **San Michele di Salvènero (Ploaghe)** stands abandoned in the middle of a series of road interchanges.

The **Santissima Trinità di Saccargia** is the most significant example of Romanesque architecture in northern Sardinia (p178).

Consecrated in 1107, **Santa Maria del Regno (Ardara)** is famous for the Retablo Maggiore di Ardara. The paintings on the altar step are by the Sardinian Giovanni Muru (1515).

↑ A decorative column capital at Santissima Trinità di Saccargia

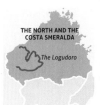

Locator Map
For more detail see p170

↑ Nostra Signora di Castro, standing on a
hill outside Oschiri

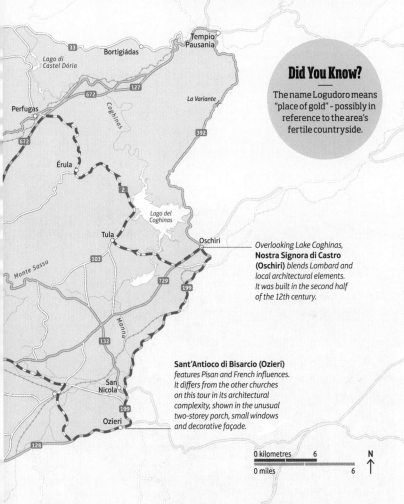

Did You Know?

The name Logudoro means "place of gold" – possibly in reference to the area's fertile countryside.

Overlooking Lake Coghinas,
Nostra Signora di Castro (Oschiri) *blends Lombard and local architectural elements. It was built in the second half of the 12th century.*

Sant'Antioco di Bisarcio (Ozieri)
features Pisan and French influences. It differs from the other churches on this tour in its architectural complexity, shown in the unusual two-storey porch, small windows and decorative façade.

0 kilometres 6
0 miles 6

N

NEED TO KNOW

Driving along the Orientale Sarda highway

BEFORE
YOU GO

Forward planning is essential to any successful trip. Be prepared for all eventualities by considering the following points before you travel.

AT A GLANCE

CURRENCY
Euro

AVERAGE DAILY SPEND

SAVE	SPEND	SPLURGE
€100	€200	€300+

BOTTLED WATER	COFFEE	BEER	DINNER FOR TWO
€1	€2	€4	€60

ESSENTIAL PHRASES

Hello	Buongiorno
Goodbye	Arrivederci
Please	Per favore
Thank you	Grazie
Do you speak English?	Parla Inglese?
I don't understand	Non capisco

ELECTRICITY SUPPLY

Power sockets are type F and L, fitting two-and three-pronged plugs. Standard voltage is 220–230v.

Passports and Visas

EU nationals and citizens of the US, Canada, Australia, and New Zealand do not need visas for stays of up to three months. Consult your nearest Italian embassy or check the **Polizia di Stato** website if you are travelling from outside these areas.
Polizia di Stato
🅦 poliziadistato.it

Travel Safety Information

Visitors can get up-to-date travel safety advice from the **UK Foreign and Commonwealth Office**, the **US Department of State**, and the **Australian Department of Foreign Affairs and Trade**.
Australia
🅦 smartraveller.gov.au
UK
🅦 gov.uk/foreign-travel-advice
US
🅦 travel.state.gov

Customs Information

Limits vary if travelling from outside the EU, so check restrictions before travelling. An individual is permitted to carry the following within the EU for personal use:
Tobacco products 800 cigarettes, 400 cigarillos, 200 cigars or 1 kg of smoking tobacco.
Alcohol 10 litres of alcoholic beverages above 22% strength, 20 litres of alcoholic beverages below 22% strength, 90 litres of wine (60 litres of which can be sparkling wine), and 110 litres of beer.
Cash If you plan to enter or leave the EU with €10,000 or more in cash (or equivalent in other currencies) you must declare it to the customs authorities prior to departure.

Insurance

It is wise to take out an insurance policy covering theft, loss of belongings, medical problems, cancellations and delays. Emergency medical care in Italy is free for all EU and Australian citizens. EU citizens should ensure they have an **EHIC** (European Health Insurance Card) and Australians should be registered to **Medicare** to receive this benefit. Visitors from outside these areas must arrange their own private medical insurance before arriving in Italy.

EHIC
🅦 gov.uk/european-health-insurance-card
Medicare
🅦 humanservices.gov.au/individuals/medicare

Vaccinations

No inoculations are required to visit Sardinia, but bring mosquito repellent, especially if you are travelling during the summer months.

Money

Most large establishments accept major credit and debit cards, but visitors should carry cash for small items such as coffee and gelato. Smaller shops, some rural tourist attractions and boat tours may only accept cash. Banks are the best place to exchange foreign currency, but opening hours are limited. ATMs, known as *bancomat*, are widespread and operate 24 hours a day.

Booking Accommodation

Sardinia offers a wide variety of lodgings, from luxury five-star hotels to budget hostels. Camping, bed and breakfasts, *agriturismo* (farmstays) and Airbnb are popular alternatives. During the peak season (July and August), accommodation is snapped up fast, and rates are at their highest. In some cities you will be charged a city tax on top of the price for the room (usually a few euros per person per night). Under Italian law, hotels are required to register guests at police headquarters and issue a receipt of payment *(ricevuta fiscale)*, which you must keep until you leave Italy.

Agriturismo
🅦 agriturismo.it

Travellers with Specific Needs

Sardinia's historic towns and cities tend to be ill-equipped for disabled access, though improvements are being made. Contact the local tourist office to find out what services are available at your chosen destination. Trenitalia *(p205)*, the national train operator, can arrange special reservations and assistance at stations.

Language

Italian is the official language but Sardinian (Sardo) is widely spoken. It still has a clear Latin base – the word *domus* is used to mean "house", for instance, instead of the Italian *casa* – and also has Arabic, Spanish and Catalan influences, reflecting the island's turbulent history. The level of English and other foreign languages spoken in Sardinia can be limited, particularly in rural areas, but locals appreciate visitors' efforts to speak Italian, even if only a few words.

Closures

Lunchtime Most churches and small businesses close for a few hours in the afternoon.
Mondays Some museums and some restaurants and cafés close for the day.
Sundays Most shops and businesses are open, but for limited hours. Restaurants are usually closed for lunch. Churches and cathedrals forbid tourists from visiting during Mass and public transport runs a reduced service.
Public holidays Shops, churches, museums and some restaurants either close early or for the entire day.

PUBLIC HOLIDAYS	
1 Jan	New Year's Day
6 Jan	Epiphany
Mar/Apr	Easter Sunday
Mar/Apr	Easter Monday
25 Apr	Liberation Day
1 May	Labour Day
2 Jun	Republic Day
15 Aug	Ferragosto
1 Nov	All Saints' Day
8 Dec	Feast of the Immaculate Conception
25 Dec	Christmas Day
26 Dec	St Stephen's Day

GETTING AROUND

Whether you are visiting for a short beach break or a rural country retreat, discover how best to reach your destination and travel like a pro.

AT A GLANCE

PUBLIC TRANSPORT COSTS

CAGLIARI

€1.30

one way
bus & tram

SASSARI

€1.30

one way
bus & tram

OLBIA

€1.30

one way
bus

TOP TIP
Avoid on-the-spot fines – be sure to stamp your ticket to validate your journey.

SPEED LIMIT

DUAL CARRIAGEWAY

110 km/h
(65mph)

NATIONAL ROADS

90 km/h
(55mph)

URBAN AREAS

50 km/h
(30mph)

Arriving by Air

The main airports in Sardinia are Cagliari's Elmas airport in the south, Alghero's Fertilia airport in the northwest and the Olbia-Costa Smeralda airport in the northeast. All three are close to their respective city centres and offer taxi services as well as public transport into town. For information on getting to and from Italy's main airports, see the table opposite.

European airlines fly from major airports and from mainland Italy to Sardinia's airports year round at reasonable prices. Long-haul passengers will almost inevitably have to change in a city on the Italian mainland or elsewhere in Europe. Often the most economical option is to take a flight to London, Berlin or Barcelona and catch a budget flight from there to the island.

Arriving by Sea

Sardinia is easily reached by ferry from Italy's mainland ports, which are accessible by train. Ferry services are more frequent and reliable in summer, but it is advisable to book in advance if travelling in July or August, especially if taking a vehicle. The crossing can be long (14 hours from Naples to Cagliari), although some ferry lines offer a faster service (5 hours from Piombino to Olbia). For overnight crossings, passengers can book a cabin.

Ferry services leave the mainland from Naples, Civitavecchia, Piombino, Livorno and Genoa. They dock in Sardinia at the tourist ports of Olbia, Golfo Aranci, Porto Torres, Arbatax and Cagliari. A number of ferries also ply the Strait of Bonifacio between Sardinia and the French island of Corsica; there are several different crossings on offer, the quickest of which is between Santa Teresa di Gallura and Bonifacio, taking around 50 minutes. Services on these and the mainland routes are run by a number of different companies; two of most reliable operators are **Moby** and **Corsica Sardinia.**
Corsica Sardinia
W corsica-ferries.co.uk
Moby
W moby.it

Airport	Distance to city	Taxi fare	Public transport	Journey time
Alghero-Fertilia	10 km (6 miles)	€25	bus	25 mins
Cagliari Elmas	8 km (5 miles)	€20	train	20 mins
Olbia-Costa Smeralda	5 km (3 miles)	€15	bus	10 mins

Train Travel

Sardinia has an efficient – if sometimes slow – railway service via Italy's **Trenitalia**. There are several daily departures from Cagliari to Sassari, Porto Torres and Golfo Aranci; the journeys take between 3 and 4 hours. Tickets can be bought online, but there are only a fixed number available so it is advisable to book ahead. Most rail journeys to the north of the island necessitate a change of train at Ozieri-Chilivani. There are also regular local trains between Cagliari, Iglesias and Carbonia, as well as between Alghero and Sassari – fares on these services can often be surprisingly cheap.

It is possible to buy tickets and passes for multiple journeys around Sardinia via **Eurail** or **Interrail**, but these are usually only economical if you are planning to embark on further travel in Italy and Europe. Note that you may still need to pay an additional reservation fee depending on which rail service you travel with. Always check that your pass is valid before boarding.

A train ride is an enjoyable and relaxing way to see the island's stunning scenery, and the **Trenino Verde** (little green train) tourist service is dedicated entirely to this purpose. Operated by Sardinia's main public transport company, Azienda Regionale Sarda Trasporti (ARST), it runs along five different routes: Palau–Tempio, Macomer–Bosa, Mandas–Sorgono, Mandas–Seui and Arbatax–Gairo. Trains operate throughout the year, with additional services laid on during the peak summer season. Prices vary according to the distance travelled.

Eurail
W eurail.com
Interrail
W interrail.eu
Trenino Verde
W treninoverde.com
Trenitalia
W trenitalia.com

Bus Travel

The **ARST** bus network covers most towns, cities, and resorts in Sardinia. Other bus companies operate within specific towns or provinces. Travel times can be slow through the island's more rural areas, and you may have to change bus on longer journeys. Tickets (biglietti) are sold at kiosks and at tobacconists, as well as at bus stations. Long-distance services often depart from outside main railway stations or from a town's main piazza.

Note that timetables can vary considerably depending on the day of the week or the season, with reduced services common on Sundays and public holidays. For more information about schedules, contact the local tourist office or check **Sardegna Mobilità**, the official information portal for public transport on the island.

Bus services within cities are efficient and user-friendly. Tickets are timed and need to be validated in the machines on the bus. Day tickets are usually cheap and are often the best option.

ARST
W arst.sardegna.it
Sardegna Mobilità
W sardegnamobilita.it

Taxis

Travelling by taxi isn't the most practical means of transport in Sardinia, but the service may come in handy when arriving at one of the airports. Taxis are not hailed so take one at an official taxi stand (usually found at the station, main piazza or close to key tourist sites), or reserve one by phone. When you order a taxi by phone, the meter will run from your call. Extra charges are added for each piece of luggage placed in the boot; for rides between 10pm and 6am, on Sundays and public holidays; and for journeys to and from airports. Taxi apps such as Uber are not yet operational in Sardinia.

ROAD JOURNEY PLANNER

This map is a handy reference for travelling between Sardinia's main cities and towns by car. The times given reflect the fastest and most direct routes available on each journey.

Alghero to Olbia	2 hrs
Alghero to Porto Torres	40 mins
Alghero to Sassari	35 mins
Cagliari to Bosa	2 hrs
Cagliari to Iglesias	1 hr
Cagliari to Oristano	1 hr
Olbia to Dorgali	1.5 hrs
Olbia to Nuoro	1 hr
Olbia to Santa Teresa Gallura	1 hr

Driving

Given Sardinia's wealth of spectacular natural scenery and sometimes limited public transport system, travelling by car is one of the best ways to become acquainted with the island.

Driving to Sardinia

Vehicles can be carried on many of the ferry services to Sardinia (p204). If you bring your own foreign-registered car into Italy, you must carry the vehicle's registration documents, have proof of insurance coverage, and have a valid driver's licence with you when driving. Driving licences issued by any of the EU member states are valid throughout the European Union, including Italy. If visiting from outside the EU, you will need to apply for an International Driving Permit (IDP) – check with your local automobile association for further information.

Driving in Sardinia

Italians have a reputation for driving fast, so make sure you are familiar with the rules of the road (see right). Many of Sardinia's roads are characterized by curves and tight bends, winding their way over hills and across plains, so allow plenty of time when planning a tour. Minor roads will often be blocked by flocks of sheep, further adding to your travel time. Road signs are not always clear and may be missing just when you need them most. Should this occur, the best thing to do is to ask someone on the way – Sardinians will happily help. Another potential problem is petrol, as there are not many filling stations in the interior. Lastly, you will often find yourself forced to take difficult dirt roads, particularly when looking for an out-of-the-way church or archaeological site. Always carry a good, up-to-date road map and download a map onto your phone, as signals cannot always be guaranteed, especially in rural areas. Keep your vehicle and identity documents (including driving licence) with you in the car at all times, as the police *(carabinieri)* often carry out spot checks.

Car Rental

Most international car rental companies are represented in Sardinia. To rent a car you must be over 21 and have held a valid driver's licence for at least a year. It is more cost-effective to have arranged a car rental in advance.

Parking

In winter, parking at the beach is normally free; throughout the rest of the year, fees may apply and a parking attendant will be present. On the streets, blue lines denote pay-and-display parking while white lines denote free parking. Yellow lines are reserved spaces, such as for local residents who have special passes. The historical centres of cities such as Cagliari, Sassari, Alghero and Oristano are pedestrianized during certain hours, so check for related signage when driving in these areas.

Rules of the Road

Drive on the right, use the left lane only for passing, and yield to traffic from the right. Seatbelts are required for all passengers in the front and back, and heavy fines are levied for using a mobile phone while driving. A strict drink-drive limit is enforced and it is illegal to throw rubbish out of the window, especially cigarette butts due to the risk of fire. Motorcyclists and moped riders must wear helmets, as must their passengers.

During the day, headlights are compulsory when you are driving on dual carriageways and on all out-of-town roads. A red warning triangle, spare tyre and fluorescent vests must be carried at all times, for use in case of an emergency. In the event of an accident or breakdown, switch on your hazard warning lights and place a warning triangle 50 m (55 yds) behind your vehicle. For breakdowns, call the Automobile Club d'Italia (**ACI**) emergency number (116) or the emergency services (112 or 113). The ACI will tow any foreign-registered vehicle to the nearest ACI-affiliated garage free of charge.

ACI
🌐 aci.it

Scooter Hire

You can rent motorcycles and scooters hourly or by the day from most towns and cities throughout the island. You must have a valid driving licence to hire a scooter or motorcycle, and you may have to leave your passport with the rental shop as a deposit. Helmets are obligatory.

Cycling

The quiet roads along the coast and through the stunning countryside in the interior are ideal for long cycling trips. Tourist offices will have suggestions for local bicycle routes, and the **Piste Ciclabili** website provides a map of bike lanes and bike-friendly itineraries for excursions. Bicycles can be rented in most towns and cities; high-visibility clothing and helmets are not obligatory, but wearing them is strongly advised.

If you prefer more arduous exercise, the steeper mountain roads are suitable for mountain bikes. Both **MTB Sardinia** and **Dolcevita Bike Tours** are experienced operators of off-road tours by mountain bike.

Cagliari has a bike sharing system called **Cabubi**, with a choice of bicycles for rent at various stations throughout the city. Models on offer include electric bikes, tandems, and bikes with baskets and cargo trailers.

Cabubi
🌐 cabubi.it
Dolcevita Bike Tours
🌐 dolcevitabiketours.com
MTB Sardinia
🌐 mtbsardinia.com
Piste Ciclabili
🌐 piste-ciclabili.com

Boat Hire

Hiring a boat is a good way to see the island away from the busy resorts. **Olbia Boat Rental** and **Sardinia Boat Charter** are two great options for boat rentals. Alternatively, you can make enquiries at any marina, where there are often rental kiosks set up for these purposes. In many ports it is possible to charter yachts. Prices vary depending on the duration, and may include a crew or simply the use of the boat.

Olbia Boat Rental
🌐 olbiaboatrental.com
Sardinia Boat Charter
🌐 sardiniaboatcharter.com

Walking and Hiking

The city centres in the majority of Sardinia's towns are usually compact, with key sites within easy reach of each other, and are best enjoyed on foot. The countryside of the interior is rugged but unspoilt and ideal for walking, hiking and more strenuous treks. However, be aware that facilities are few and far between, clearly signposted footpaths are rare, and there are very few refuges or stopping places. It is always advisable to carry an up-to-date map and to take plenty of water and food when hiking, as it is possible to walk for kilometres without stumbling across a village.

PRACTICAL
INFORMATION

A little local know-how goes a long way in Sardinia. Here you will find all the essential advice and information you will need during your stay.

AT A GLANCE

EMERGENCY NUMBERS

GENERAL EMERGENCY	STATE POLICE
112	**113**

AMBULANCE	FIRE SERVICE
118	**115**

TIME ZONE
CET/CEST. Central European Summer Time runs from the last Sun in Mar to the last Sun in Oct.

TAP WATER
Unless stated otherwise, tap water in Sardinia is safe to drink

TIPPING

Waiter	Not expected
Hotel Porter	€1 a bag
Housekeeping	€1 a day
Bar Staff	Round up bill
Taxi Driver	Not expected

Personal Security

On the whole, Sardinia is a safe place for visitors and only a few basic precautions are needed for a pleasant stay. Beware of pickpockets in the busy passenger terminals of the ports and in cities and do not leave valuables in your car if the parking place is unsupervised. If you have anything stolen, report the crime as soon as possible to the nearest police station. Get a copy of the crime report in order to claim on your insurance.

During the summer, forest fires are a serious problem in Sardinia, so make sure you know how to contact the local police or firemen in case an emergency should arise.

Health

In tourist areas, the Guardia Medica (emergency treatment centre) provides medical services for visitors in summer. These seasonal surgeries are closed in low season, so in winter you will have to go to a hospital instead. Sardinia has a good network of hospitals and casualty departments (pronto soccorso). Emergency medical care in Italy is free for all EU and Australian citizens. If you have an EHIC card (p203), be sure to present this as soon as possible. You may have to pay for your treatment and reclaim the money later. For visitors from outside the EU and Australia, payment of medical expenses is the patient's responsibility. As such it is advisable to arrange comprehensive medical insurance. For medicinal supplies and advice for minor ailments, visit a pharmacy (farmacia); these are widespread throughout the island.

Smoking, Alcohol and Drugs

Smoking is banned in enclosed public places and the possession of illegal drugs could result in a prison sentence. Italy has a strict limit of 0.05 per cent BAC (blood alcohol content) for drivers. This means that you cannot drink more than a small beer or a small glass of wine if you plan to drive. For drivers with less than three years' driving experience the limit is 0.

ID

By law you must carry identification with you at all times in Italy. A photocopy of your passport photo page (and visa if applicable) should suffice. If you are stopped by the police you may be asked to present the original document within 12 hours.

Responsible Tourism

Sardinians are very eco-conscious, especially when it comes to preserving their beaches and their landscape. Staying at a family-run guest house or an *agriturismo*, shopping at the local markets and businesses, and visiting rural locations are great ways to support the local economy. **Ecobnb** lists Sardinian bed and breakfasts run by green-conscious hosts, while **Sardinia Slow Experience** offers sustainability-focused tours that support local communities. Also be mindful to respect the wildlife by not approaching or feeding wild animals, and note that it is illegal to take sand and shells from any of the beaches in Sardinia.

Ecobnb
W ecobnb.com
Sardinia Slow Experience
W sardiniaslowexperience.com

LGBT+ Safety

Homosexuality is legal and widely accepted in Sardinia, particularly in larger cities such as Cagliari and Olbia. However, smaller towns and rural areas are often traditional in their views, and overt displays of affection may receive a negative response from locals.

Visiting Churches and Cathedrals

Strict dress codes apply: cover your torso and upper arms, and ensure shorts and skirts cover your knees. Shoes must be worn. Do not talk loudly or use cameras or mobile devices without first asking permission.

Mobile Phones and Wi-Fi

Wi-Fi is generally available throughout Sardinia, and cafés and restaurants will usually give you the password for their Wi-Fi on the condition that you make a purchase. Visitors travelling to Sardinia with EU tariffs are able to use their devices abroad without being affected by roaming charges – users will be charged the same rates for data, SMS and voice calls as they would pay at home. Visitors from other countries should check their contracts before departure to avoid unexpected charges.

Post

Stamps (*francobolli*) are sold in kiosks and tobacconists (*tabacchi*). Letters and postcards can take anything between four days and two weeks to arrive, depending on the destination.

Taxes and Refunds

VAT (called IVA in Italy) is usually 22 per cent, with a reduced rate of 4–10 per cent on some items. Non-EU citizens can claim an IVA rebate subject to certain conditions. It is easier to claim before you buy (you will need to show your passport to the shop assistant and complete a form). If claiming retrospectively, present a customs officer with your purchases and receipts at the airport. Receipts will be stamped and sent back to the vendor to issue a refund.

Discounts

For those under 18 years of age and over 65, many museums and attractions will offer a discounted admission. Student discounts are also often available, especially in larger cities such as Cagliari and Sassari.

WEBSITES AND APPS

www.italia.it
   Website of Italy's tourist board.
www.sardegnaturismo.it
   Official website for Sardegna Turismo, Sardinia's tourist board.
www.cagliariturismo.it
   Tourist information for visitors to the island's capital.
CTM BusFinder
   Official app for Cagliari's public bus system.

INDEX

PHRASE BOOK

IN AN EMERGENCY

Help!	Aiuto!	eye-**yoo**-toh
Stop!	Ferma!	fair-**mah**
Call a doctor.	Chiama un medico	kee-**ah**-mah oon meh-dee-koh
Call an ambulance.	Chiama un' ambulanza	kee-**ah**-mah oon am-boo-**lan**-tsa
Call the police.	Chiama la polizia	kee-**ah**-mah lah pol-ee-**tsee**-ah
Call the fire brigade.	Chiama i pompieri	kee-**ah**-mah ee pom-pee-**air**-ee
Where is the telephone?	Dov'è il telefono?	dov-eh eel teh-**leh**-foh-noh?
The nearest hospital?	L'ospedale più vicino?	loss-peh-**dah**-leh pee-oo vee-**chee**-noh?

COMMUNICATION ESSENTIALS

Yes/No	Si/No	see/noh
Please	Per favore	pair fah-**vor**-eh
Thank you	Grazie	**grah**-tsee-eh
Excuse me	Mi scusi	mee **skoo**-zee
Hello	Buon giorno	bwon **jor**-noh
Goodbye	Arrivederci	ah-ree-veh-**dair**-chee
Good evening	Buona sera	**bwon**-ah **sair**-ah
morning	la mattina	lah mah-**tee**-nah
afternoon	il pomeriggio	eel poh-meh-**ree**-joh
evening	la sera	lah **sair**-ah
yesterday	ieri	ee-**air**-ee
today	oggi	**oh**-jee
tomorrow	domani	doh-**mah**-nee
here	qui	kwee
there	la	lah
What?	Quale?	**kwah**-leh?
When?	Quando?	**kwan**-doh?
Why?	Perchè?	pair-**keh**?
Where?	Dove?	**doh**-veh?

USEFUL PHRASES

How are you?	Come sta?	**koh**-meh stah?
Very well, thank you.	Molto bene, grazie.	**moll**-toh **beh**-neh grah-tsee-eh
Pleased to meet you.	Piacere di conoscerla.	pee-ah-**chair**-eh dee coh-**noh**-shair-lah
See you later.	A più tardi.	ah pee-oo **tar**-dee
That's fine.	Va bene.	va **beh**-neh
Where is/are...?	Dov'è/Dove sono...?	dov-eh/dov-eh **soh** noh?
How long does it take to get to...?	Quanto tempo ci vuole per andare a...?	**kwan**-toh **tem**-poh chee voo-**oh**-leh pair an-**dar**-eh ah...?
How do I get to...?	Come faccio per arrivare a...?	koh-meh **fah**-choh pair arri-**var**-eh ah...?
Do you speak English?	Parla inglese?	**par**-lah een-**gleh**-zeh?
I don't understand.	Non capisco.	non ka-**pee**-skoh
Could you speak more slowly, please?	Può parlare più lentamente, per favore?	pwoh par-lah-reh pee-oo len-ta-**men**-teh pair fah-**vor**-eh?
I'm sorry.	Mi dispiace.	mee dee-spee-**ah**-cheh

USEFUL WORDS

big	grande	**gran**-deh
small	piccolo	**pee**-koh-loh
hot	caldo	**kal**-doh
cold	freddo	**fred**-doh
good	buono	**bwoh**-noh
bad	cattivo	kat-**tee**-voh
enough	basta	**bas**-tah
well	bene	**beh**-neh

open	aperto	ah-**pair**-toh
closed	chiuso	kee-**oo**-zoh
left	a sinistra	ah see-**nee**-strah
right	a destra	ah **dess**-trah
straight on	sempre dritto	**sem**-preh **dree**-toh
near	vicino	vee-**chee**-noh
far	lontano	lon-**tah**-noh
up	su	soo
down	giù	joo
early	presto	**press**-toh
late	tardi	**tar**-dee
entrance	entrata	en-**trah**-tah
exit	uscita	oo-**shee**-ta
toilet	il gabinetto	eel gah-bee-**net**-toh
free, unoccupied	libero	**lee**-bair-oh
free, no charge	gratuito	grah-**too**-ee-toh

MAKING A TELEPHONE CALL

I'd like to place a long-distance call.	Vorrei fare una interurbana.	vor-**ray far**-eh oona in-tair-oor-**bah**-nah
I'd like to make a reverse-charge call.	Vorrei fare una telefonata a carico del destinatario.	vor-**ray far**-eh oona teh-leh-fon-**ah**-tah ah **kar**-ee-koh dell dess-tee-nah-**tar** ree-oh
I'll try again later.	Ritelefono più tardi.	ree-teh-**leh**-foh-noh pee-oo **tar**-dee
Can I leave a message?	Posso lasciare un messaggio?	**poss**-oh lash-**ah**-reh oon mess-**sah**-joh?
Hold on.	Un attimo, per favore	oon ah-tee-moh, pair fah-**vor**-eh
Could you speak up a little please?	Può parlare più forte, per favore?	pwoh par-**lah**-reh pee-oo for-teh, pair fah-**vor**-eh?
local call	telefonata locale	te-leh-fon-**ah**-tah oh-cah-leh

SHOPPING

How much does this cost?	Quant'è, per favore?	kwan-**teh** pair fah-**vor**-eh?
I would like...	Vorrei...	vor-**ray**
Do you have...?	Avete...?	ah-**veh**-teh...?
I'm just looking.	Sto soltanto guardando.	stoh sol-**tan**-toh gwar-dan-doh
Do you take credit cards?	Accettate carte di credito?	ah-chet-**tah**-teh kar-teh dee **creh**-dee-toh?
What time do you open/close?	A che ora apre/chiude?	ah keh **or**-ah **ah**-preh/kee-oo-deh?
this one	questo	**kweh**-stoh
that one	quello	**kwell**-oh
expensive	caro	**kar**-oh
cheap	a buon prezzo	ah bwon **pret**-soh
size, clothes	la taglia	lah **tah**-lee-ah
size, shoes	il numero	eel **noo**-mair-oh
white	bianco	bee-**ang**-koh
black	nero	**neh**-roh
red	rosso	**ross**-oh
yellow	giallo	**jal**-loh
green	verde	**vair**-deh
blue	blu	bloo

TYPES OF SHOP

antique dealer	l'antiquario	lan-tee-**kwah**-ree-oh
bakery	il forno/il panificio	eel forn-oh/eel pan-ee-**fee**-choh
bank	la banca	lah **bang**-kah
bookshop	la libreria	lah lee-breh-**ree**-ah
butcher	la macelleria	lah mah-chell-eh-**ree**-ah
cake shop	la pasticceria	lah pas-tee-chair-**ee**-ah
chemist	la farmacia	lah far-mah-**chee**-ah
delicatessen	la salumeria	lah sah-loo-meh-**ree**-ah

department store	il grande magazzino	eel *gran-deh* mag-gad-*zee*-noh
fishmonger	il pescivendolo	eel pesh-ee-*ven*-doh-loh
florist	il fioraio	eel fee-or-*eye*-oh
greengrocer	il fruttivendolo	eel froo-tee-*ven*-doh-loh
grocery	alimentari	ah-lee-men-*tah*-ree
hairdresser	il parrucchiere	eel par-oo-kee-*air*-eh
ice cream parlour	la gelateria	lah jel-lah-tair-*ree*-ah
market	il mercato	eel mair-*kah*-toh
newsstand	l'edicola	leh-*dee*-koh-lah
post office	l'ufficio postale	loo-*fee*-choh pos-*tah*-leh
shoe shop	il negozio di scarpe	eel neh-*goh*-tsioh dee *skar*-peh
supermarket	il supermercato	eel su-pair-mair-*kah*-toh
tobacconist	il tabaccaio	eel tah-bak-*eye*-oh
travel agency	l'agenzia di viaggi	lah-jen-*tsee*-ah dee vee-*ad*-jee

SIGHTSEEING

art gallery	la pinacoteca	lah peena-koh-*teh* kah
bus stop	la fermata dell'autobus	lah fair-*mah*-tah dell *ow*-toh-booss
church	la chiesa	lah kee-*eh*-zah
	la basilica	lah bah-*seel*-i-kah
closed for holidays	chiuso per le ferie	kee-*oo*-zoh pair leh *fair*-ee-eh
garden	il giardino	eel jar-*dee*-no
library	la biblioteca	lah beeb-lee-oh-*teh*-kah
museum	il museo	eel moo-*zeh*-oh
railway station	la stazione	lah stah-tsee-*oh*-neh
tourist information	l'ufficio di turismo	loo-*fee*-choh dee too-*ree*-smoh

NUMBERS

1	uno	*oo*-noh
2	due	*doo*-eh
3	tre	treh
4	quattro	*kwat*-roh
5	cinque	*ching*-kweh
6	sei	*say*-ee
7	sette	*set*-teh
8	otto	*ot*-toh
9	nove	*noh*-veh
10	dieci	dee-*eh*-chee
11	undici	*oon*-dee-chee
12	dodici	*doh*-dee-chee
13	tredici	*tray*-dee-chee
14	quattordici	kwat-*tor*-dee-chee
15	quindici	*kwin*-dee-chee
16	sedici	*say*-dee-chee
17	diciassette	dee-chah-*set*-teh
18	diciotto	dee-*chot*-toh
19	diciannove	dee-chah-*noh*-veh
20	venti	*ven*-tee
30	trenta	*tren*-tah
40	quaranta	kwah-*ran*-tah
50	cinquanta	ching-*kwan*-tah
60	sessanta	sess-*an*-tah
70	settanta	set-*tan*-tah
80	ottanta	ot-*tan*-tah
90	novanta	noh-*van*-tah
100	cento	*chen*-toh
1,000	mille	*mee*-leh
2,000	duemila	*doo*-eh mee-lah
5,000	cinquemila	*ching*-kweh *mee*-lah
1,000,000	un milione	oon meel-*yoh*-neh

TIME, DAYS, MONTHS, SEASONS

one minute	un minuto	oon mee-*noo*-toh
one hour	un'ora	oon *or*-ah
half an hour	mezz'ora	medz-*or*-ah
a day	un giorno	oon *jor*-noh
a week	una settimana	oona set-tee-*mah*-nah
Monday	lunedí	loo-neh-*dee*
Tuesday	martedí	mar-teh-*dee*
Wednesday	mercoledí	mair-koh-leh-*dee*
Thursday	giovedí	joh-veh-*dee*
Friday	venerdí	ven-air-*dee*
Saturday	sabato	*sah*-bah-toh
Sunday	domenica	doh-*meh*-nee-kah
January	gennaio	jen-*nah*-yo
February	febbraio	feb-*bra*-yo
March	marzo	*mar*-tzo
April	aprile	a-*pree*-leh
May	maggio	*mah*-jo
June	giugno	*joo*-nyo
July	luglio	*loo*-lyo
August	agosto	ag-*os*-toh
September	settembre	set-*tem*-bre
October	ottobre	ot-*toh*-bre
November	novembre	no-*vem*-bre
December	dicembre	dee-*chem*-bre
Spring	primavera	pree-mah-*veh*-ra
Summer	estate	es-*tah*-te
Autumn	autunno	ow-*toon*-noh
Winter	inverno	een-*vair*-no
Christmas	Natale	nah-*tah*-le
Christmas Eve	la Vigilia di Natale	vee-*jee*-lya dee nah-*tah*-le
Good Friday	Venerdí Santo	ven-air-*dee* san-toh
Easter	Pasqua	*pas*-kwa
New Year	Capodanno	kah-poh-*dan*-noh
New Year's Eve	San Silvestro	san seel-*ves*-tro
Whitsun	Pentecoste	pente-*kos*-te

TRAVELLING

adult	l'adulto	ad-*ool*-toh
airport	l'aeroporto	a-air-oh-*por*-toh
baggage claim	il ritiro bagagli	ree-*tee*-roh bah-*gal*-yee
boarding card	la carta d'imbarco	*kar*-tah deem-*bar*-koh
boat	la barca	*bar*-kah
booking office	la biglietteria	beel-yet-teh-*ree*-ah
bus	l'autobus	*ow*-toh-booss
bus stop	la fermata dell'autobus	*fer*-*mah*-tah del-*ow*-toh-booss
check-in desk	l'accettazione	achet-ah-*tzyoh*-neh
luggage	i bagagli	bah-*gal*-yee
child (male)	il bambino	bam-*bee*-noh
child (female)	la bambina	bam-*bee*-nah
coach (bus)	la corriera	kor-ee-*air*-ah
connection	la coincidenza	ko-een-chee-*den*-tza
couchette	la cuccetta	koo-*chet*-tah
customs	la dogana	doh-*gah*-nah
delay	ritardo	ree-*tar*-doh
domestic	nazionale	natz-yoh-*nah*-leh
exit gate	l'uscita	oo-*shee*-tah
fare	la tariffa	tah-*reef*-fah
ferry	il traghetto	trah-*get*-toh
first class	prima classe	pree-*mah klas*-seh
flight	il volo	*voh*-loh
left luggage	il deposito bagagli	deh-*poh*-zee-toh bah-*gal*-yee
lost property	l'ufficio oggetti smarriti	oof-*fee*-cho *ojet*-tee zmar-*ree*-tee
luggage trolley	il carrello	kar-*rel*-loh
non-smoking	non fumatori	*noh*-n foo-mah-*toh*-ree

passport	il passaporto	pas-sah-**por**-toh
platform	il binario	bee-**nah**-ree-o
railway	la ferrovia	fer-roh-**vee**-a
reservation	la prenotazione	pre-noh-**tatz**-yoh-neh
return ticket	andata e ritorno	an-**dah**-tah ay ree-**tor**-no
seat	il posto	**poss**-toh
second class	seconda classe	sek-**on**-da klas-seh
single ticket	solo andata	soh-loh an-**dah**-tah
smoking	fumatori	foo-mah-**toh**-ree
station	la stazione	statz-**yoh**-neh
supplement	il supplemento	soop-leh-**men**-toh
taxi	il taxi	**tak**-si
ticket	il biglietto	beel-**yet**-to
timetable	l'orario	oh-**rah**-ry-oh
train	il treno	**treh**-noh
underground	la metropolitana	met-roh-poh-lee-**tah**-nah

MOTORING

Fill it up	il pieno	eel **pyeh**-noh
Do you do repairs?	Effettua riparazioni?	ef-**fet**-tua ree-paratz-**yoh**-nee?
I'd like to hire a car	Vorrei noleggiare una macchina	vor-**ray** noh-ledg-**ah**-re oona **mah**-keena
automatic	con il cambio automatico	kon eel **kam**-bee-oh ow-toh-**mah**-tee-koh
boot	il portabagagli	porta-bah-**gal**-yee
car	l'automobile, la macchina	ow-toh-moh-**bee**-leh **mah**-kee-nah
car ferry	il traghetto	trah-**geh**-to
diesel oil	gasolio	gaz-**oh**-lyo
garage (repairs)	il meccanico	mek-**ah**-neeko
four-star petrol	benzina super	ben-**dzee**-na **soo**-per
licence	la patente	pah-**ten**-teh
motorbike	la motocicletta	moh-toh-chee-**kleh**-ta
motorway	l'autostrada	ow-toh-**strah**-da
petrol	la benzina	ben-**dzeena**
petrol station	la stazione di servizio	statz-**yoh**-neh dee sair-**veetz**-yo
ring road	raccordo anulare	rak-**or**-do an-oo-**lah**-re
road	la strada	**strah**-da
traffic lights	il semaforo	sem-**ah**-foh-roh
unleaded petrol	benzina senza piombo	ben-**dzeena** sen-dza **peeom**-boh

SIGNS YOU MAY SEE ON THE ROAD

accendere i fari	ach-**en**-deh-reh ee **fah**-ree	headlights on
caduta massi	kah-**doo**-tah **mah**-see	falling rocks
divieto di accesso	dee-**vyeh**-toh dee ach-**eh**-so	no entry
divieto di sosta	dee-**vyeh**-toh dee **sos**-tah	no stopping
dogana	dog-**ah**-nah	customs
escluso residenti	es-**kloo**-so reh-zi-**den**-ti	residents only
ghiaccio	**gyah**-cho	ice
lavori in corso	lah-**voh**-ree een **kor**-so	roadworks
nebbia	**neb**-bya	fog
parcheggio a pagamento	par-**kej**-yo a pah-gah-**men**-toh	paying car park
parcheggio custodito	par-**kej**-yo koo-sto-**dee**-toh	car park with attendant
pedaggio	peh-**daj**-oh	toll
pericolo	peh-**ree**-koh-loh	danger
rallentare	rah-lehn-**tah**-reh	reduce speed
senso unico	**sen**-tzo oo-nee-ko	one way
uscita camion	oo-**shee**-tah **kah**-myon	works exit
zona pedonale	**dzoh**-na peh-doh-**nah**-leh	pedestrian area

STAYING IN A HOTEL

Do you have any vacant rooms?	Avete camere libere?	ah-veh-teh kah-mair-eh **lee**-bair-eh?
double room	una camera doppia	oona kah-mair-ah **doh**-pee-ah
with double bed	con letto matrimoniale	kon **let**-toh mah-tree-moh-nee-**ah**-leh
twin room	una camera con due letti	oona kah-mair-ah kon **doo**-eh **let**-tee
single room	una camera singola	oona kah-mair-ah **sing**-goh-lah
room with a bath, shower	una camera con bagno, con doccia	oona kah-mair-ah kon **ban**-yoh, kon **dot**-chah
I have a reservation.	Ho fatto una prenotazione.	oh **fat**-toh oona preh-noh-tah-tsee-**oh**-neh
balcony	balcone	bal-**coh**-neh
breakfast	prima colazione	**pree**-ma coh-lah-**tzyoh**-neh
key	la chiave	lah kee-**ah**-veh
porter	il facchino	eel fah-**kee**-noh
room service	servizio in camera	ser-**vitz**-yoh een **cah**-meh-rah

EATING OUT

Have you got a table for...?	Avete un tavolo per...?	ah-veh-teh oon **tah**-voh-loh pair...?
I'd like to reserve a table.	Vorrei riservare un tavolo.	vor-**ray** ree-sair-**vah**-reh oon **tah**-voh-loh
the bill, please.	il conto, per favore.	**kon**-toh pair fah-**vor**-eh
I am a vegetarian.	Sono vegetariano/a.	**soh**-noh veh-jeh-tar-ee-**ah**-noh/nah
beer	la birra	**bee**-rah
bread	il pane	**pah**-neh
bottle	la bottiglia	bot-**teel**-yah
breakfast	la prima colazione	pree-mah koh-lah-tsee-**oh**-neh
butter	il burro	**boor**-roh
carafe	la caraffa	kah-rah-**fah**
child's portion	una porzione per bambini	portz-**yoh**-neh pair bam-**bee**-nee
coffee	il caffè	kaf-**feh**
cover charge	il coperto	koh-**pair**-toh
cup	la tazza	**tat**-zah
dessert	il dessert	des-**ser**
dinner	la cena	**cheh**-nah
dish of the day	il piatto del giorno	pee-**ah**-toh dell or-no
first course	il primo	**pree**-moh
fixed price menu	il menù a prezzo fisso	meh-**noo** ah **pret**-soh **fee**-soh
fork	la forchetta	for-**ket**-tah
glass	il bicchiere	bee-kee-**air**-eh
half-litre	da mezzo litro	da met-zoh **lee**-troh
knife	il coltello	kol-**tel**-loh
litre	un litro	**lee**-troh
lunch	il pranzo	**pran**-tsoh
main course	il secondo	seh-**kon**-doh
medium (meat)	al punto	al **poon**-toh
menu	il menù	meh-**noo**
milk	il latte	**lat**-teh
pepper	il pepe	**peh**-peh
plate	il piatto	p-**yat**-toh
rare (meat)	al sangue	al **sang**-gweh
receipt (in bars)	lo scontrino	skon-**tree**-noh
(in restaurants)	la ricevuta	ree-cheh-voo-tah
restaurant	il ristorante	rees-toh-**ran**-teh
salad	l'insalata	een-sah-**lah**-tah
salt	il sale	**sah**-leh
sandwich	il panino	pan-ee-noh
serviette	il tovagliolo	toh-val-**yoh**-loh
snack	lo spuntino	spoon-**tee**-noh
soup	la minestra	mee-**nes**-trah
spoon	il cucchiaio	koo-kee-**eye**-oh

arter	l'antipasto	an-tee-**pas**-toh	cavolfiore	kavol-**fyoh**-reh	cauliflower
ugar	lo zucchero	**dzoo**-keh-roh	cavolo	**kah**-voh-loh	cabbage
a	il tè	teh	cefalo	**che**-fah-loh	grey mullet
aspoon	il cucchiaino	kook-yah-**ee**-noh	cernia	**cher**-nya	grouper (fish)
o	la mancia	**man**-cha	ciambella	cham-**bella**	ring-shaped cake
egetables	il contorno	eel kon-**tor**-noh	cicoria	chih-**kor**-ya	chicory
aitress	la cameriera	kah-mair-ee-**air**-ah	ciliege	chil-**yej**-eh	cherries
aiter	il cameriere	kah-mair-ee-**air**-eh	cioccolata	choc-oh-**lah**-tah	chocolate
ater	l'acqua	**ak**-wah	cipolle	chip-**oh**-leh	onions
izzy/still	gassata/naturale	gah-**zah**-tah/ nah-too-**rah**-leh	coniglio	kon-**ee**-lyo	rabbit
			contorni	kon-**tor**-nee	vegetables
ell done (meat)	ben cotto	ben **kot**-toh	coperto	kop-**er**-toh	cover charge
ine	il vino	**vee**-noh	coppa	**koh**-pah	cured pork, sliced finely and eaten cold
ine list	la lista dei vini	**lee**-stah day **vee**-nee	cordula	**kor**-doo-lah	Sardinian spit-roasted plaited lamb entrails

MENU DECODER

bbacchio	ab-**ak**-yoh	spring lamb	cotoletta	kot-oh-**let**-ta	pork or lamb chop
cciughe	ach-**oo**-geh	anchovies	cozze	**kot**-zeh	mussels
ceto	ach-**eh**-toh	vinegar	crema	**kreh**-mah	custard dessert
cqua minerale	**ah**-kwah mee-**nair**- **ah**-leh gah-**zah**-tah/ nah-too-**rah**-leh	mineral water	crespella	**kres**-pel-lah	savoury pancake
gassata/ naturale		fizzy/still	crostata di frutta	kros-**tah**-tah dee **froo**-tah	fruit tart
glio	al-**ee**-oh	garlic			
gnello	ah-**niell**-oh	lamb	datteri	**dat**-eh-ree	dates
forno	al **for**-noh	baked	digestivo	dee-jes-**tee**-voh	digestive liqueur
la griglia	ah-lah **greel**-yah	grilled	dolci	**dol**-chi	desserts, cakes
bicocche	al-bee-**kok**-eh	apricots	espresso	es-**pres**-soh	strong black coffee
nanas	**an**-an-ass	pineapple	fagiano	fah-**jah**-noh	pheasant
natra	**an**-at-rah	duck	fagioli	fah-**joh**-lee	beans
nguria	an-**goo**-rya	water melon	fagiolini	fah-joh-**lee**-nee	long, green beans
ntipasti	ahn-ti-**pas**-ti	starters	fegato	**feh**-gah-toh	liver
peritivo	apeh-ree-**tee**-voh	aperitif	fettuccine	feh-too-**chee**-neh	ribbon-shaped pasta
ragosta	ara-**goss**-tah	lobster	fichi	**fee**-kee	figs
rancia	ah-**ran**-cha	orange	filetto	fee-**leh**-toh	fillet (of beef)
ringa	ah-**reen**-gah	herring	finocchio	fee-**noh**-kyo	fennel
rrosto	ar-**ross**-toh	roast	formaggio	for-**maj**-yo	cheese
sparagi	as-**pah**-rah-ji	asparagus	fragole	**frah**-goh-leh	strawberries
accalà	bak-al-**la**	dried cod	frappé	frap-**eh**	whisked fruit or milk drink with ice
asilico	bas-**ee**-lee-ko	basil			
esciamella	besh-ah-**mel**-ah	white sauce	fregula	**freh**-goo-lah	small, granular pasta
rra	**beer**-rah	beer	frittata	free-**tah**-tah	type of omelette
stecca	bees-**tek**-ka	steak	fritto	**free**-toh	deep fried
ottarga	bot-**ahr**-gah	salted mullet roe	fritto misto	**free**-toh **mees**-toh	seafood in batter
ranzino	bran-**zee**-no	sea bass	frittura di pesce	free-**too**-rah dee **pesh**-eh	variety of fried fish
rasato	bra-**sah**-toh	braised beef			
resaola	breh-**sah**-oh-lah	slices of cold, wind-dried beef with oil and lemon	frutta	**froo**-tah	fruit
			frutta secca	**froo**-tah sek-kah	dried fruit
rioche	bri-**osh**	type of croissant	frutti di mare	**froo**-tee dee **mah**-reh	seafood
rodo	**broh**-doh	clear broth	funghi	**foon**-g-ee	mushrooms
udino	boo-**dee**-noh	pudding	gamberetti	gam-beh-**reh**-tee	shrimps
urro	**boor**-oh	butter	gamberi	**gam**-beh-ree	prawns
affè	kah-**feh**	espresso coffee	gamberoni	gam-beh-**roh**-nee	king prawns
affè corretto	kah-**feh** koh-**reh**-toh	espresso coffee with a dash of liqueur	gelato	gel-**ah**-toh	ice cream
affè lungo	kah-**feh** **loon**-goh	weak espresso coffee	gnocchi	**nyok**-ee	small flour and potato dumplings
affè macchiato	kah-**feh** mak-**yah**-toh	espresso coffee with a dash of milk	gorgonzola	gor-gon-**zoh**-lah	strong, soft blue cheese
affè ristretto	kah-**feh** ree-**streh**-toh	strong espresso coffee	granchio	**gran**-kyo	crab
affelatte	kah-**feh**-lah-teh	half coffee, half milk	granita	gra-**nee**-tah	drink with crushed ice
alamari	kah-lah-**mah**-ree	squid	grissini	gree-**see**-nee	thin, crisp breadsticks
alzone	kal-**zoh**-neh	folded pizza filled with tomato and mozzarella	insalata	een-sah-**lah**-tah	salad
			involtini	een-vol-**tee**-nee	meat rolls stuffed with ham and herbs
amomilla	kah-moh-**mee**-lah	camomile tea			
annella	kan-**el**-ah	cinnamon	lamponi	lam-**poh**-nee	raspberries
annelloni	kan-eh-**loh**-nee	stuffed pasta tubes	latte	**lah**-teh	milk
appuccino	kap-oo-**chee**-noh	coffee with foaming milk	lattuga	lah-**too**-gah	lettuce
			leggero	leh-**jeh**-roh	light
arciofi	kar-**choh**-fee	artichokes	legumi	leh-**goo**-mee	pulses
arne	**kar**-neh	meat	lenticchie	len-**teek**-yeh	lentils
arote	kar-**roh**-teh	carrots	lesso	**less**-oh	boiled
astagne	kas-**tan**-yeh	chestnuts	lepre	**leh**-preh	hare
			limone	lee-**moh**-neh	lemon
			lingua	**leen**-gwa	tongue
			macedonia	mach-eh-**doh**-nya di frutta dee **froo**-tah	fruit salad

Italian	Pronunciation	English
maiale	mah-**yah**-leh	pork
mandarino	man-dah-**ree**-noh	mandarin
mandorla	**man**-dor-lah	almond
manzo	**man**-dzo	beef
mascarpone	mah-skar-**poh**-neh	soft, sweet cheese
mela	**meh**-lah	apple
melanzane	meh-lan-**zah**-neh	aubergines
melone	meh-**loh**-neh	melon
menta	**men**-tah	mint
merluzzo	mer-**loo**-tzoh	cod
minestrone	mee-nes-**troh**-neh	thick vegetable soup
mirtilli	meer-**tee**-lee	bilberries
more	**mor**-eh	blackberries
nasello	nah-**seh**-loh	hake
nocciole	noch-**oh**-leh	hazelnuts
noce moscata	**noh**-che mos-**kah**-tah	nutmeg
noci	**noh**-chi	walnuts
olio	**oh**-lyo	oil
orata	oh-**rah**-tah	gilthead bream
origano	oh-**ree**-gah-noh	oregano
ossobuco	os-oh-**boo**-ko	stewed shin of veal
ostriche	**os**-tree-keh	oysters
pane	**pah**-neh	bread crisp, circular
carasau	cah-rah-**sahw**	bread
panino	pah-**nee**-noh	filled roll
panna	pah-**nah**	cream
parmigiana	par-mee-**jah**-nah dee	aubergine, tomato,
di melanzane	meh-lan-zah-neh	mozzarella and
		parmesan bake
parmigiano	par-mee-**jah**-noh	parmesan cheese
pasticcio	pas-**tich**-oh	pasta and meat bake
patate	pah-**tah**-teh	potatoes
pecorino	peh-coh-**ree**-noh	strong, hard ewe's
		milk cheese
penne	peh-**neh**	pasta quills
pepe	**peh**-peh	pepper (spice)
peperoncino	peh-peh-**ron**-chee-noh	cayenne pepper
peperoni	peh-peh-**roh**-nee	peppers
pera	**peh**-rah	pear
pesca	**pes**-kah	peach
pesce	**pesh**-eh	fish
piselli	pee-**seh**-lee	peas
polenta	poh-**len**-tah	boiled cornmeal with
		meat or vegetables
pollo	**poh**-loh	chicken
polpette	pol-**peh**-teh	meatballs
polpettone	pol-**peh**-toh-neh	meatloaf
pomodori	poh-moh-**doh**-ree	tomatoes
pompelmo	pom-**pel**-moh	grapefruit
porceddu	por-**ched**-doo	roast suckling pig
porri	**poh**-ree	leeks
prezzemolo	pretz-**eh**-moh-loh	parsley
primi piatti	**pree**-mee **pyah**-tee	first courses
prosciutto	pro-**shoo**-toh	ham cooked/cured
cotto/crudo	**kot**-toh/**kroo**-doh	
prugne	**proo**-nyeh	plums
radicchio	rah-**deek**-yo	red chicory
ragù	rah-**goo**	mince and tomato
		sauce
ravanelli	rah-vah-**neh**-lee	radishes
ravioli	rah-vee-**oh**-lee	square-shaped
		egg pasta filled
		with meat
razza	**rah**-tzah	skate
ricotta	ree-**kot**-tah	white, soft cheese
ripieno	**ree**-pyeh-noh	stuffed
riso	**ree**-soh	rice
risotto	ree-**soh**-toh	rice cooked in stock
rognone	ron-**yoh**-neh	kidney
rosato	roh-**sah**-toh	rosé wine
rosolato	roh-soh-**lah**-toh	fried
rosmarino	ros-mah-**ree**-noh	rosemary
salame	sah-**lah**-meh	salami
sale	**sah**-leh	salt
salsa	**sal**-sah	sauce
salsiccia	sal-**see**-cha	sausage
salvia	**sal**-vya	sage
scaloppine	skah-loh-**pee**-neh	veal escalopes
seadas	say-**ah**-dahs	sweet cheese and
		lemon fritters
secco	**seh**-koh	dry
secondi piatti	seh-**kon**-dee **pyat**-ee	main courses
sedano	**seh**-dah-noh	celery
selvaggina	sel-vah-**jee**-nah	game
semifreddo	**seh**-mee-**freh**-doh	ice cream and
		sponge dessert
senape	**seh**-nah-peh	mustard
seppie	**sep**-pee-eh	cuttlefish
servizio	ser-**vitz**-yo	service charge
compreso	com-**preh**-soh	included
servizio	ser-**vitz**-yo	service charge not
escluso	es-**cloo**-so	included
sogliola	**sol**-yoh-lah	sole
sorbetto	sor-**bet**-oh	sorbet
speck	sp-**ek**	cured, smoked ham
spezzatino	spetz-ah-**tee**-noh	stew
spiedini	spyeh-**dee**-nee	meat or fish on a spit
spinaci	spee-**nah**-chee	spinach
spremuta	spreh-**moo**-tah	freshly squeezed
		juice
spumante	spoo-**man**-teh	sparkling wine
stufato	stoo-**fah**-toh	casserole
tacchino	tak-**ee**-noh	turkey
tagliatelle	tah-lyah-**teh**-leh	flat strips of
		egg pasta
tartine	tar-**tee**-neh	small sandwiches
tartufo	tar-**too**-foh	ice cream covered
		in cocoa
tè	**teh**	tea
tiramisù	tee-rah-mee-**soo**	dessert of coffee-
		soaked sponge,
		Marsala and
		mascarpone
tisana	tee-**zah**-nah	herbal tea
tonno	toh-**noh**	tuna
torta	**tor**-tah	tart, cake
torta salata	**tor**-tah sah-**lah**-tah	savoury flan
tortellini	tor-teh-**lee**-nee	stuffed pasta shapes
triglia	**tree**-lya	red mullet
trippa	tree-**pah**	tripe
trota	**troh**-tah	trout
uova	oo-**wo**-va	eggs
uova sode	oo-**wo**-va **soh**-deh	hard-boiled eggs
uva	**oo**-va	grapes
verdura	ver-**doo**-rah	vegetables
vino	**vee**-noh	wine
vino bianco	**vee**-noh **byan**-ko	white wine
vino da dessert	**vee**-noh dah deh-**ser**	dessert wine
vino da pasto	**vee**-noh dah **pas**-toh	table wine
vino da tavola	**vee**-noh dah **tah**-voh-lah	table wine
vino rosso	**vee**-noh **ros**-soh	red wine
vitello	vee-**tel**-loh	veal
vongole	**von**-goh-leh	clams
zafferano	zah-fair-**ah**-noh	saffron
zucca	**dzoo**-kah	pumpkin
zucchero	**dzoo**-kair-oh	sugar
zucchine	dzoo-**kee**-neh	courgettes
zuppa	dzoo-**pah**	soup
zuppa inglese	dzoo-**pah** een-**gleh**-seh	trifle

ACKNOWLEDGMENTS

The publisher would like to thank the following for their kind permission to reproduce their photographs:

Key: a-above; b-below/bottom; c-centre; f-far; l-left; r-right; t-top

4Corners: Alessandro Addis 90t, 195br; Marco Arduino 188-9b; Pietro Canali 188clb; Franco Cogoli 176-7.

Alamy Stock Photo: age Fotostock / Carles Soler 128tl, / Guido Cozzi 24t; Agencja Fotograficzna Caro / Sorge 40-1t; Claudio H. Artman 111br; Dorin Marius Balate 22t, 42br; Lorenzo Bassetti 74clb; Bernard Bialorucki 148-9t; blickwinkel / S. Meyers 31cr; Eva Bocek 67tl, 102-3t; Milena Boeva 22-3ca; Michael Brooks 16, 54-5, 56-7, 138-9, 183tr; David Burton 154t; Andy Christiani 41cla; CHROMORANGE / Lothar Hinz 77bl; Chronicle 52clb; Rebecca Cole 191br; Roger Cracknell 01 / classic 194t; Ian Dagnall 22-3t; Gabriele Dessì 107b; Didi 35cla; Martin A. Doe 76-7t; Adam Eastland 12-3b; FALKENSTEINFOTO 50br; Faraway Photos 140b; Paolo De Faveri 147cra; Massimiliano Finzi 49tl; funkyfood London - Paul Williams 126t, 179tr; Gianluigibec 8cl; Renato Granieri 46cla; hemis.fr / Leroy Francis 71tr, / Bruno Morandi 31b, 122tl, / Philippe Renault 22ca, 70cr; Nicola Iacono 80tr; Image Professionals GmbH / TravelCollection 40-1b; Image Source / David Fettes 12t; imageBROKER / Peter Giovannini 47cr, 153tr, 158t, 178bl, 187br; Reinhard Hölzl 18cb; Alexander Pöschel 50-1t, / Joerg Reuther 152cr, / Konrad Wothe 102b, 190-1t, 134-5; Wendy Johnson 173br; Jon Arnold Images Ltd / Alan Copson 193t; Attila Kleb 33cla; Tomasz Koryl 200-1; Luis Leamus 26tl; Yadid Levy 11cr, 38bl; Melvyn Longhurst 13br; Lorenza photography 24ca, 26-7b; M.Sobreira 64b; Dorina Maisto 47crb; Francesco Maltinti 156-7b; MARKA / claudio ciabochi 159b; mauritius images GmbH / Christian Bäck 68-9t; 165t, / ClickAlps 174cr, / JIRI 83bl; MAWPIX 27cl; Serge Mouraret 116t; Graham Mulrooney 20t; Nature Picture Library / Kristel Richard 36bl; North Wind Picture Archives 48crb; Panther Media GmbH 184-5t; Massimo Piacentino 65br, 110cl, 121br, 127br, 155tr, 164tr, / sculpture by Francesco Cadeddu 162-3b; Prisma Archivo 50tl; Realy Easy Star 43cl, / Toni Spagone 51tr, 62-3t, 63ca, 88bl, 150ca, 150bl,151tr, 164bl, 180bl, 180-1t, 182clb, 182b; REDA &CO srl 157br, / Enrico Spanu 20crb; REDA &CO srl / Luca Picciau 10-1b; 97bl; REDA &CO srl / Fabiano Caddeo 86-7b, 175br, / Massimiliano Maddanu 106tr, / Renato Valterza 37br; robertharding / Oliviero Olivieri 47tr, / ProCip 18tl, 112-3; RooM the Agency Mobile / Snapper 131; Chris Rout 157tl; Grega Rozac 198bl; Witold Skrypczak 96-7t, 104-5b; Mauro Spanu 10clb, 70-1b, 119t, 160bl; Wolfgang Steiner 47cl; David Towers 11br; Travel Wild 30-1t; Travelwide 24-5t; Universal Images Group North America LLC / DeAgostini / DEA / A. Vergani 45br, / G. Carfagna 185clb; Chris Willemsen 45tr; Jan Wlodarczyk 29cl, 43br, 125tr, 172b; Tim Wright 99cra.

Aquafantasy Park: 39crb.

AWL Images: Katja Kreder 120-1t; Doug Pearson 178-9t; Ken Scicluna 25tr.

Bridgeman Images: 52crb; © Look and Learn 52cr, / Illustrated Papers Collection 48bc; © Luisa Ricciarini 49bc.

Dreamstime.com: Alkan2011 186-7t; Steve Allen 147tl; Filippo Arena 30bl; Stefano Argenti 75; Blitzkoenig 174-5t; Eva Bocek 38-9t, 82-3t, 141tl; Damaisin1979 13cr; Dorinmarius 196-7b; Dirk Ercken 98-9b; Erix2005 8clb, 28-9t, 53tr; Petr Goskov 35br; Janmarijs123 11t; Jorisvo 50cb; Kasto80 29br; Kuvona 128bc; Miroslav Liska 8cla; Marcosborne 142-3; Milosk50 27t, 153cra, 199tr; Poike2017 2-3; Antonio Scarpi 74cb; Toldiu74 60-1t; Unclejo978 46cl; Alessandro Vallainc 20cr, 97cb; Vinciber 109; Hilda Weges 145br.

Getty Images: 500Px Unreleased Plus / Jean-Luc Bohin 100b; Alinari Archives Florence 52tl, / George Tatge 49tr; AlKane 73bl; Atlantide Phototravel 147tr; Corbis Documentary / Atlantide Phototravel 152-3b, 166-7t; Corbis Historical / Vittoriano Rastelli 53clb; De Agostini Picture Library / DEA 48t, 62bl, / Archivio J Lange 49clb, / G. Barone 86tr, / M. Carrieri 49cla, 71tl, / G. Cozzi 65tr, / V. Giannella 73clb, / P. Jaccod 12clb, / L. Romano 78tl; / EyeEm / Dariusz Oczkowicz 8-9b; hemis.fr / Lionel Montico 96ca; Lonely Planet Images / Witold Skrypczak 6-7, 79b, 153tc; Moment / Ellen van Bodegom 23tr; Photodisc / Buena Vista Images 53bc; Photolibrary / Andrea Pistolesi 19, 168-9; Witold Skrypczak 117br; Stockbyte Unreleased / Michael Pasdzior 129b; ullstein bild Dtl. / Heinrich Hoffmann 52-3t; Universal Images Group / AGF / Giorgio Evangelista 160-1t; / Marka 13t, 46cra, / Prisma 51bl, / REDA&CO / Fabiano Caddeo 101tr, 119cra, 132, 185b, 186br, / Max Cavallari 45clb, / Riccardo Lombardo 192b, / / Massimiliano Maddanu 41crb, 42-3t, 99tl, / Mira Sardegna 123b, / Giuseppe Sedda 36-7t, 37cb, / Enrico Spanu 17, 32t, 34-5t, 44tl, 69tr, 73crb, 74b, 80-1b, 89t, 92-3, 163crb, / Mauro Spanu 124b; Westend61 72-3t; 91br.

iStockphoto.com: al_foto 105tr; E+ / xenotar 84-5; garnet71 47tl; Natalia_Glynkina 34b; imantus 20bl, 66cla; mammuthone 46crb; Gabriele Sotgiu 189t; Travel Wild 10ca.

Jebel Sardinia: 32-3b.

Library of Congress, Washington, D.C.: 51crb.

Parco Museo S'Abba Frisca: Alessandro Spanu 39cla.

Rassegna dei Vini Novelli Milis: 47clb.

Ristorante Mirage: 24-5ca.

Robert Harding Picture Library: Enrico Spanu 4.

Sherden Overtone Singing School: 33crb.

Shutterstock: Marco Alien 28br; Paolo Certo 44b, 46cr; Ekaterina Pokrovsky 46clb.

Front Flap images
Alamy Stock Photo: Gianluigibec bl; Image Source / David Fettes c; Jon Arnold Images Ltd / Alan Copson br;
Dreamstime.com: Eva Bocek cla; Milosk50 cra;
iStockphoto.com: Gabriele Sotgiu t.

Cover images
Front and Spine: **iStockphoto.com:** Gabriele Maltinti.
Back: **Alamy Stock Photo:** agefotostock / Guido Cozzi, Michael Brooks cl; **iStockphoto.com:** Gabriele Maltinti b;
Robert Harding Picture Library: Enrico Spanu.

For further information see: www.dkimages.com

Main Contributors Lisa Voormeij, Fabrizio Ardito

Senior Editor Ankita Awasthi Tröger

Senior Designer Tania da Silva Gomes

Project Editor Elspeth Beidas

Designers Jordan Lambley, Stuti Tiwari Bhatia, Bharti Karakoti

Factchecker Carol King

Editor Matthew Grundy Haigh

Proofreader Stephanie Smith

Indexer Hilary Bird

Senior Picture Researcher Ellen Root

Picture Research Susie Watters, Jen Veall, Sumita Khatwani, Rituraj Singh, Vagisha Pushp

Illustrators Giorgia Boli, Alberto Ipsilanti, Daniela Veluti, Nadia Viganò

Cartographic Editor James Macdonald

Cartography Asutosh Ranjan Bharati, Rajesh Chhibber, Paul Stafforda

Jacket Designers Jordan Lambley, Bess Daly, Maxine Pedliham

Senior DTP Designer Jason Little

DTP Designer Rohit Rojal

Technical Prepress Manager Tom Morse

Image Retouching Steve Crozier

Producer Kariss Ainsworth

Managing Editor Rachel Fox

Managing Art Editor Bess Daly

Art Director Maxine Pedliham

Publishing Director Georgina Dee

The information in this
DK Eyewitness Travel Guide is checked regularly.
Every effort has been made to ensure that this book is as up-to-date as possible at the time of going to press. Some details, however, such as telephone numbers, opening hours, prices, gallery hanging arrangements and travel information, are liable to change. The publishers cannot accept responsibility for any consequences arising from the use of this book, nor for any material on third party websites, and cannot guarantee that any website address in this book will be a suitable source of travel information. We value the suggestions and suggestions of our readers very highly. Please write to: Publisher, DK Eyewitness Travel Guides, Dorling Kindersley, 80 Strand, London, WC2R 0RL, UK, or email: travelguides@dk.com

First edition 1998

Published in Great Britain by Dorling Kindersley Limited, 80 Strand, London, WC2R 0RL

Published in the United States by DK Publishing, 1450 Broadway, Suite 801, New York, NY 10018

A CIP catalog record for this book is available from the British Library.

A catalog record for this book is available from the Library of Congress.

ISSN: 1542 1554
ISBN: 978 0 2414 1131 5

Printed and bound in China.

www.dk.com